Alfred Portale's
Gotham
Bar and Grill
Cookbook

Alfred Portale's
Gotham
Bar and Grill
Cookbook

Doubleday ✳ **New York** ✳ **London** ✳ **Toronto** ✳ **Sydney** ✳ **Auckland**

Text by Andrew Friedman

Photography by Gozen Koshida

Recipes tested by Rick Rodgers

Published by Doubleday

a division of Bantam Doubleday Dell Publishing Group, Inc.
1540 Broadway, New York, New York 10036

Doubleday and the portrayal of an anchor with a dolphin are trademarks of Doubleday, a division of Bantam Doubleday Dell Publishing Group, Inc.

Book design by Marysarah Quinn

Library of Congress Cataloging-in-Publication Data

Portale, Alfred.
    Alfred Portale's Gotham Bar and Grill cookbook /
Alfred Portale.
        p.   cm.
    Includes index.
    1. Cookery.   I. Gotham Bar and Grill.
TX714.P67   1997
641.5'097471—dc21   97-6611
                                                    CIP

ISBN 0-385-48210-8

October 1997

FIRST EDITION

10 9 8 7 6 5 4 3 2 1

I dedicate this book to Helen,

who has always been my inspiration.

Who's Who in
Alfred Portale's Gotham Bar and Grill Cookbook

Alfred Portale is the chef/owner of the Gotham Bar and Grill. He resides in New York City with his wife and two daughters.

Andrew Friedman is an aspiring screenwriter who lives in Greenwich Village, New York. He is also a public relations executive with Kratz & Company, Inc.

Gozen Koshida is a professional photographer who resides in Tokyo, Japan, with his wife and three children. He has worked professionally in the United States, France, and Japan.

Rick Rodgers is a professional recipe tester, cookbook author, cooking teacher, and radio and television personality. He resides in Jersey City, New Jersey.

Acknowledgments

The following people made special contributions to this project:

David Kratz, my publicist, agent, and friend, who helped conceptualize the book and get it to the right people;

David Gernert, formerly of Doubleday, who first believed in the book;

My excellent business partners, especially Jerry Kretchmer;

Marysarah Quinn, Doubleday's talented design director;

Judy Kern, my editor at Doubleday, for her great notes and constant support;

Jacinto Guadarama, my sous chef of the last ten years, who helped me test recipes and prepare for the photographs in the book;

Wonyee Tom, Gotham's pastry chef, who helped develop many of the dessert recipes and contributed her advice and experience to that chapter;

Bill Telepan, another sous chef at Gotham for five years, whose great sense of humor and attitude kept us going through the arduous and painstaking recipe testing;

Helen Chardack, who lent a critical eye to the all-important second edit of the recipes;

Andrew Friedman, my coauthor, who came into the project rather late and helped pull it all together. He happily penned several drafts before hitting on the "voice" that I felt expressed my point of view;

Saundra Blackman, for her special help in keeping me organized;

Laurie Tomasino, the Gotham's invaluable service director, who brought her keen aesthetic sense and style to the project;

Hiromi Hayashi, from tête, inc., new york, who was an invaluable member of the photography team;

. . . and my undying appreciation to the entire staff at the Gotham, who have kept us successful for more than twelve years.

Contents

Introduction

Cookbooks have always been an integral part of my life in the kitchen. In fact, it was a cookbook that first interested me in becoming a professional chef. I still vividly remember the day I leafed through *Modern French Culinary Art* by Henri-Paul Pellaprat . . . and something deep inside me said, *This is what I want to do.*

Today, the shelves of my study are lined with cookbooks, hundreds of them. Some were bought at auction years ago, others were bought last week. Some remind me of chefs with whom I've worked or have admired. Others are mementoes of *one* exceptional meal, with a note from the chef-author scrawled on the inside cover. Scores of these books were purchased at times when I was working to make a new recipe in an unfamiliar style, like when I wanted to master curry sauce and basmati rice for a Thai/Indian dish I had in mind, and bought a small stack of cookbooks so that I could absorb the best advice each had to offer. Many of my books are written in German, Italian, and Japanese—languages I don't speak—but the photographs inspire me.

Dinner Party Déjà Vu

These books are to me what travel publications are to globe-trotters—the closest one can come to experiencing, or reexperiencing, a place without actually "visiting" it. Indeed, good food is a lot like travel. It stimulates and surprises. It satisfies our craving for the exotic and the unknown. Good food is an adventure.

That is how I think about it every day. Because cooking isn't just a job to me; it's something for which I feel a real passion and an insatiable curiosity. I've always believed that one of the most important realizations at which an aspiring cook can arrive is how much he or she doesn't know. The fear and respect of this fact have been the driving forces in my development as a professional chef—I see myself on a perpetual quest for knowledge. This is what keeps my work fresh and allows me to begin each day feeling highly motivated. I work *very* hard to stay curious and informed, looking for new and stimulating pleasures whenever possible.

Discovering these new pleasures, or even finding the time just to look for them, can be very difficult for a professional chef, and even harder for a home cook. Consequently, a lot of people become arrested in their culinary development because of what I've taken to calling the "Dinner Party Cycle." Many people make the same dish every time they entertain, returning continually to the recipes they know and have mastered. I grew up watching my parents serve the same pasta with artichokes and peas, or another favorite, fillet of sole topped with a mixture of bread crumbs and parsley, each time we had company. And today I have friends who frequently host dinner parties using a recurring series of menus, including special drinks and canapés.

While these dishes keep cooking from becoming stressful, they also prevent home cooks from growing by denying them the opportunity for trial and error that must be a part of any learning process.

Professional chefs face the same dilemma. The dishes on our menus represent items from our "repertoires," the recipes we've got down cold, that delight *our* guests, and that people *expect* us to make. These become known as our "signature dishes," the culinary equivalent of a hit single. But, like songwriters, chefs seek to expand their repertoires. We gather new influences from whatever sources inspire us, such as meals we've eaten in restaurants here and abroad, or from cookbooks we know and respect. We appreciate, scrutinize, and absorb what the world of food has to offer, developing our own personal style so that we may offer our guests a constantly evolving selection of new and intelligent dishes.

There are two primary advantages a professional chef enjoys over the home cook. One is that most chefs have attended a cooking school and/or spent years learning on the job, so new influences are viewed through the lens of tradition. Another advantage of professional chefs is that we spend all of our working time surrounded by food, thinking about new dishes, honing our personal style, and expending our repertoire.

I'd like to help you overcome the "Dinner Party Cycle" by giving you the tools to develop your own expanded repertoire—sharing the product of the time *I've* spent learning and creating. Since I believe the best way to teach is by example, I hope this book will provide some instructive examples to follow.

If you look ahead at the recipes, you will notice that most of the dishes are comprised of three or four components—a primary element, a sauce, and two or three accompaniments—each with its own recipe. My hope is for you to be able to master these recipes and use them confidently in a variety of dishes and contexts of your own design, perhaps creating your own signature dishes.

For example, there's a roast lobster dish on page 231 that features beet couscous and baby bok choy. After preparing that entrée, you will have learned not only how to roast lobster—a technique that will allow you to grill or smoke it with exceptional results—but also how to prepare a port ginger sauce that may be used to complement just about any type of seafood. And the beet couscous alone might become the inspiration for a dozen salads of your own design. These recipes, like the others in the book, are supplemented by a range of advice, suggestions, and observations that make them interactive, encouraging, and that show you how to adapt them to express your own personal style and taste.

These comments will also help demonstrate one of the most difficult things for an inexperi-enced cook to understand—why certain flavor combinations work and others don't. Because my food is primarily rooted in Mediterranean cuisine, the flavors are intense, clean, and balanced, and the combinations of ingredients are usually tradi-tional. Of course, personal interpretation figures into all the decisions you will make, but I believe that classic references offer the best guidance. Knowing and understanding the cuisine of the past is an important first step in creating future dishes. These culinary basics have survived the test of time for a reason, after all. Most modern artists first learned the rules of classic technique before they began breaking them. Picasso, for ex-ample, mastered portraiture before becoming a cubist. The same approach is absolutely crucial in cooking.

In addition to the advice and instruction this book provides, there is also an array of pho-tographs illustrating the steps involved in prepar-ing certain recipes as well as showing you many of the finished dishes themselves. The procedural photos are meant to help you master the tech-niques in the book, so that you can use them in whatever context you'd like. The finished dishes are intended to show my restaurant style of pre-sentation and, in some cases, a more relaxed, everyday style, which is certainly more practical for the home cook. They also serve another crucial function: they help whet your appetite and get you excited about creating the dishes, to make you want to take part in the "adventure."

My ultimate goal is for this book to become a starting point, for the recipes and techniques to become the building blocks and inspiration for your own creations. I also hope that it will provide some guidance, so that you will go forward with an understanding of the logical foundation on which the recipes are built.

For example, I'd like you to read the recipe for

the Ratatouille Risotto (page 172) and absorb the *technique* for making risotto so that, months later, if you happen to open your refrigerator to find an abundance of mushrooms, you can use the methodology to prepare a well-made and deeply satisfying mushroom risotto. Or that you develop a sense of how to combine flavors so that you can build a variety of menus around the Grilled Leg of Lamb with Roasted Garlic, Braised Escarole, and Chick-pea Puree (page 299), pairing it one summer evening with the Summer Tomato Salad with Ricotta Salata and Creamy Garlic Vinaigrette (page 96) and the Champagne Granité with Strawberries and Grand Marnier (page 365) for a dinner party in the country.

I also hope that the constant emphasis on variation and presentation might inspire you. As one gains more and more knowledge and cooking experience, it becomes a far less daunting task to create, or to experiment successfully. For me, this is where the great pleasures continue to be born.

Finally, I hope that this book itself—its recipes, anecdotes, and photographs—will offer some simple pleasure to you, your family, and friends. If, over the years, you find it to be a reassuring presence in your kitchen, one that you turn to equally for reading pleasure and culinary advice, it will have achieved its goal.

—ALFRED PORTALE
New York City
April 1997

Alfred Portale's
Gotham
Bar and Grill
Cookbook

1 Gotham Bar and Grill: The Making of a Restaurant

The Road to the Gotham

I haven't always practiced what I'm preaching. When I first heard of our nation's lesser-known CIA (the Culinary Institute of America), I was intrigued by the idea of a "chef college," where you went in a know-nothing and came out a world-class cook. But most of all, I was attracted to the speed with which you could achieve this transformation—only two years!

At the time, I was in my early twenties and planning to become a jewelry designer. I had taken classes in drawing and painting since the age of ten. While honing my craft, I made a living selling small pieces. Do you remember spoon rings? Well, they provided much of my livelihood for a few years, along with such items as hair combs, bracelets, and silver buckles set with semiprecious stones. I was, however, growing frustrated by the quest for a way to make a good living, and I took it as an omen when my scheme to mass produce my designs came to a screeching halt with the theft of my proofs—at a trade show no less. The Gods of the Industry, I decided, were trying to tell me something, and I went looking for a new vocation.

At about this time, I first heard of the CIA, and—following some primal instinct—mentioned it to a friend, who showed me a set of classical French cookbooks, including Henri-Paul Pellaprat's and *Larousse Gastronomique,* the bible of the craft. I was intrigued. To a young man who had been raised on basic Italian-American fare in Buffalo, New York, the pictures in these books depicted an unknown world of food to be explored and conquered.

I think it was at that moment I decided I wanted to be a chef, though not the one I eventually became. My imagination filled with images of myself, twenty-four months down the road, as an accomplished "serious" chef—which to me, at the time, meant amazing bystanders with beautiful ice sculptures and elaborate buffet presentations ("Step right up, folks, and see the Great Alfred Portale, *chef extraordinaire!*").

Fortunately, the CIA has a safeguard against such ill-founded fantasies—they turn away applicants with no experience and suggest that they work in a restaurant kitchen for a year. And that's what I did. I got a job at a popular Italian restaurant in Buffalo, and my first day there marked the beginning of an eight-year period of nonstop learning . . . and exhaustion.

You might be surprised to know how much chronically useful information one can pick up in a few months in a Buffalo kitchen. Under the auspices of a French-Canadian chef, I mastered several dozen sauces, the preparation of a wide range of fresh pastas (spinach, wild mushroom, etcetera), and even a host of Italian specialties that the restaurant featured once a year during the Feast of Saint Joseph. I also picked up a primer on the equally important rules of how a kitchen is organized, especially how to cook to meet the requirements of restaurant service, timing dishes to get to each table at the right time. We also catered a lot of local parties and banquets, so I *did* get to help create ornate buffets and sculptures.

This was hard work, but from the start of each morning to the end of each day, I loved every second of it. And while the CIA seemed closer and closer every day, I just couldn't wait . . . I bought some cookbooks and began teaching myself at home . . . until my mother scolded me for using up all the pots and pans and banished me from her kitchen, delaying my practical education even longer.

Nevertheless, I managed to develop a base of knowledge that qualified me for a job at the most renowned restaurant in Buffalo, owned by a well-respected local restaurateur named Michael Delmont. Delmont's restaurant had a broader, continental focus, and, working under a chef who was a graduate of the CIA, I took my skill set to the next level. After several months, I was hired to work in San Francisco at a country French restaurant, cooking for two chef-owner brothers from Brittany. Arriving at this restaurant was like entering heaven after looking in through the gates for nearly a year. Here, we did *everything*—all the basics of French cooking—from classic stocks and sauces to charcuterie. We baked bread for the restaurant daily, and made all the desserts, ice creams, and sorbets. To say I learned a lot would be an understatement—I had a crash course of which many American culinary students at the time would have been envious.

I had become a working professional cook.

And *then* they let me into school.

The CIA, based in Hyde Park, New York, is, at the time of this writing, the most revered cooking school in the country. But in 1979, when I enrolled, it didn't yet enjoy the reputation it does today. "Star chefs" weren't even a concept yet, so there were no famous graduates. But it was a fabulous place to learn. It was also an exciting time for the school, since its new president, Ferdinand Mets, was beginning to take the institute in new directions, attracting high-profile instructors and rounding out the curriculum. In addition to honing the techniques I had developed earlier in the restaurants, I worked very hard in classes on the French language itself, and also at such practical courses as costing and restaurant accounting. Neither of these came very naturally to me, but I recognized them as a prerequisite to any future success I hoped to enjoy.

The cooking classes were another story. I couldn't get enough of them. I was never more certain that I had selected the right path than when I would hit the kitchen/classroom every morning. My hunger for knowledge was insatiable; I devoured everything each instructor had to offer. I also spent countless hours at the institute's culinary library—one of the best in the country—reading all the classic cookbooks. They even had a video library (a real novelty at the time) where you could watch tapes that demonstrated a host of techniques, such as boning a leg of lamb.

Two years later, hard work and passion paid off (as they always do)—I received the highest rank in the class, and won the "Most Outstanding Student" Award.

Then, as before, I had to find a job. Just prior to graduation, I had answered to an ad to "work for a chef who worked for Michel Guérard." Though the ad was vague, Guérard—widely acknowledged as the father of modern spa cuisine—was one of my idols, so I answered it. Before too long, I found myself presented with the opportunity to be part of the cooking team at a new start-up gourmet shop at Bloomingdale's—a classic French charcuterie in midtown Manhattan not

unlike the upscale gourmet take-out establishments that have proliferated in major American cities over the last ten years.

I was hired, and showed up on the first day only to be greeted by Guérard himself, accompanied by Michel Troisgros (son of Pierre, half of the legendary Troisgros brothers of Roanne). Talk about being in the right place at the right time! I couldn't believe it.

Because I had worked in a French restaurant in San Francisco, I knew the language well enough to translate for Guérard (who didn't speak English all that well), and help him navigate New York's culinary world, sourcing hard-to-find items and doing all the ordering. Something unique about this job was that it was all production, with no service. There were no waiters, no "waves" of customers with which to contend. We simply cooked all day long, preparing foods to be sold over the counter. It

was like attending a paid graduate school with one of the best chefs in the world at the blackboard.

After about a year, Michel Troisgros helped me and my friend Helen Chardack (who had also worked at the Bloomingdale's shop) secure jobs at his family's restaurant in France. When we first arrived, we leased a car and spent some time touring the countryside, eating at every restaurant of any renown. It took six weeks to cover Paris alone. On the wall of my apartment there, I hung a map that was dotted with push pins representing every town, vineyard, and restaurant we visited. (By the time I left France, one year later, it was pretty well crammed with push pins.)

I spent six months of my year in France working in the Troisgros brothers' restaurant, at the time one of the most famous contemporary dining establishments in France. Just one of many re-

markable aspects of the restaurant was the highly social atmosphere. Despite their fame, the Troisgros brothers were extremely down-to-earth, and when Helen and I first arrived, we were warmly welcomed by the entire family, including Michel's grandmother. As the new American in the kitchen, my participation in the staff's weekly basketball game, which took place between shifts on Monday afternoons, was *not* optional, even after I began working. Can you imagine, after six consecutive double shifts, having to play two hours of full-court basketball?

The tone the Troisgros brothers set was that of a real working "family," and they became my first role models for a management style that combined a demanding professionalism with fairness and respect for the employees. We felt like one big team.

The Troisgros brothers' kitchen is one of the most beautiful in France. I worked the fish station as *poissonier*. The French system is truly grueling, and—despite their personal touch—Jean and Pierre's restaurant was no exception. There were twenty-five cooks turning out one hundred meals, lunch and dinner, six days a week. This was exhausting, and I would often nap between shifts, and stay in bed all day on Tuesday when the restaurant was closed, listening to the rest of Roanne enjoying the sidewalks, cafés, and parks. It was extremely hard work, but for an aspiring young cook, it was a dream situation. I left with a profound respect for wine and food, especially seafood, with all of its possibilities.

Immediately after this *stage* (the French term for a time spent apprenticing in the kitchen), I spent six months working at Guérard's restaurant, first on the *dressage* station (the name literally means to dress each plate), and later as *entremettier,* preparing vegetables, grains, and legumes. My last several weeks, I served as *garde-manger,* which is the cold appetizer station. To give you a sense of just how complex the food could be at Guérard's, there were six of us working this station, and often four cooks at once would labor over two plates. I studied Guérard's flair for graceful presentation, which relied on an abundant use of fresh herbs, as hard as I had studied anything in school. One of my favorite tasks was picking fresh herbs from the restaurant's garden; twice a day I would take to the one-acre patch with a basket in hand and clip fresh herbs for the next meal. Another of my fondest memories of those days is of all the local farmers who would show up at the restaurant's back door every day with fresh greens, vegetables, and mushrooms from their gardens.

I also learned quite a bit about ducks—the best way to cook them, how to prepare *foie gras* and confit, and other lessons. And I learned it from

one of the best chefs in the world. It was a price-less year.

Homesick for the States, I returned to New York in 1984, eager to round out my experience and to hone my management skills. I was soon invited to work for another French luminary, Jacques Maximin, at his new restaurant, Tucano, on the East Side of Manhattan. I was very familiar with Maximin's influence for a number of reasons: I had eaten at his restaurant in France, which was at the time the hottest thing in Europe; the chef who took over the shop at Bloomingdale's when Guérard returned to France had been one of Maximin's sous chefs; and I had met Maximin himself at the Hotel Negresco in Nice. Best of all, the position I was offered, *saucier,* is one of the most coveted jobs in any kitchen because it's the most prestigious. It requires the most experience and training to achieve and is widely considered a launching pad to becoming sous chef or *chef de cuisine.*

Tucano had all the elements of a hot New York restaurant. It was designed by the renowned Adam Tihany, had a fashionable address, and boasted one of the world's most famous chefs at the helm. But it was an expensive restaurant to run for many reasons, including the cost of frequently flying chefs in from France, as was Maximin's wont. Still, it was a profitable experience for me: By the time the restaurant closed, about one year later, I had graduated to the position of sous chef, learning as much about management as I did about sauces. Another sensational experience.

At this time, I was first feeling up to the task of designing my own menu and heading my own kitchen. Soon after, an acquaintance of mine gave me a tip—"I hear the Gotham Bar and Grill is auditioning for a new chef."

The Gotham Bar and Grill. I knew the room and loved it—thought it would be an ideal backdrop for

the style I was developing. A few days later, I phoned the restaurant to schedule an interview.

Gotham Bar and Grill

The Gotham Bar and Grill is nestled among a row of apartment houses and boutique offices on the south side of East 12th Street in Greenwich Village, New York. Twelfth is a relatively quiet, tree-lined street, and—in a city known for theatricality—the Gotham has provided the requisite dose between Fifth Avenue and University Place since 1984.

From the street, an expansive window looks in on the Gotham's high-ceilinged space, comprised of a multitude of levels and recesses, which extends deep into the block and is adorned with softly spectacular, billowy "parachutes" that hang from the heavens overhead.

During the day, sunlight sparkles in through the back windows, washing the entire room in a soothing, natural brightness. At night, the room is lit sensationally with a combination of bulbs embedded in the recesses, glowing through the furled parachute fabric, and even atop the torch held high by the replica of the Statue of Liberty that stands proudly beside our western wall. In the evenings, a cumulative glow hovers like a blanket over the dining room, much the way street lamps seem to meld into a river of light when viewed from apartment balconies overlooking the streets of New York.

In fact, you might say that the entire room, its combination of density and privacy, recalls the city—people living practically atop one another yet somehow finding comfort and serenity while basking in the grandeur of their surroundings.

And if the diners in their seats, or customers at the bar, offer a metaphor for the city at rest, the

festive, ordered frenzy of the staff—palpable even from the street—mirrors the bustle of pedestrians during a morning rush hour (though our staff is a *bit* more courteous than the average rush-hour pedestrian). Gazing in from outside, it's difficult to resist at least a peek inside our doors.

The Gotham Experience

Since I wasn't with the Gotham when it first opened in 1984, I must compliment my business partners, Jerry Kretchmer, Jeff Bliss, and Richard and Robert Rathe, for creating a space so perfectly designed to drum up energy and excitement.

Enter the restaurant and you pass a small checkroom before stepping up onto an elevated plane that actually looks down just a few feet on the main dining room. Surveying the restaurant from here is like looking down into a busy swimming pool full of people at play . . . just before diving in. From this spot, you can best appreciate the effect of those billowy parachutes—softening the spectacular space and making the seventeen-foot ceilings seem quite celestial.

So much seemingly spontaneous activity takes place on the service floor that it's easy to forget how carefully orchestrated the staff is and how much work goes into making the whole place run

smoothly. If you were to stand at this spot for just one hour, you would be amazed at how the action literally never stops. It's a nightly triumph that dishes don't drop, servers keep their calm, and customers can move freely from one end of the room to another without being knocked off their feet. It's also remarkable that as soon as you sit down at your table, you feel at ease, as though the mere act of sitting had somehow separated you from the frenzy.

Every restaurant has its own system for achieving this effect. Ours was designed by Laurie Tomasino, our service director, who was at the Gotham the year before I became chef and who has gone on to design a brilliant service program that has become a model for other American restaurants. (This is not just my sentiment, but one shared by *The New York Times* restaurant critic Ruth Reichl.) Laurie has been an indispensable ingredient in the Gotham's recipe for success.

Among the steps we take to keep the Gotham on its toes is a nightly family meeting. (Restaurants often use the word *family* to refer to themselves. The nightly staff dinner, for example, is the "family meal.") Every day at about five o'clock, the service staff gathers in a circle at the end of the bar—some sitting, some standing—to receive their nightly briefing from the manager. (A similar meeting takes place before lunch.) It's a great moment in the day—an energetic cross between a theater troupe's "warm up," a schoolroom lecture, and a police department's roll call. It's the moment at which the entire staff becomes focused on the work ahead of them.

At this meeting, every aspect of service is reviewed. If something went wrong the previous evening, it is discussed, along with methods of remedying it. If any special guests are expected, the entire staff is notified. The dining-room manager also reviews his or her notes on the floor check for the night, reminding the appropriate people to

replace a torn linen or to put fresher flowers on a particular table. If I'm debuting a new dish, I'll present it to the group at this meeting, explain its ingredients and preparation, and let them have a taste, so that they'll be able to describe it properly to the clientele. (We also create a written description complete with wine suggestions, and keep a complete menu description book available at the service station.)

The Gotham's reservation system is also noteworthy, and we have been improving it year by year for a decade.

Simply put, the Gotham's reservation system has been designed to maximize the capacity of our dining room without overtaxing the kitchen and without overbooking, which would cause customer waits. Rather than adhering to the traditional quota of two seatings per meal, we began experimenting with a new system years ago, determining the maximum number of seatings we could accommodate every thirty minutes. In order

to anticipate cancellations and "no-shows," we mark advance reservations differently than we do same-day reservations (same-days are more likely to cancel). We also leave a few "hold" tables clear every night so that we can accommodate last-minute requests for reservations without displacing any customers.

The most personal touch in our system: To keep ourselves on our toes, we write the number of people served on each date the previous year, along with the weather on that date, at the top of the same day's page for the current year. If we aren't matching or surpassing those numbers consistently, we know we're doing something wrong.

While this is a highly evolved system, we continue to improve it even today, tracking no-show rates, and calling customers to confirm. Reservation confirmations are a delicate business, and we have a "reservationist" devoted solely to managing the reservation book from ten in the morning until we close late at night. When we take a reservation, we issue a reservation number to the customer, and ask that he or she call the day before to confirm. If we do not hear from the customer, we call him. If he does not return the call, we place the reservation on an unconfirmed list and hold it until the prearranged time. Only once the actual reservation time has elapsed do we give up the table to another customer.

We also employ up-to-the-minute technology to aid the reservationist in servicing customers as best

she can. Our service director actually carries a pocket computer to keep track of vital statistics about regular customers, such as their favorite dishes, their anniversaries and birthdates, what we might have sent out to them as a gift from the kitchen on their last visit so as not to repeat a menu.

The Meal

As soon as you are settled at your table, you are greeted by a waiter or waitress, most of whom have undergone years of training. We try to hire people who share a real passion for food, wine, the restaurant business in general, and the Gotham in particular. This passion is all-important, and we will actually hire an inexperienced wait person if he or she demonstrates genuine enthusiasm.

Because many of our staff members have been with the restaurant for years, there is a real sense of a large team, so the term "family" is really quite appropriate. All of them possess a degree of style, but no pretension. We also try to hire people who have a good intuition for how much attention a customer wants from their wait person, so they can sense whether to converse with the customer, recommending dishes and so forth, or simply to take that person's order and move on. A lot of people, both customers and industry profession-als, have described our service as "invisible," which is harder to achieve than it might sound. Because what might be "invisible" to one person can seem "neglectful" to another.

To ensure that the staff is up to speed, we give them periodic written tests about the food; those who score less than 90 percent are taken off the service floor until they *can* pass the test, which they may take over as soon as the next day. We go to similar lengths to keep the staff educated about the wines we serve, conducting tastings two or three times a week. We also keep a small "library" of wine reference books (actually a dedicated book shelf) in the Gotham office.

Our menu looks like the menu at most restaurants, but there are some distinctions. One is that the dish descriptions are very simple, indicating only ingredients and, sometimes, cooking methods, with no descriptive text. The other is that we *never* run nightly specials. I've never been comfortable "testing" new dishes on our customers; we stick to dishes we know work and only debut new ones when they've been carefully thought out and thoroughly tested.

After you place your order, your waitperson enters it into a computer off to the side of the dining room, and it is then printed downstairs in the kitchen.

In the Kitchen

To the first-time visitor, the Gotham kitchen is a mind-blowing and somewhat intimidating experience. And with good reason. There are fifteen cooks focused on nothing but the dish at hand; burners, ovens, saucepans, and pots emitting steam and flame all over the room, like tiny eruptions that threaten to singe the uninitiated. It's sort of a culinary version of the cave Indiana Jones had to navigate at the beginning of *Raiders of the Lost Ark.*

Another telltale detail of our kitchen is the constant motion: one cook squeezing past another to pull a piece of fish off its flame at just the right moment; another dashing a pinch of salt over some potatoes just as the plate is passed down the line and placed on the serving rack; a line of servers waiting for a table's next course, loading it onto their trays and carrying it at shoulder level up the flight of stairs that leads back up to the dining room. It's a constant shifting of people, equipment, and food that doesn't let up from the beginning of service until late in the evening.

The cooking team is divided into two parts—the hot line and the cold line. When an order arrives, each team gets a copy immediately and begins determining the sequence in which they should prepare the dishes.

The orchestration of the kitchen staff is something to behold. Though there are often more than two hundred people in our dining room, the

Our system varies from the one I learned in France, in which every cook has a very specific task and gets only one day off a week; there's no sense of teamwork at all. At the Gotham, the cooks are all cross-trained so that if we get, say, six orders for sautéed softshell crabs at once, several cooks can pitch in and help. This system also allows for greater flexibility in scheduling, so an employee can take a day off if he or she needs one, and it keeps each person's work from becoming too familiar or tired.

As for the pastry station, most of the production takes place before service, so during service the cooks there are primarily plating desserts. But the ice cream machine runs fourteen hours a day.

The constant maintenance of this system and the dedication of the cooking team are essential to the success of every plate turned out by the kitchen. The effort is reflected in each part of your meal, from the first course to the petits fours that are presented with the check.

At the end of the meal, you are sent off as enthusiastically as you were welcomed, as each staff person you pass wishes you a good afternoon or evening. This isn't just their training; all of us delight in serving everyone who comes into our restaurant, and look forward to entertaining them again.

kitchen is always deadly quiet during service, except for myself or my sous chef of the last ten years, Jacinto Guadarrama. We call orders out to the line, "conducting" the team, and fussing over each plate before it leaves the kitchen. The entire staff keeps the amount of noise in the room to a minimum so that the line cooks can really focus on their work.

Being the chef (or sous chef) is like coaching. As with any leadership role, you want to get the best work out of your people, but to motivate by example rather than intimidation. I favor a supportive, calm tone. If we really get slammed with a rush of orders, I'll add a little urgency to it. Neither I nor any of the line cooks leave the line during service. The entire team stays put, for hours at a time. It's a very intense environment.

2 How to Use This Book

Cooking Like a Chef at Home

This book offers the next best thing to working a day in the kitchen at the Gotham Bar and Grill, which would be a great learning opportunity for anyone interested in cooking, if I do say so myself. (In fact, the actual experience of working at the restaurant has turned out to be just that for a number of the best-known chefs in New York who began their careers at the Gotham.) Though the restaurant is known for its role in New American Cuisine, most of what we do there is actually founded on classic French technique, with a few notable Asian exceptions.

The success of most Gotham dishes comes from our adhering to traditional culinary logic but modernizing and sometimes introducing unexpected flavor variations into that context. A good example of this is the Lobster Gazpacho with Cilantro and Cumin (page 113), which varies a traditional gazpacho, using diced vegetables rather than a puree, and adding lobster and cumin to the mix. This book will teach you how to operate on both sides of this equation, offering many of my more popular contemporary recipes, and explaining the classic traditions on which they are based.

Many of these recipes can be time consuming, but there's simply no shortcut to achieving a certain level of flavor. Additionally, I've tried to select recipes that offer universal lessons, so that the effort of cooking each dish is rewarded two-fold. Many dishes are comprised of several components that constitute an entire main course—meat, poultry, or fish, plus a vegetable and a starch. If time is limited, try cooking just the principal element, such as the Loin of Venison with Rosemary Poached Pears (page 317) without the Root Vegetables and Pumpkin Puree, or the Striped Bass with Champagne Vinaigrette (page 184), saving the Sweet Corn Custard for another time.

In addition, this book will teach you some useful rules to follow in designing a dish, keeping the range of flavors and elements to a minimum while still making the range interesting. With regard to the Squab Salad with Couscous, Currants, and Curry Vinaigrette (page 85), for example, I might point out that while the warm squab complements the flavors of the couscous and currants, the importance of the Apricot-Cherry Chutney in this context cannot be overstated for two reasons: It plays the classic role of offsetting the curry with a cooling effect, and the combination of apricot and cherry adds an uncommonly sweet counterpoint of flavor.

So, imagine yourself at the restaurant at the height of service. As dishes go by, I'll describe them and their preparation or give you thorough instructions for how to adjust each recipe in order to prepare it at home.

Because the average home cook doesn't have the resources or time of a restaurant chef (thirty line cooks, for example), I'll tell you how to simplify each dish. And, because home kitchens are so different from their restaurant counterparts, I have cooked every recipe in this book in a corner of the Gotham's kitchen, which we temporarily adjusted to replicate a home environment.

In addition to addressing the mechanics of how to prepare each dish at home, if a recipe features a component—from a vegetable to a sauce to a custard—I will tell you how to use that component in other dishes and how you might adjust it to work in a different season, or with different ingredients in case some are unavailable.

At the end of the night, I'll send you off with the recipes and notes themselves. I hope that by the time we're through, and you've spent some time reflecting on what we've discussed, you'll be on your way to developing your own repertoire and creating your own signature dishes at home.

In order to make this process as user-friendly as possible, this book is broken down into the following sections:

Chapter Introductions

This book is divided into chapters that cover broad categories of foods—soups and sandwiches, salads and starters, meats, poultry, fish and seafood, and desserts. Each chapter is preceded by an introduction that explains why some of the recipes were selected. The introductions also explain important techniques featured in each chapter, as well as the occasional piece of special equipment you might need. In addition, they include definitions and additional information about key components of the topic (skate, for instance, in the "Fish and Shellfish" chapter), which form the book's informal, intermittent glossary. The chapter introductions are also where I'll share any general thoughts I might have on subjects contained within the chapter recipes, such as ingredients, traditions, or unique cooking methods.

Recipes

This book features approximately 100 dishes, comprised of a total of about 200 recipes. It includes numerous methods for creating vinaigrettes, sauces, and side dishes or accompaniments. I've tried to design it so that each recipe is a valuable learning experience communicating a universal lesson that may be applied to many other dishes. I've also selected dishes that feature highly versatile components, and have supplied notes that will leave you with an understanding of why these components work well together and how you might use some of them in other contexts. (To facilitate this, I've placed the recipes for the more versatile components, such as sauces and vinaigrettes, *after* the recipe for the dish itself. In cases where I feel you are less likely to use the component in another context, such as the Artichoke Sauce in the Salmon with Artichokes *à la Grecque* on page 202, I've left it in the body of the recipe. Principal elements, such as meats, poultry, and fish, are *always* included in the main body of the recipe. An index of "Recipes Within Recipes" is featured on page 373.)

The headnote, or introduction, to each recipe summarizes the lesson you might take from it, which can range from noting an unusual flavor combination to emphasizing a particular technique, to explaining how I first conceived the dish—which might help inspire you to create a dish of your own by demonstrating how a flash of inspiration can be converted into a workable, log-

ical recipe. These introductions also point out ideal seasons, and/or particularly appropriate occasions, in which to serve dishes.

The "Thinking Ahead" section that follows most, but not all, of the headnotes offers options for preparing certain elements of a dish in advance or, in some cases, points out elements (i.e., marinades, braised meats) that *must* be made in advance of the final preparation. (This section does *not* indicate basics that might be kept on hand such as a good chicken stock—called for by many recipes in the book—that can be made ahead and frozen. Nor does it mention items that are commonly made ahead, such as vinaigrettes.) See *"Mise en Place,"* below, for some further thoughts on how to maximize the "Thinking Ahead" information.

Some of the recipes are very long and complex, but if you plan ahead and organize yourself properly, you will find that you can make every recipe in the book. Read each one several times, very closely, until you have a sense of the entire process before you begin.

Mise en Place

The French term *mise en place* ("everything in place") is a concept adhered to in every professional kitchen, from three- and four-star restaurants in New York and Paris, to greasy spoon diners around the world. In order to turn out the number of meals any establishment must generate in the course of a day or evening, it's crucial that as much work as possible be done in advance and kept within arm's reach or just inside a refrigerator door.

If you walk into the Gotham's kitchen at 5 P.M., you'll find a flurry of activity taking place just before service: Fish is scaled and filleted; meat is

let, you should be making sure of the proper doneness and not trying to steam the vegetables, stir the rice, and finish the sauce, all at the same time.

Doing some of the work ahead of time is *not* "cheating." There is nothing wrong, for example, with precooking vegetables and legumes and re-heating them properly. Great restaurants do it every day. *Though seafood, meat, and poultry are always cooked and served immediately, and never reheated.*

It's a myth that everything is cooked *à la minute* (at the last minute).

Trying to finish too many things at the same time will only create inconsistencies and mistakes in cooking temperatures and seasoning. It's simply too difficult to keep your mind on these things if you're also worrying about chopping herbs in time to garnish the dish, or locating the right serving platter when you've got a fish sitting in a hot pan longer than it should. By making these decisions and doing this work ahead of time, cooking can actually be a relaxing, meditative endeavor, rather than a study in stress.

In a home setting, you might also convert your guests into line cooks, assigning such tasks as peel-ing, chopping, stirring, and grilling to friends and family, and making the cooking itself a communal experience. While this obviously would not be ap-propriate for a formal occasion, it can make cook-ing much more fun and add an extra dimension to your socializing. (A rule we enforce when enter-taining *very* good friends: Those who are unwill-ing to cook must clean up.)

Designing Your Own Dishes

Most recipes in this book are followed by one or more supplemental sections, which are intended

trimmed and portioned; vegetables are peeled and blanched; herbs are cut and placed in stainless-steel containers. Pots of water are brought to a boil well before the first pasta order is even placed.

Most of the work in most restaurants happens at the same time most of the work happens in other businesses—during the course of the day. If I'm cooking at home, I look at the work and plan it in a very organized and meticulous way, just as I do at the restaurant. Can I arrange things on plates ahead of time and have them out on the counter? Can things be kept warm? I make a timing list on a piece of paper to organize my schedule.

All home cooks would be well advised to adopt this system in their own kitchens by doing as much of the work as possible before the actual cooking time. When you're cooking, you should be focused completely on how each component is progressing—if you're making a risotto, you should have all of your ingredients in bowls in front of you so you can tend to the stirring and concentrate on how much of the stock has been absorbed by the rice; if you're sautéeing a fish filto empower you to learn as much as possible about a particular dish and how to embellish it, adjust it, or use its components in different settings. This is the most important, most interactive section of the book. These sections will help teach you to think like a chef once you have mastered the basic techniques. They will free you from recipe dependence while revealing the building blocks of dish composition and, I hope, encourage you to improvise. In short, they will allow *you* to control the dish you are creating at home and help you become more adroit and comfortable in the kitchen.

These sections are:

VARIATIONS

These are suggestions on how to vary a dish to accommodate different tastes, occasions, or season and ingredient availability. For example, the **Variations** that accompany the recipe for Farfalle with Prosciutto di Parma, Pea Leaves, and Parmigiano (page 141) suggests substituting arugula for pea leaves, or using sliced mushrooms in addition to, or in place of, the prosciutto. The one that accompanies Seared Tuna with Caponata, Pappardelle, and Red Wine Sauce (page 217) explains how to use the tuna in a salad, or how to toss the caponata with pasta for an easy sauce.

FLAVOR BUILDING

These are suggestions for boosting or augmenting each dish's flavors for maximum impact. It will let you know how to take a dish from the everyday to something truly exceptional. In cases where we have simplified the original restaurant recipe, this section will explain how to reincorporate the elements we have left out.

PRESENTATION

The food at the Gotham Bar and Grill is known

for presentation as much as flavor. But presentation takes time, which is something for which all of us are often at a loss. In hopes of accommodating everyone, I've provided two options for presenting many of the recipes in this book. For those of you who want to really "go for it," the **Gotham Presentation** offers a step-by-step guide to plating the dish the way we do at the restaurant. If, however, you're hosting a more casual dinner, or simply have no interest in an elaborate visual style, I've provided **Everyday Presentation** suggestions for serving many of the dishes "family," or buffet, style. In cases where only one presentation makes sense, there is only one format provided.

Focus on Flavor: A Culinary Philosophy

If you asked me to name the one underlying trait of my cooking, the hub around which my culinary philosophy is centered, it would have to be the respect I have for the flavor and texture of each individual ingredient that comprises a dish. To me, cooking is primarily about flavors—isolating them, maximizing them, and combining them. Although high-quality ingredients often need nothing more than salt and pepper and a quick cooking to unlock their flavor potential, one of the greatest tasks a chef can face is solving the puzzle of how to coax full flavor out of less-savory ingredients. A good example of this is American pork, which isn't as tasty as its Italian counterpart. But if you slow-cook it, and season it with a range of aromatics, its flavor comes to the fore. Take a moment and look at the recipe for Braised Pork Roast with Mustard Spaetzle and Poached Lady Apples (page 309) and you'll see what I mean. Another good example is Confit Tomatoes (page 46), which offers a good method for using fresh tomatoes out of season, because slow roasting amplifies their flavor.

Every ingredient you might use in a dish presents a similar decision. Let's say, for example, that you want to use parsnip as a filling for ravioli. In order for this vegetable to stand out against the noodle that will envelop it and the broth or sauce in which it will be placed, it must be roasted, which amplifies its distinct flavor. The Duck Soup with Turnip and Roasted Parsnip Ravioli (page 108) illustrates this principle.

Some ingredients with very strong flavors offer a similar, but more complicated, decision. Take garlic, for example. Minced, crushed, or sliced, the flavor of garlic can infuse a sauce or a broth with a hearty undercurrent, while slow-roasting garlic cloves, or even a full head of garlic, makes a sweet, mellow, interactive component of a dish, allowing the diner to add whatever amount they desire to each mouthful.

Combining Flavors: Composing a Dish

It's important to understand these principles because how you employ them will make the crucial difference in whether or not your ingredients are used to create maximum impact. The flavors in a dish should be harmonious, either balancing or providing contrast to one another, but they should never be superfluous or jarring. Have you ever eaten a dish and felt that the chef put too many items on the plate? If you had this sensation, you were probably right; if every ingredient were contributing something positive, the thought never would have occurred to you.

Keeping this basic rule in mind will start you on the way to "cooking smart." As you eat in restaurants, or prepare the recipes in this book and others, try to develop your own "taste memory"—the skill of being able to remember a flavor, or combination of flavors, and to be able to conjure them up. When you taste new dishes, try to isolate why you enjoy each one. As you start to recognize your preferences, ideas will simply occur to you—new combinations, or ways to vary a meal you enjoyed in a restaurant. Eventually, you might find inspiration from simply tasting one ingredient and imagining other foods that would accompany it in a new, unusual, *and* logical way.

A Delicate Balance

The dilemma one faces in attempting to create a great dish is to offer enough variety of flavors and textures to avoid boring the palate while keeping the flavors harmonious, creating a balance that prevents any one flavor from dominating the dish. For an example of this principle, take a moment to look at the recipe for Butternut Squash Risotto, Maple-Smoked Bacon, and Sage (page 157). If you read that recipe closely, you'll notice that the instructions very precisely indicate that you should not stir the squash in early, but that you should wait until the last second and then *gently* fold the squash cubes into the risotto. This is to keep the cubes separate so that they *punctuate* the risotto rather than overwhelm it, making each forkfull slightly different. The small bits of smoked bacon, the sweet squash, and the rice (which is perfumed with a delicate spiced butter) all maintain their very distinct identities.

The way the squash punctuates this risotto also offers an example of *pacing,* which many people overlook when thinking about food. Consider for a moment how many elements of a dish are "in flux" when they arrive at the table. If you place cheese on a hot dish, it will melt as the diner eats it. If you "stratify" your ingredients by stacking them, the diner will work his or her way through them, his palate accumulating more and more flavors as he moves along. If you don't understand this point, take a look at the recipe and headnote for Fettuccine, Braised Veal Shanks, and Herbed Ricotta (page 136). Imagine the vast difference in flavors and textures that exists on the plate from when the dish first arrives at the table to the last moments a diner spends with it.

A dish is not a finished piece. There is a "dialogue" that takes place between the diner and the dish. In Loin of Venison with Rosemary Poached Pears, Root Vegetables, and Pumpkin Puree (page 317), for example, the diner is presented with a range of flavors and textures to mix and match as he or she sees fit: sweet, tart pear and red onion marmalade; soft, seasonal pumpkin puree; gamey venison, and a peppery *poivrade* sauce. Because each item is separate on the plate, the diner may alternate varying combinations throughout the meal, which has a lot to do with the overall enjoyment of a dish.

Don't Stray Too Far

A lot of chefs today seem hell-bent on breaking all the rules in order to create something *truly* original, and this has inspired home cooks to follow suit. But we should all accept the fact that you can only be *so* original.

It's important to keep in mind the capacity of your diners to appreciate and enjoy the unfamiliar. Very often, when designing a new dish, I'll try to create a strong link between the flavors, to keep both myself and the diner from feeling disoriented. Roast Lobster with Beet Couscous and

Baby Bok Choy (page 231) offers a prime example of this. That dish—comprised of Asian ingredients—is something of a departure for me, but the components are united by the familiar combination of ginger, scallions, cilantro, and garlic. The original and inventive element in the dish, the beet couscous, is grounded by these traditional surroundings.

Presentation

As for presentation, it can make a tremendous first impression, but it's by far the least important aspect of a dish. (One doesn't, after all, eat with one's eyes.) In fact, the origins of the Gotham style, which has become so well-known, were

based in large part on necessity. For example, in order to keep the cooking time down to facilitate the production of certain fish entrées, we began cutting the fish in half. Rather than placing the two fillet halves on a plate, we stacked them. Similarly, in a restaurant setting, where there's an almost assembly-line process at work, the presentation for which we're known was first employed to compartmentalize and standardize each component of a plate and ensure that every dish was prepared the same way every time. No single element of a dish is left to a cook's individual interpretation, which might open the door to creative chaos, or inconsistency at the least. The truth is that when I cook at home I almost never use elaborate presentations. Because presentation for presentation's sake is not important. Taste is everything.

Where presentation can occasionally play an important role is when you want to make something special out of a simple combination of ingredients, say a combination of tomatoes and basil at their peak of flavor, or give new interest to an old standard. In cases like these, an unexpected plating technique might be enough to make the selection seem inspired. Take a look at the Autumn Salad of Pears, Gorgonzola, and Walnut Vinaigrette (page 88) and note the presentation. It makes a stunning impact.

The plates themselves should be chosen to focus as much attention as possible on the food. The best analogy I can think of is a picture frame. Sometimes an ornate picture frame can bring out additional beauty in a painting. Sometimes a plain wood frame is enough. A good decision-making factor then is the complexity of the food itself: With very few exceptions, simple food can support a more elaborate plate, while more complex presentations are usually best presented against a simple, or solid, background. I've included some photographs in the book that demonstrate how both approaches can be equally stunning.

3 A Few Gotham Basics

White Chicken Stock

Brown Chicken Stock

Double Turkey Stock

Duck Stock

Clam Broth

Fish Stock

Vegetable Stock

How to Chop and Julienne Vegetables

Cleaning and Chopping Fresh Herbs

Notes on Fresh Foie Gras

Confit Tomatoes

Roasted Garlic

Roasted Peppers

Because professional chefs work in supremely stocked professional kitchens, we thrive on being able to experiment with the highest quality ingredients and on being able to select the ideal oil or stock for each dish. We have everything we could possibly desire at our fingertips. But this is not the case for most home cooks. Recognizing the limited pantry size by which most home chefs are constrained, and in hopes of making this book more accessible and practical for you, I've attempted to scale down and reduce the number of complex preparations and esoteric ingredients required to prepare the recipes.

This is especially true of basic ingredients; if I were to suggest that you have on hand the selection of basics that we do, your pantry would overflow. At the Gotham, for example, our stockpot runs twenty-four hours a day, seven days a week. We make squab, lobster, clam, white veal, brown veal, white chicken, brown chicken, venison, and duck stocks. For this book, however, I tested or adapted most of the sauces with relatively fast-cooking chicken stock. But when you need a real viscosity and a greater depth of flavor, my brown chicken stock recipe provides plenty of meat "extract" and a mahogany color. (This "stock" is actually more of a demiglace.) For seafood recipes, I recommend a simple clam stock.

Following are some notes on basic ingredients, all of which should be as carefully considered and chosen as any other component of a dish.

Salt and Pepper

The right amount of salt can make or break a dish. Yet, because of the different types of salt available, and to allow for individual taste, the recipes in this book call for seasoning with salt and pepper "to taste" (a very common instruction). In general, though, I find home cooks rarely cook with enough salt. Most people would be shocked at the amount of salt used in professional kitchens, where we season every component of a dish carefully, and then combine them. A recipe cannot be cooked without salt and then sprinkled with salt at the table—it simply doesn't work. For flavor's sake, I believe that most cooks should experiment with increasing the amount of salt they use for seasoning. Season lightly and carefully, tasting often, until you achieve the right flavor for the dish—the desired effect is a heightened sense of the flavor of the ingredient itself without too much awareness of the flavor of the salt.

I always cook with coarse kosher salt, which is processed without additives and has a purer saline taste than iodized table salt. It is also easier to handle when cooking because its texture facilitates sprinkling. A second choice is *fine* sea salt, available at natural food stores and in many supermar-

kets. (Don't buy the coarse sea salt, unless you own a salt mill.) Both kosher and sea salts taste less salty than iodized, so don't be surprised if you have to use more of them to season your dish. (Approximately 2 teaspoons of kosher or sea salt is equal to 1 teaspoon of table salt.)

Freshly ground pepper, produced with a pepper mill, is the proper pepper for *any* purpose, so you should have a good pepper mill in your kitchen. I use white pepper in most of my dishes to avoid marring the appearance, but I will use black pepper whenever a dish needs the more pungent taste of black peppercorns.

Stocks

If you've never used a homemade stock in your own cooking, try it once and you'll be sold on the merits of planning ahead to always have some on hand.

The one stock I keep at home at all times is a chicken stock, which I store in the freezer. Before freezing, reduce your stock by half so it takes up less space, and reconstitute it by adding an equal amount of water. For a simple preparation, say for cooking vegetables, I will sometimes use a canned low-sodium broth. But for a special dish that depends on the richness and consistency of a reduced stock, enriched by the gelatin released from the bones, it is imperative to use your own.

In many cases, a recipe will yield bones or trimmings that may be used to create a stock to complement that dish. In these instances, I provide instructions to create such a stock, as I do in the recipe for Duck Breast with Chinese Five-Spice Powder and Asian Vegetables (page 260).

Oils

More and more, oils are used not just as cooking mediums, but as condiments in their own right. For the recipes in this book, a selection of basic oils will suffice, though I do occasionally suggest such luxurious ingredients as white truffle oil to finish a dish.

For simplicity's sake, I've kept the suggested range of oils in the book to a minimum.

Canola Oil

This oil has the lightest, most neutral flavor of all the vegetable or seed oils, and can be subjected to very high temperatures without smoking—a valuable attribute in a restaurant kitchen, where many dishes are cooked quickly over a high flame. Canola oil is made from rapeseed, an important Canadian export, and "canola" is a marketing expert's contraction of "Canadian oil."

Olive Oil

I recommend two types throughout the book—regular and extra virgin. Regular olive oil is very versatile. Light-bodied, with a mild olive flavor, it can be used either for sautéing or as the main ingredient in vinaigrettes and mayonnaise. While Italian olive oils have a formidable reputation, there are some good Spanish and French imports, so choose oil based on taste. Extra-virgin olive oil (sometimes called "cold pressed") has more olive impact, and like a fine wine, it varies in taste from maker to maker. Some brands are fruity, some spicy. The distinctive-tasting, expensive estate-bottled oils should be saved for uses where their high quality can be appreciated, such as to dress vegetables.

Nut Oils

Nut oils are made most often from walnuts or hazelnuts. Buy French brands, and store them in the refrigerator after opening, as they turn rancid quickly.

White Truffle Oil

White truffle oil is olive oil flavored with white truffles. This relatively expensive luxury is drizzled over a dish just before serving, so the diner can appreciate its earthy aroma. Since white truffle oil is an investment, try to taste it before buying, or at least get a firm recommendation from a friend or purveyor. Unfortunately, there is often no correlation between price and quality. Freshness, however, is a factor, so purchase white truffle oil where you believe there is a brisk turnover of product. Store it in the refrigerator.

Wine Vinegar

Wine vinegar is available in red or white wine varieties. Superior vinegars are slowly fermented from good wine aged in wood. Supermarket varieties are made quickly and will yield inferior vinaigrettes and sauces, particularly when the vinegar is reduced by boiling. The acidity of the vinegar varies from brand to brand and is indicated on the label, with the better vinegars being the more acidic (6 or 7 percent), so don't be surprised if you have to adjust a recipe's acidity to taste.

Balsamic Vinegar

Balsamic vinegar is available in a wide range of prices and qualities, from moderately priced, factory-made supermarket versions to the handmade, extravagantly expensive, aceto balsamico tradizionale made by traditional Italian methods perfected by artisans around Modena. The classic aceto balsamico ("healthful vinegar") is the result of a long process during which sweet grape juice is aged in successive barrels of oak, chestnut, cherry, locust, ash, mulberry, and juniper. As the juice evaporates and ferments over the years (this can take up to fifty years or more for the finest balsamico), the barrels get smaller, and the vinegar increases in sweetness and picks up the wood flavors. No wonder this lovingly made condiment is often packaged in crystal decanters and garners high prices. It is reserved for special occasions or dishes where just a few drops can go a long way. Fine Italian restaurants will often serve it drizzled over veal chops, for example. Factory-made balsamic vinegar is made from boiled, caramelized grape juice and spends much less time aging in wood. There's nothing wrong with this product, but buy the best one you can afford. If possible, taste and look for a mellow balance between sweet and sour with a hint of wood flavor. The best, and therefore most expensive, balsamic vinegar is available in twenty-five-, fifty- and one hundred-year-old bottlings.

Herbs and Spices

It's reassuring to see major supermarkets offering a large assortment of fresh herbs, which was unusual even five years ago. With the exception of bay leaves, do not use freeze-dried, spice-rack variety herbs; they bear little resemblance to their fresh counterparts. The best way to keep herbs fresh is in Ziploc bags. Chives, basil, and parsley should not be stored wet, so dry them in a salad spinner if they've been recently cleaned. (If you're only using a few leaves, simply pat them dry with paper towels.) I recommend growing herbs in pots on window sills, porches, or sun decks, or—if you're fortunate enough to have one—in a garden. Not only will this give you easy access to herbs, it will also encourage you to experiment. Also, home gardening is extremely economical—you can grow pots of herbs from a bag of seeds that costs just pennies. I've included seed sources on page 375; they are the same sources from which I buy the seeds I use to grow herbs at my weekend home.

Soft-leaved herbs such as parsley, basil, and tarragon, should be stacked and cut into a chiffonade. However you chop or mince herbs, be sure to use a *very* sharp knife so that you don't mash the leaves.

White Chicken Stock

MAKES ABOUT 2 ½ QUARTS

Thinking Ahead: The stock may be prepared up to 4 days in advance, cooled, covered, and refrigerated; or it may be frozen for up to 3 months.

6 pounds chicken bones, coarsely chopped (substitute wings if bones or carcasses are unavailable)

4 quarts cold water, or as needed

1 large onion, chopped

1 small carrot, coarsely chopped

1 small celery rib, coarsely chopped

1 head garlic, halved crosswise

2 sprigs thyme

2 sprigs flat-leaf parsley

1 teaspoon whole black peppercorns

1 dried bay leaf

Place the chicken in a large stockpot, and add the cold water to cover by 2 inches. Bring to a boil over medium-high heat, skimming off any foam that rises to the surface. Add the remaining ingredients. Reduce the heat to low and simmer uncovered gently for at least 6 hours or overnight.

Strain the stock into a large bowl, and cool completely. Skim off and discard the clear yellow fat that rises to the surface. Or, refrigerate the stock until the fat chills, about 4 hours, then scrape it off with a large spoon.

THIS IS THE MOST useful stock to have on hand at all times. See "Chicken Stock Tips" (page 36) for more information.

To make a simple herb sauce, boil 3 cups White Chicken Stock until reduced by half and intensely flavored. Swirl in 2 or 3 tablespoons unsalted butter to enrich the sauce and give it some body. Season with salt and pepper, and add whatever finely chopped herbs you wish.

I specify dried imported bay leaves for this book. I always prefer fresh herbs, but fresh bay leaves are an exception—they have a medicinal flavor that I don't like. (I also use dried oregano for some dishes, as it has a different, somewhat more pronounced Mediterranean flavor than fresh.)

Brown Chicken Stock

MAKES ABOUT 3 CUPS

THIS RECIPE ACTUALLY produces what the French call a *demiglace* (a stock that is highly reduced to create a "half glaze"), but in the Gotham kitchen we refer to it simply as "brown chicken stock." Every serious cook should invest in a large stockpot for recipes like this; It can be made in two 6-quart pots, but the stockpot is most efficient. Even though this recipe yields only 3 cups, the intense flavor of the stock is worth the effort.

Thinking Ahead: The brown stock may be prepared up to 1 week in advance, cooled, covered, and refrigerated; or it may be frozen for up to 3 months.

Special Equipment: a very large stockpot, with at least a 12-quart capacity

10 pounds chicken bones, coarsely chopped (substitute wings if bones and carcasses are unavailable

2 tablespoons canola oil

1 large onion, chopped

1 small carrot, coarsely chopped

1 small celery rib, coarsely chopped

8 quarts water, or as needed

1 head garlic, halved crosswise

2 sprigs thyme

2 sprigs flat-leaf parsley

1 teaspoon whole black peppercorns

1 dried bay leaf

Preheat the oven to 450° F. Place the chicken in 2 large roasting pans. Roast, stirring occasionally, until the chicken is evenly browned, 40 minutes to 1 hour. Halfway through roasting, pour off and discard any accumulated fat.

Meanwhile, heat the oil in a very large stockpot over medium-high heat. Add the onion, carrot, and celery. Cook, stirring often, until golden brown, about 10 minutes. Reduce the heat to medium and continue cooking, stirring often, until very well browned, about 10 minutes.

Transfer the chicken bones to the stockpot. Place the roasting pans on 2 burners on top of the stove over high heat. Add $\frac{1}{2}$ cup of the water to each pan. Bring to a boil, scrape up the browned bits on the bottom of the pan, and pour into the stockpot.

Add enough water to the stockpot to cover the ingredients by 2 inches. Bring to a boil over medium-high heat, skimming off any foam that rises to the surface. Add the garlic, thyme, parsley, peppercorns, and bay leaf. Reduce the heat to low and simmer uncovered gently for 8 to 10 hours, the longer the better. As the stock evaporates, add water to keep the ingredients barely covered. Strain the stock into a large bowl or container, pressing hard on the solids. Let stand for 5 minutes, until the fat rises to the surface. Then skim off and discard the fat.

Clean the pot. Return the strained stock to the pot and bring to a boil over high heat. Boil until the stock reduces to a rich consistency, 1 to 1½ hours, depending on the size of the pot. You should have about 3 cups. Pour the brown stock into the container you plan to store it in (it will gel as it cools) and cool completely.

To transform Brown Chicken Stock into a versatile sauce that goes with just about any poultry, game, or meat dish (and even a few fish entrées), bring the stock to a boil. Remove from the heat, and whisk in some butter to "soften" the flavor (about 1 tablespoon for every ¾ cup sauce). Season with salt and pepper, and if you wish, add chopped herbs of your choice.

You can increase the yield of this recipe by using a technique called *remoullage,* which simmers the strained stock ingredients a second time. Return them to the stockpot, and add enough water to barely cover. Simmer over low heat for 1 hour, strain again, and combine with the first batch of stock. Bring to a boil over high heat and reduce the stock until it reaches a rich consistency, 1½ to 2 hours, depending on the size of the pot. Pour the stock into the container you plan to store it in (it will gel as it cools) and cool completely.

Chicken Stock Tips

Tip: Most stocks include classic seasoning vegetables (chopped garlic, onions, carrots, and celery, called a "mirepoix"), but use them in moderation to allow the flavor of the meat to dominate.

Tip: Caramelize the seasoning vegetables for a brown stock on top of the stove in the stockpot or in a large sauté pan, not in the oven along with the bones. (They give off steam that inhibits browning and soak up fat. The stovetop method allows more control over the caramelizing process.)

Tip: A good stock simmers uncovered for *at least* 6 hours—the longer the better, and if you can manage to simmer a stock overnight, you should definitely do so.

Tip: The chicken parts (wings or backs) should be chopped into large pieces with a heavy cleaver or knife to get a small, more complete extraction of their flavor.

Tip: Always start a white stock with cold water. While bringing the broth to a simmer, skim off the foam that rises to the surface. Be sure most of the foam has stopped rising to the surface (about 20 minutes) before adding the mirepoix and aromatics. This foam is nothing more than proteins being released from the bones, but it should be removed in order to yield a clear stock.

Tip: Purchase a heavy stockpot with at least a 12-quart capacity to make large batches of stock for freezing. (This huge pot will also come in handy for cooking lobsters.) Stock is very easy to make, and making large batches saves time.

Tip: If you don't have the freezer room to store a lot of stock, simply boil the strained batch of stock down until it is reduced by half. Pour the concentrated stock into containers and freeze. Reconstitute the stock with an equal amount of water when cooking with it to return it to its original volume.

Double Turkey Stock

MAKES ABOUT 1 ½ QUARTS

Thinking Ahead: The stock may be prepared up to 3 days in advance, cooled, covered, and refrigerated; or it can be frozen for up to 3 months.

USE THIS STOCK TO ADD depth of flavor to risotto, as well as with the Roast Turkey on page 277. .

3 pounds turkey wings, chopped into 2-inch pieces

2 quarts White Chicken Stock (page 33)

3 cups water, or as needed

½ cup chopped onion

¼ cup chopped celery

¼ cup chopped carrot

3 garlic cloves, peeled and crushed

2 sprigs thyme

2 sprigs flat-leaf parsley

1 teaspoon whole black peppercorns

Place the turkey wings and stock in a large stockpot, and add enough cold water to cover by 2 inches. Bring to a boil over medium-high heat, skimming off any foam that rises to the surface. Add the remaining ingredients. Reduce the heat to low and simmer the stock until well-flavored, 3 to 4 hours.

Strain the stock into a large bowl, and cool completely. Skim off and discard the clear yellow fat that rises to the surface. Or, refrigerate the stock until the fat chills, about 4 hours, then scrape the fat off with a large spoon.

Duck Stock

MAKES ABOUT 1 ½ CUPS

Thinking Ahead: The stock may be prepared up to 4 days in advance, cooled, covered, and refrigerated; or it can be frozen for up to 3 months.

Reserved trimmings, necks, carcasses, wing tips, and giblets (no livers) from 2 Muscovy ducks, including drumsticks

2 tablespoons canola oil

1 small onion, chopped

1 small celery rib, chopped

1 small leek, washed and chopped

1½ cups dry red wine

1½ quarts water, or as needed

1 whole head garlic, halved crosswise

½ teaspoon whole black peppercorns

¼ teaspoon caraway seeds

5 sprigs thyme

2 dried bay leaves

Position the rack in the top third of the oven and preheat to 400° F. Using a heavy cleaver or knife, coarsely chop the neck and carcass. Spread the duck parts in a large roasting pan. Roast, stirring several times, until lightly browned, about 30 to 40 minutes.

Meanwhile, heat the oil in large stockpot over medium heat. Add the onion, celery, and leek. Cook, stirring occasionally, until they're nicely browned, 7 to 10 minutes. Remove from the heat.

Transfer the duck to the stockpot. Discard any fat from the roasting pan. Place the roasting pan on top of the stove over medium-high heat. Add the wine, bring to a boil, and scrape up the browned bits on the bottom of the pan. Pour into the stockpot.

Add enough water to cover the solids by 2 inches. Bring to a boil, skimming off any foam that rises to the surface. Add the garlic, peppercorns, caraway seeds, thyme, and bay leaves. Reduce the heat to low and simmer gently for at least 2¹/₂ hours and up to 6 hours, the longer the better. Add water to the stock if the water level evaporates below the surface of the ingredients.

Strain the stock into a large bowl or container, pressing on the solids to extract all the flavor. Let stand for about 5 minutes, until the fat rises to the surface. Skim off and discard the fat. You should have about 1¹/₂ quarts of stock.

In a medium saucepan, bring the stock to a boil over high heat and cook until it reduces to a rich, syrupy consistency, 20 to 30 minutes. You should have about 1¹/₂ cups. Immediately pour the stock into the container you plan to store it in (the stock will gel as it cools), and cool completely.

Clam **Broth**

MAKES ABOUT 3 CUPS

Thinking Ahead: The broth may be prepared up to 2 days in advance, cooled, covered, and refrigerated; or it may be frozen for up to 3 months.

1 dozen large clams, preferably chowder (quahog)

3 tablespoons vegetable oil

1 cup chopped onion

$1/4$ cup chopped celery

$1/4$ cup chopped leek, white part only

4 garlic cloves, unpeeled and crushed

1 cup dry white wine

1 teaspoon black peppercorns

4 sprigs flat-leaf parsley

1 sprig thyme

$1^1/2$ cups water

Variation: You may substitute 2 dozen cherrystone clams for the chowder clams, since chowder clams are sometimes difficult to find outside of coastal cities. However, it would be a waste to discard the clam meat, so be sure to save it for another use. (You might, for example, combine it with cooled, cooked rice, chopped tomatoes, and basil, and dress it with Lemon Vinaigrette, page 60, for a quick salad.)

Scrub the clams well under cold running water. Discard any clams that feel much heavier than the others (they may be filled with sand), or that remain open after washing.

In a large pot, heat the oil over medium-low heat. Add the onion, celery, leek, and garlic. Cover and cook without browning until the vegetables are soft, about 7 minutes. Add the wine, peppercorns, parsley, and thyme and boil until reduced by half, about 5 minutes. Add the clams and the water, then cover. Cook, shaking the pot occasionally, until the clams open, about 6 minutes. Discard any unopened clams.

Strain the broth into a large bowl or container and cool completely.

Fish **Stock**

MAKES ABOUT 1 ½ QUARTS

Thinking Ahead: The broth may be prepared up to 2 days in advance, cooled, covered, and refrigerated; or it can be frozen for up to 3 months.

2 to 3 pounds assorted fish bones (frames and heads, gills removed by snipping with kitchen shears or scissors) from white-fleshed fish, such as snapper, cod, halibut or flounder

3 tablespoons canola oil

1 cup chopped onion

¼ cup chopped celery

¼ cup chopped leek, white part only

4 garlic cloves, unpeeled and crushed

1 teaspoon black peppercorns

4 sprigs flat-leaf parsley

1 sprig thyme

1 cup dry white wine

1½ quarts water, or as needed

WHILE I LIKE TO USE clam broth in my fish recipes, there is certainly nothing wrong with a good fish stock. I am supplying this recipe just in case you find it easier to obtain fish bones than chowder clams. Fish stock cooks in much less time than other stocks because the bones are more delicate. Don't be tempted to simmer it longer than 30 minutes, or the flavor will become muddled. The real trick to a good fish stock is to rinse the bones well under cold running water to refresh their flavor and remove any traces of blood. Don't use bones from oily-fleshed fish, such as salmon, bluefish, or mackerel.

Using a heavy knife or a cleaver, chop the bones into large pieces. Place them in a large bowl in the sink, and let a thin stream of cold water run into the bowl for 20 minutes. Drain.

In a large pot, heat the oil over medium-low heat. Add the onion, celery, leek, garlic, peppercorns, parsley, and thyme. Cook without browning until soft, about 7 minutes. Add the drained fish bones and cook, stirring occasionally, for 10 minutes. Add the wine, increase the heat to high, and cook until the wine reduces by half, about 5 minutes. Add water to cover the ingredients by 1 inch. Bring to a boil, removing any foam that rises to the surface. Reduce the heat to low and simmer for 30 minutes.

Remove from the heat and let stand for 20 minutes. Strain the broth into a large bowl or container. Cool completely.

Vegetable **Stock**

MAKES ABOUT 2 QUARTS

THIS STOCK IS PROVIDED as a vegetarian option for White Chicken Stock (page 33). If making ahead and freezing, *do not* reduce for easier storage, since boiling negatively affects the flavor.

Thinking Ahead: The stock may be prepared up to 2 days in advance, cooled, covered, and refrigerated; or it can be frozen for up to 3 months.

2 tablespoons olive oil

2 medium onions, thinly sliced

2 medium zucchini, thinly sliced into rounds

2 small leeks, trimmed, split lengthwise, rinsed, and thinly sliced

1 medium fennel bulb, halved and thinly sliced

1 large beefsteak tomato, halved

1 head garlic, halved crosswise

2 large shallots, thinly sliced

Coarse salt to taste

2 quarts cold water

2 sprigs thyme, coarsely chopped

2 sprigs basil, coarsely chopped

2 sprigs flat-leaf parsley, coarsely chopped

Variation: To make a Brown Vegetable Stock, try caramelizing the vegetables in the oil as described in the recipe for Brown Chicken Stock (page 34) and adding 1 tablespoon tomato paste before adding the other ingredients.

In a large saucepan, warm the oil over medium heat. Add the onions, zucchini, leeks, fennel, tomato, garlic, and shallots, and season with salt. Cover and cook without browning until the vegetables are soft, about 10 minutes.

Add the water and bring to a boil over high heat. Reduce to medium-low and simmer, uncovered, for 20 minutes. Add the herbs and simmer for 10 minutes. Remove from the heat and let steep for 10 minutes. Strain the stock into a large bowl or container and cool completely.

How to Chop and Julienne Vegetables

Right, top to bottom:

To julienne bell peppers

1. Halve the peppers and remove the seeds. Lay a pepper half flat, inside up, and remove the ribs with a sharp knife
2. Cut into julienne strips
3. Place the strips in a bowl of ice water to create pepper curls

Left: Plates left to right show vegetables chopped into small, medium, and large dice.

Cleaning and Chopping Fresh Herbs

Rinse the herbs under cold water, if necessary, to remove any dirt or grit. Shake off the excess moisture or spin dry.

For herbs with woody stems, such as rosemary, tarragon, and thyme, strip the leaves from the stems by holding the tip in one hand and running your fingers back down the stem in the other direction. Chop the leaves with a very sharp knife, as dull knives will bruise, not chop, the herbs.

Tender or large-leaved herbs, such as basil, sage, cilantro, parsley, and chervil, should be picked from their tougher stems before chopping. Chives should be gathered up into a bundle, and finely cut.

"Chiffonade" is a term for thin strips of herbs. Large herb leaves, such as basil or sage, are stacked, rolled lengthwise into a cylinder, and cut into very thin ($^1/_{16}$ inch) "ribbons."

Chop herbs as close to when they will be needed as possible. If necessary, store them, covered, in the refrigerator.

Notes on Fresh Foie Gras

French foie gras comes from specially raised ducks and geese, whose entire lives are dedicated to being fed a high-calorie diet that gives them plump livers with an extraordinary texture and flavor. In America, foie gras is mainly produced in the New York Hudson Valley from Moulard ducks, a cross between Muscovy and Pekin. Fine butchers may carry fresh foie gras, or be able to special-order it for you. (To mail-order it yourself, see the sources on page 375.) Ask specifically for fresh foie gras, or you may get canned foie gras terrine or pâté. Fresh foie gras will come vacuum-packed, and if left unopened and refrigerated, should last about ten days.

These duck livers are quite large, weighing about 1½ pounds. Purchase Grade A, the highest grade, which is easier to clean and free of bruises. For a terrine that uses a whole foie gras, the veins should be removed. For the grilled foie gras recipe on page 81 (or other recipes that call for sautéed foie gras), you only need to slice the liver on a slight bias into thick slices with a warm knife.

Let fresh foie gras stand unopened at room temperature for 1 hour before cleaning and deveining. It may crack if you try to work with it while too cold.

Grilled and sautéed dishes require quick cooking at high temperatures to scar the outside while leaving the inside medium-rare. Terrines, however, call for low temperatures. An instant-read thermometer is imperative to check the internal temperature. Any of the deep yellow fat rendered during cooking can be saved. Use it as you would butter, to add a special flavor when cooking savory foods. Covered and refrigerated, it will last two weeks.

To begin, rinse the foie gras and pat it dry with a kitchen towel. To keep the liver from sliding around while you are working with it, place it on the kitchen towel on the work surface. Work gently, trying to keep the lobes as intact as possible.

Carefully pull apart the two lobes (one large and one small). Using a small sharp knife, cut away any extraneous fat and green spots and pull off any membranes.

Starting with the inner side of the small lobe, use your fingers or the edge of a spoon to expose the large vein that runs through the center. Carefully pull it out, using the tip of the knife to help. Remove any smaller veins that branch out from it, as well.

The larger lobe has a more complicated network of veins. Again, locate the large central vein, using the tip of the knife when necessary. Remove it and any attached smaller veins.

Confit Tomatoes

MAKES 16 CONFIT TOMATOES

SLOW-COOKING IS AN effective method of coaxing intense flavor from off-season tomatoes. Plan ahead to use them, since they require several hours to cook. The amount of tomatoes may be adjusted as needed, but I think it's worth making a lot at one time as you will find many uses for them. (Most American chefs would refer to these tomatoes as "oven-roasted." *Confit,* or *confiture,* means to preserve or preserves and, indeed, if these tomatoes were stored in olive oil, they would keep in your refrigerator for weeks. I prefer, however, to use them within a day or two.)

Thinking Ahead: These tomatoes must be allowed to cook for *at least* 8 hours.

8 large tomatoes, peeled, halved horizontally, squeezed gently to remove seeds

2 tablespoons extra-virgin olive oil

1½ teaspoons chopped fresh thyme

3 medium garlic cloves, thinly sliced

Coarse salt and freshly ground white pepper to taste

Preheat the oven to 200° F. Place the tomatoes, cut sides down, on a lightly oiled baking sheet or shallow roasting pan. Brush with the oil, then sprinkle with the thyme, garlic, salt, and pepper. Bake very slowly until they have shrunken to about one half their original size, 8 to 12 hours or overnight. At first the tomatoes will release a lot of liquid, but as they continue to cook and lose their moisture, they will darken and concentrate in flavor. Serve at room temperature, or heated as part of a dish.

For an easy pasta sauce, chop confit tomatoes and toss with spaghetti, chopped basil, and olive oil. Serve hot or at room temperature.

46 Gotham Bar and Grill Cookbook

Roasted Garlic

MAKES 20 ROASTED GARLIC CLOVES

Thinking Ahead: Roasted garlic may be prepared up to 2 days in advance, covered, and refrigerated.

20 large garlic cloves, unpeeled (choose fresh heads of garlic that are firm and not sprouting)

1 tablespoon extra-virgin olive oil

1 tablespoon water

Coarse salt and freshly ground white pepper to taste

SLOW-ROASTING MELLOWS and sweetens the impact of raw garlic and transforms it into a versatile ingredient, allowing cooks to add a subtle wave of garlic flavor to butters, oils, soups, vinaigrettes, and sauces.

Preheat the oven to 325° F. Place the garlic in a small baking dish and toss with the oil, water, salt, and pepper. Cover with aluminum foil and bake until the garlic is tender (squeeze a clove to check), 25 to 35 minutes.

Roasted Garlic Purée is made by pressing the cooked garlic out of its skin into a bowl, and mashing it with a fork. One large head of garlic will yield about 3 tablespoons of puree.

Roasted Peppers

ALL PEPPERS START OUT green, but as they mature, their flavor deepens and they change color to red, orange, yellow, or purple. Roasting mature peppers intensifies their flavor, softens the flesh, and helps loosen the tough skin. Red and yellow peppers are best for roasting; immature green peppers can be bitter.

If using a grill, place the peppers over medium-hot coals, turning them as the skin blackens and blisters, 10 to 15 minutes. Remove immediately to avoid overcooking the flesh. If using a broiler, place the peppers on a rack positioned about 6 inches from the preheated source of heat and turn frequently to blacken all sides. If using a gas burner: Place the peppers on the burner racks directly over the flame and proceed in the same fashion. Adjust the heat if necessary or raise the peppers away from the flame by stacking 2 racks together.

Transfer the roasted peppers to a large bowl and cover tightly with plastic wrap. Let them steam for 10 to 15 minutes. Using a small knife, cut away the stems. Open the peppers up and remove the seeds and membranes. Wipe the work surface clean with a damp towel whenever necessary. Scrape away the charred skin.

4 Starters, Salads, and Small Meals

Gotham Seafood Salad

Hot Smoked Salmon with Corn Cakes and Crème Fraîche

Grilled Salmon and Potato Salad with Black Olive Vinaigrette

Skate with Eggplant Caviar and Citrus Vinaigrette

Red Snapper Seviche

Tuna Tartare with Herb Salad and Ginger Vinaigrette

Smoked Duck Breast with Basmati Rice Salad and Apricot-Cherry Chutney

Duck Salad with Beets, Endive, Arugula, and Walnut Vinaigrette

Duck and Foie Gras Terrine with Lentil Salad and Pickled Cipollini Onions

Grilled Foie Gras with Grilled Mango Salad and Balsamic Vinaigrette

Squab Salad with Couscous, Currants, and Curry Vinaigrette

Autumn Salad of Pears, Gorgonzola, and Walnut Vinaigrette

Asparagus Salad with Beets, New Potatoes, and Mustard Vinaigrette

Endive, Parsley, and Shallot Salad

Creamy Polenta, Chanterelle Mushrooms, and White Truffle Oil

Summer Tomato Salad with Ricotta Salata and Creamy Garlic Vinaigrette

Frisée Salad with Roquefort Croutons and Caesar Vinaigrette

When I go out to eat, I will often order two or three "first course" dishes rather than one appetizer and one main course. In contemporary American restaurants like the Gotham Bar and Grill, first courses offer the greatest opportunity for the chef to experiment, so two or more people sampling a handful of appetizers might enjoy a greater range of flavors (and surprises) than they probably would in the more conventional pairing of a salad and a main course.

In today's restaurants, the definition of what constitutes a "salad" has expanded considerably, so what was traditionally a salad course has become a breeding ground for new ideas, many of them cross-cultural. Even at the Gotham, with its strong Mediterranean orientation, we feature a variety of international influences in our first courses, ranging from a classic French Duck and Foie Gras Terrine with Lentil Salad (page 77) to the Asian-influenced Tuna Tartare with Herb Salad (page 69) to the

French/Indian hybrid, Smoked Duck Breast with Basmati Rice Salad and Apricot-Cherry Chutney (page 73).

But we have stayed true to tradition, as well. We often feature our own interpretations of classic salads, modernizing them with contemporary presentations. For example, the Frisée Salad with Roquefort Croutons and Caesar Vinaigrette (page 98) replaces the traditional Caesar's romaine lettuce with tender, slightly bitter vines of frisée and adds croutons spread with creamy Roquefort, altering the familiar flavor of this standard. Similarly, the Gotham Seafood Salad (page 55) varies a traditional Italian seafood salad by keeping the ingredients separate, so that they maintain their individual colors, textures, and flavors. It also presents them in dramatic, stratified form, making a simple combination of ingredients look very special.

The range of flavors and options that some of these dishes pack into their relatively small scale offers one great advantage to home cooks: In everyday use, many of them, such as the Skate with Eggplant Caviar and Citrus Vinaigrette (page 65), are substantial enough to qualify as a small meal. For those salads that are not, I've offered suggestions on how to augment them to serve this purpose. The Flavor Building note that accompanies the Endive, Parsley, and Shallot Salad (page 93), for example, explains how to add shrimp and/or avocado to render the salad a viable main course.

(On the other hand, if you are serving a three-course meal to guests, be sure that you're sharing the shopping and cooking responsibilities with another person when including one of these more complex salads as part of an evening's menu.)

Drying and Seasoning Greens

I've noticed a few common errors that many home cooks make when preparing salads, and which I thought I would mention here.

In home settings, as well as in many restaurants—often people do not properly dry lettuces. If the leaves are wet, the vinaigrettes that dress them become diluted and the salad tastes thin and watery. You should use a salad spinner to dry greens, but if you don't have one, use the following, very effective method: Place the greens on a large, clean bath towel; gather up the ends; be sure there's nobody standing nearby . . . and whirl the impromptu salad sack over your head. The greens will be spun dry after a minute or two.

I've also noticed that many home cooks do not make their vinaigrettes assertive enough. With the exception of arugula, the greens in this book are sturdy lettuces that can stand up to a thorough cleaning and a flavorful dressing. After they are washed, dried, and well chilled, dress the greens and season them carefully with salt and fresh ground pepper. Then taste. If the salad seems flat, add a dash of vinegar or lemon juice to lift the flavor.

When tasting vinaigrettes on their own, you must keep in mind that they are going to be used to dress another ingredient. Think of a vinaigrette as you would a condiment, mustard for example. If you taste mustard out of the jar, you will find it unbearably strong; much too strong to eat a spoonful of it. But spread out on a ham and cheese sandwich, its flavor registers in proper balance.

Vinaigrettes operate under the same principle. If it makes it easier to appreciate this, taste your vinaigrettes with a component of the dish it will dress . . . a lettuce leaf, an asparagus spear, a piece of shrimp, whatever you can spare.

Herb Salads

A number of the following dishes feature herb salads. While most herb salads served in restaurants are comprised entirely of herbs, I find this to be impractical for two reasons. First of all, the cost is very high, so for home cooks they are especially prohibitive. Second, they're often not palatable because there's nothing to moderate the strong flavor of the herbs. I usually comprise my salads with about half whole herbs and half frisée lettuce, ideally using the small, yellow centers, which contain the most delicate leaves. This ratio makes the salad more palatable and gives it a greater volume so it won't wilt when dressed.

Sherry Vinaigrette: This is the Gotham Bar and Grill's house dressing. In a small bowl, whisk 2 tablespoons aged sherry vinegar and $1^1/_2$ teaspoons Dijon mustard. Gradually whisk in $^1/_2$ cup extra-virgin olive oil until emulsified. Season with salt and pepper. This makes about $^2/_3$ cup dressing, enough for 6 servings.

Gotham Seafood Salad

MAKES 4 SERVINGS

Thinking Ahead: The seafood and dressing may be prepared up to 8 hours in advance, covered, and kept at room temperature. Do not dress the seafood until just before serving, or the acids in the vinaigrette will ruin the flavor and texture of the salad.

BRAISED OCTOPUS

6 cups water

3 cups dry white wine

1 medium onion, chopped

1 medium celery rib, chopped

1 medium leek, white part only, chopped

1 head garlic, halved horizontally

6 sprigs flat-leaf parsley

1 sprig thyme

1 dried bay leaf

1 teaspoon whole black peppercorns

Coarse salt to taste

1 medium (2-pound) octopus, cleaned (see page 235)

In a large pot, bring all the ingredients except the salt and octopus to a boil over high heat. Taste and add salt accordingly. Add the octopus. Place a plate or pie dish that fits into the pot directly over the octopus to keep it submerged. Reduce the heat to low. Simmer, uncovered, until the octopus is tender, 2 to 2½ hours. Remove from the heat and cool in the liquid.

Drain the octopus. Using a clean kitchen towel or paper towels, rub off the skin and remove the suction cups from the octopus. Cut it into ½-inch pieces. Place in a medium bowl.

AT A RESTAURANT THAT'S famous for presentation, this signature dish is one of the most difficult ones to plate correctly. In fact, it's become something of a litmus test for cooks when they are applying for a job and get to the point where they "trail" a shift in the kitchen. Although there are a host of other criteria, if a person can plate this dish correctly by the end of his or her first night, that's usually enough to leave me fairly impressed.

The salad grew out of my frustration with seafood salads at Italian restaurants in New York in which the seafood is dressed well in advance with oil and vinegar, ruining its texture and flavor. In order to highlight the identity of each ingredient in the Gotham Seafood Salad, each is cooked until just underdone and kept separate. Then, just before serving, the ingredients are combined with a simple dressing that keeps all the individual flavors intact. At the Gotham, we use *tako* (steamed octopus), which you might find at a Japanese fish market. If you're lucky

(continued)

enough to find this, by all means use it—otherwise, I've provided a method for braising octopus at home.

This is an example of a simple combination of ingredients elevated by a dramatic presentation.

POACHED SEAFOOD

2^1/$_2$ quarts water

1 tablespoon vinegar, preferably white wine

Coarse salt to taste

6 ounces cleaned squid

1^1/$_4$ pounds sea scallops

1 (1^1/$_4$-pound) live lobster

In a large pot, bring the water and vinegar to a boil over high heat. Add salt to taste, actually tasting the liquid to be sure it has a salty edge. Reduce the heat to medium-low to keep the water at a gentle boil. Add the seafood separately, using a large skimmer or slotted spoon to transfer it to a plate to cool when cooked.

Squid: Cook, uncovered, until opaque, about 1 minute. Cut the body sacs crosswise into ^{1}/$_4$-inch-thick rings. Cut the tentacles in half vertically.

Scallops: Cook, uncovered, until opaque, 2 to 3 minutes. Slice crosswise into ^{1}/$_4$-inch-thick rounds.

Lobster: Cook, covered, until the shell is tinged with red, about 6 minutes. Remove the lobster meat from the tail and claws, and cut into ^{1}/$_4$-inch slices and cubes.

Transfer all the cooked seafood to the bowl of octopus.

ASSEMBLY

Lemon Vinaigrette (recipe on page 60)

1 ripe Hass avocado

1 head baby frisée, washed, dried, and separated into leaves

1 head lolla rossa (curly red-leaf) lettuce, washed, dried, and separated into leaves

1 head red oak-leaf lettuce, washed, dried, and separated into leaves

Coarse salt and freshly ground white pepper to taste

1 tablespoon minced shallot

^{1}/$_4$ cup gently packed basil leaves cut into chiffonade (page 44)

Red and yellow bell pepper julienne (page 43—optional)

4 teaspoons finely chopped fresh flat-leaf parsley leaves

Don't assemble the salads any longer than 10 minutes ahead, or the lemon vinaigrette may affect the texture of the seafood.

Cut the avocado in half vertically. Remove the pit.

Cut avacado in half lengthwise and remove pit with the heel of a knife. Remove skin, then cut again lengthwise to make quarters.

Using a sharp, thin-bladed knife, cut each quarter lengthwise into thin slices about ⅛ inch thick, keeping the slices attached at the top of each quarter.

In a medium bowl, toss the lolla rossa, red oak-leaf lettuce, and frisée with 1½ tablespoons of the lemon vinaigrette. Season with salt and pepper.

Add the remaining vinaigrette, the shallot, basil, red and yellow julienned peppers, and the parsley to the seafood and toss well. Season with salt and pepper.

On 4 chilled dinner plates, arrange fans of the lolla rossa lettuce. Place a tall mound of the seafood salad in the center of each plate.

Fan out the slices of each avocado quarter. Wrap the avocado fan around the seafood salad mound.

Insert a bouquet of the dressed lettuces in the center of each mound.

Everyday Presentation: For informal service, place the dressed seafood on a bed of dressed lettuce and avocado slices in the center of a large chilled plate.

Variations: Substitute 1 pound large shrimp (cooked, peeled, and deveined, then cut into ½-inch dice) for the lobster. At the restaurant, we also add an additional texture and a hint of salinity by flinging some flying fish roe at the side of this salad just before serving.

LEMON VINAIGRETTE

2 tablespoons fresh lemon juice

1 tablespoon red wine vinegar

$^{1}/_{2}$ teaspoon Dijon mustard

$^{2}/_{3}$ cup extra-virgin olive oil

Coarse salt, freshly ground white pepper, and cayenne to taste

In a blender, combine the lemon juice, vinegar, and mustard. With the machine running, gradually add the oil until emulsified. Season with salt, pepper, and a pinch of cayenne.

Hot Smoked Salmon with Corn Cakes and Crème Fraîche

MAKES 4 SERVINGS

Thinking Ahead: The salmon can be smoked, and the vegetable garnish prepared, up to 3 hours in advance, then covered and refrigerated. The corn cakes are best freshly made, but they can be reheated on a baking sheet in a 350° F. oven for 5 to 10 minutes.

SMOKED SALMON

1 cup alderwood or other hardwood chips, soaked in water to cover for 30 minutes, drained, wrapped in foil, the foil pierced in several places (see Sidebar, page 60)

1 pound salmon fillets

Coarse salt and freshly ground white pepper to taste

Build a charcoal fire banked on one side of an outdoor grill. Place a disposable aluminum pan on the other side of the grill and add enough water to come ½ inch up the sides of the pan. Let the coals burn until they are covered with white ash and you can hold your hand over the coals for 3 or 4 seconds (the coals should be medium hot). Place the wood chips packet on the coals and let them begin to smolder. Lightly oil the grill grate.

Season the salmon with salt and pepper, and place it on the grill over the pan. Cover the grill and smoke the salmon until it is barely opaque in the center, about 20 minutes. The heat inside the grill should be about 180° to 225° F. If your grill cover has a thermometer, that's the most efficient, otherwise place an oven thermometer next to the salmon.

Cool the salmon until easy to handle. Using a small sharp knife, peel off and discard the skin. Scrape away the thin layer of grayish fat under the skin. Gently flake the salmon into 1-inch pieces. Cover and refrigerate until ready to use.

THIS DISH LENDS ITSELF to entertaining because all of the components—smoked salmon, lemon vinaigrette, crème fraîche, and corn cakes—may be made ahead of time. The salmon is highlighted by a lemon vinaigrette and then piled on a warm corn cake that contains whole kernels, lending it more texture. This is a popular first course at the Gotham, but it would be a suitable main course for brunch or lunch, as well. You do not need a special smoker for the salmon; it's simple to make in an outdoor grill.

LEMON VINAIGRETTE

1½ tablespoons fresh lemon juice

1½ tablespoons red wine vinegar

½ teaspoon Dijon mustard

6 tablespoons extra-virgin olive oil

Coarse salt and freshly ground white pepper to taste

In a small bowl, whisk together the lemon juice, vinegar, and mustard (or use a hand blender). Gradually whisk in the oil. Season with salt and pepper. Set aside.

CORN CAKES

1½ cups fresh corn kernels (from about 3 ears corn)

Coarse salt

⅓ cup stone-ground yellow cornmeal

⅓ cup all-purpose flour

½ teaspoon baking powder

⅛ teaspoon freshly ground white pepper

⅔ cup heavy cream

2 large egg yolks

2 tablespoons unsalted butter, melted

2 tablespoons finely minced fresh chives

In a pot, cook the corn kernels in boiling salted water over high heat until tender, about 2 minutes. Drain well.

In a medium bowl, whisk together the cornmeal, flour, baking powder, ¼ teaspoon salt, and the pepper. In another bowl, whisk the heavy cream and eggs until combined. Pour into the dry ingredients and stir just until smooth. Stir in the butter, then the corn. Cover and set aside for 30 minutes.

Preheat the oven to 200° F. Lightly oil a 6-inch nonstick sauté pan and heat over medium-high heat. Stir the chives into the batter. Ladle a generous ½ cup of batter into the pan, and tilt the pan so the batter evenly coats the bottom. Cook, adjusting the heat if necessary, until the cake edges are browned, about 3 minutes. Turn the corn cake and continue cooking until the other side is golden brown, about 1½ minutes. Place on a baking sheet and keep warm in the oven. Repeat the procedure with the remaining batter.

While wood chips are widely available at specialty food and hardware stores, I prefer larger wood chunks, or even scraps of hardwood from my wood shop. My favorite woods for hot-smoking salmon are cherry, apple, and oak. I just wrap the unsoaked wood (the larger pieces do not require soaking) in heavy-duty aluminum foil and poke a few holes in the foil. Place the wrapped wood on the edge of the coal bank, and give it a few minutes to start smoldering and smoking.

ASSEMBLY

1 medium red bell pepper, seeded and cut into very fine julienne (page 43), soaked in ice water for 1 hour to crisp and curl, and well drained

2 medium scallions, thinly sliced on the bias

2 red pearl onions or cipollini, thinly sliced into rounds; or 2 tablespoons finely minced red onion

1 tablespoon finely minced fresh chives

1 tablespoon finely chopped shallot

Coarse salt and freshly ground white pepper to taste

1 tablespoon fresh lemon juice, or to taste

3 tablespoons crème fraîche or sour cream, plus more for garnish, at room temperature

8 sprigs cilantro

In a medium bowl, combine the smoked salmon, half the red pepper julienne, half the scallions, half the red pearl onion rings, the chives, and shallot. Add the lemon vinaigrette and fold together gently, breaking up the salmon as little as possible. Season with salt and pepper, adding a little lemon juice if needed to lift the flavor.

Place each warm corn cake on a large dinner plate and spread each corn cake with about 2 teaspoons crème fraîche. Arrange equal portions of the smoked salmon on top. Scatter the remaining red peppers, scallions, and red pearl onion rings over each serving, then garnish with the cilantro and a few random drizzles of crème fraîche.

Flavor Building: Garnish each serving with a spoonful of salmon roe or sevruga caviar. If using sevruga, substitute chervil for the cilantro.

While the salmon is smoking, roast an ear of unhusked corn directly over the coals, turning it occasionally until the husks are blackened on all sides and the kernels are tender, about 20 minutes. Remove the husks and silks, then cut the roast kernels off the cob. Scatter the corn kernels over the plate as an additional garnish.

Grilled Salmon and Potato Salad with Black Olive Vinaigrette

MAKES 4 SERVINGS

THIS RECIPE IS INCLUDED in the book to demonstrate how adding tapenade into a vinaigrette and softening the acidity with stock will yield a versatile sauce for seafood that is both complex in flavor and very dramatic-looking. Tapenade is an olive, anchovy, and caper paste, which has long been synonymous with Mediterranean cuisine.

Thinking Ahead: The potato salad and asparagus can be prepared as much as 3 hours in advance.

POTATO-SHALLOT SALAD

8 ounces creamer or new potatoes

3 tablespoons extra-virgin olive oil

1 tablespoon aged red wine vinegar

2 tablespoons thinly sliced shallot

Coarse salt and freshly ground white pepper to taste

In a pot of boiling salted water, cook the potatoes over high heat until tender when pierced with the tip of a sharp knife, 15 to 20 minutes. Cool in the cooking liquid. Slice into ¼-inch-thick rounds and place in a bowl. Add the oil, vinegar, and shallots and fold gently, so as not to break the potatoes. Season with salt and pepper.

ASSEMBLY

12 asparagus spears, ends trimmed, spears peeled with a vegetable peeler

1 medium Vidalia or red onion, cut into ¼-inch-thick rounds

2 tablespoons olive oil

Coarse salt and freshly ground white pepper to taste

4 (6-ounce) skinless salmon fillets

1 (6-ounce) bunch arugula, tough stems removed, washed, and dried

1 cup Herb Salad (page 69) (optional)

Black Olive Vinaigrette (recipe follows)

In a large saucepan of boiling salted water, cook the asparagus over high heat until just tender, 2 to 3 minutes. Drain, then rinse under cold running water to set the color. Cut each spear in half crosswise.

In an outdoor grill, build a charcoal fire, keeping the coals to one side of the grill. Let the coals burn until covered with white ash.

Brush the onion rings with 1 tablespoon of the oil and season with salt and pepper. Grill the rings, turning once, until lightly browned on both sides, about 8 minutes. Move the onions to the side of the grill opposite the coals to keep warm.

Brush the salmon fillets with the remaining tablespoon of oil and season with salt and pepper. Grill the salmon for about 4 minutes. Turn and continue grilling until the salmon is barely opaque in the center, about 3 minutes. Transfer the salmon and onions to a warmed platter. Cover with foil to keep warm.

In the center of 4 dinner plates, place spoonfuls of the potato salad. Add a few onion rings, then equal amounts of the arugula. Place the salmon fillets on the arugula (the heat of the salmon will wilt the arugula), then top with more onions, the asparagus, and some (optional) herb salad. Spoon 3 tablespoons of Black Olive Vinaigrette over and around the ingredients on each plate and serve remaining vinaigrette on the side.

Variation: To simplify the cooking process, grill the asparagus spears, brushed with oil and seasoned with salt and pepper, with the onions, until tender, about 5 minutes.

Black Olive Vinaigrette

MAKES ABOUT 1 ¼ CUPS

½ cup Clam Broth (page 40) or bottled clam juice

¼ cup fresh lemon juice

¼ cup extra-virgin olive oil

4 tablespoons Tapenade (recipe follows)

2 ripe plum tomatoes, peeled, seeded, and cut into ¼-inch dice

2 tablespoons finely chopped parsley

1 tablespoon finely chopped shallot

1 small garlic clove, finely chopped

Coarse salt and freshly ground white pepper to taste

In a medium bowl, whisk the clam stock and lemon juice. Gradually whisk in the oil until emulsified. Just before serving, stir in the tapenade, tomatoes, parsley, shallot, and garlic. Season with salt and pepper.

Tapenade

MAKES ABOUT ¾ CUP

THIS THICK OLIVE PASTE with anchovies and capers makes a great spread for sandwiches and hors d'oeuvres.

2 whole salt-packed anchovies

1 cup pitted niçoise or kalamata olives

2 teaspoons capers, rinsed

1 teaspoon fresh lemon juice

1 teaspoon Cognac or brandy

1 small garlic clove, minced

Freshly ground white pepper to taste

Place the anchovies in a small bowl and cover with cold water. Let stand for 10 minutes to remove the salt. Drain. Using a small knife, lift the anchovy fillets from their bones.

In a food processor fitted with the metal blade or blender, pulse the anchovy fillets with the remaining ingredients until coarsely chopped. Transfer to a small bowl and mix well. Serve at room temperature.

Salt-packed anchovies are found at Italian and Mediterranean grocers. They are superior to oil-packed canned anchovies. If necessary, substitute 2 oil-packed anchovy fillets for each whole salt-packed anchovy.

Skate **with Eggplant Caviar and Citrus Vinaigrette**

MAKES 4 SERVINGS

Thinking Ahead: The eggplant caviar may be prepared up to 2 hours in advance and kept covered at room temperature.

Eggplant Caviar

MAKES ABOUT 1 1/2 CUPS

2 medium eggplants (2 1/2 pounds total)

2 medium red bell peppers, roasted, seeded, and cut into 1/8-inch dice (see Roasted Peppers, page 48)

2 large garlic cloves, mashed to a paste with a sprinkle of salt

2 tablespoons chopped fresh basil

2 tablespoons fresh lemon juice

2 tablespoons extra-virgin olive oil

Coarse salt and freshly ground white pepper to taste

Position a rack in the center of the oven and preheat to 400° F. Place the eggplants on a baking sheet. Bake until the eggplants are extremely tender, and collapse, 40 to 50 minutes. Cool completely.

Carefully cut open the eggplants and discard as many seeds as possible. Scoop out the tender eggplant flesh and discard the skin. Coarsely chop the eggplant and transfer it to a medium bowl. Stir in the remaining ingredients. Serve at room temperature.

SKATE WINGS AND ASSEMBLY

1/4 cup vegetable oil

4 (6-ounce) skate fillets

Coarse salt and freshly ground white pepper to taste

8 sprigs cilantro

QUICKLY SAUTÉING SKATE wings coaxes out a nutty flavor and crisp texture that is very different from poaching, which requires more skill and effort. I envisioned this dish one summer morning while trying to imagine the most sunny, sensual ingredients possible to accompany this fish on my summer menu. The flesh and juice of lemons and oranges are blended with extra-virgin olive oil to create a creamy, brilliant sauce that complements the fish very well. Drizzled onto a plate, the pale orange citrus vinaigrette creates a stunning visual effect.

This dish knows no season, nor fixed place on the menu. It works equally well as a starter or as an entrée.

THIS CREAMY EGGPLANT salad is made by mashing charred eggplant with olive oil, garlic, and lemon juice to heighten the flavors. Use it to complement a variety of dishes such as Grilled Leg of Lamb with Moroccan Spices (page 302).

In a 12-inch sauté pan, heat the oil until very hot but not smoking. Season the skate on both sides with salt and pepper. In batches, if necessary (or using 2 pans), cook the fish until golden and crispy, about 2 minutes. Turn and cook just until the flesh is opaque in the center, about 30 seconds. Transfer the skate to a plate and cover to keep warm.

On each of 4 dinner plates, place a large spoonful of the eggplant caviar. Set a piece of skate next to the caviar. Spoon the vinaigrette around the plate, then garnish with the cilantro sprigs.

CITRUS VINAIGRETTE

1 small juice orange

1 small lemon

$1/2$ cup extra-virgin olive oil

Coarse salt and freshly ground black pepper to taste

$1/8$ teaspoon cayenne

Using a sharp, thin-bladed knife, cut off and discard the peel and white pith from the orange and lemon. Working over a small bowl to catch the juices, cut between the membranes to remove the orange and lemon segments, placing the segments in the bowl. Squeeze any juice from the membranes into the bowl.

Transfer to a blender and with the machine running, gradually add the oil. Season with salt, pepper, and cayenne.

Variations: To replace the skate, grill some jumbo shrimp in the shell and serve them stacked on individual plates. Or sear jumbo scallops, cooking them quickly until they're just warm inside, and serve 2 or 3 on each plate. These shellfish will work better in this dish than substituting another fish for the skate.

If you'd like to replace the vinaigrette, brown butter is a traditional accompaniment to skate; my own Brown Butter Sauce (page 230) replaces half the butter with cream, increasing the milk solids, and therefore the rich nutty flavor, tenfold. Mix it briefly in the blender (to break down the cream's larger solids), squeeze a fresh lemon into it, and you've created a simple yet intensely flavored sauce. The Brown Butter Sauce makes the sensibility of this dish more French, so replace the cilantro with basil to complete the transformation.

White Port and Ginger Sauce (page 234) is a light, foamy butter sauce that's also easy to prepare. Made with a reduction of white port for a touch of sweetness, it complements the skate. Notice that all of these alternative sauces feature a citrus component. This is an essential ingredient in fish accompaniments because the acidity of the citrus enhances the natural flavor of the fish.

Flavor Building: White Bean Salad (page 155) adds a brilliant third taste and texture to the plate. Add a small herb salad to each plate.

Red Snapper Seviche

MAKES 6 SERVINGS

Thinking Ahead: You *must* marinate the fish for 3 hours.

RED SNAPPER SEVICHE

1 cup fresh orange juice

$1/2$ cup fresh lemon juice

$1/2$ cup fresh lime juice

$1/2$ cup coarsely chopped red onion

$1/2$ cup coarsely chopped red bell pepper

1 fresh hot green chile pepper, such as jalapeño, seeded and sliced into thin rounds

$1^1/2$ teaspoons sweet Hungarian paprika

3 sprigs cilantro

Coarse salt and freshly ground white pepper

$1/8$ teaspoon cayenne

$1^1/2$ pounds red snapper fillets, skin removed, cut across the grain into $1/8$-inch-thick slices

2 tablespoons extra-virgin olive oil

1 ripe medium tomato, peeled, seeded, and chopped into $1/4$-inch dice

IN A SEVICHE, SEAFOOD is "cooked" by the acid of the fruits in which it is marinated, traditionally limes and/or lemons. We depart from convention with the addition of extra-virgin olive oil, which balances the acidity. Don't overmarinate the fish, or it will lose its texture.

It's absolutely imperative that you use freshly squeezed fruits in the marinade. Also, because the marinating vegetables' flavor is depleted, I prefer to garnish the dish with fresh ones.

In a medium, nonreactive bowl, combine the orange, lemon, and lime juices, the red onion, bell and chile peppers, paprika, and cilantro. Taste and be sure the mixture isn't too acidic; if so, balance it with additional orange juice. Season with salt to taste, $1/4$ teaspoon white pepper and the cayenne.

Place the red snapper fillets in a shallow nonreactive dish, pour the marinade over the fish, and cover tightly. Refrigerate, turning the snapper occasionally in the liquid so it marinates evenly, just until the snapper turns opaque and loses its raw look, about 3 hours.

Using a slotted spoon, transfer the snapper to a medium bowl, removing as much of the marinade ingredients as possible. Strain the liquid through a wire sieve into a medium bowl. Discard the vegetables. Gradually whisk in the oil, then stir in the tomato. Season with salt and pepper to taste. Set the dressing aside.

ASSEMBLY

2 medium red bell peppers, cut into $1/4$-inch dice

$1/4$ cup thinly sliced scallion rounds

1 small red onion, finely minced

1 tablespoon chopped fresh cilantro leaves, plus additional whole leaves, for garnish

Coarse salt to taste

Hot red pepper sauce to taste

1 ripe Hass avocado, pitted, peeled, and cut into 6 wedges

1 head baby oak-leaf lettuce, rinsed, dried, and torn into separate leaves

1 head Bibb lettuce, rinsed, dried, and torn into separate leaves

$1/2$ small head radicchio, rinsed, dried, and torn into 1-inch pieces

$1/4$ cup pitted niçoise olives

To the snapper, add the bell peppers, scallions, red onion, and chopped cilantro. Moisten with a few tablespoons of the dressing, taste, and season with salt and the hot pepper sauce to taste.

Using a small sharp knife, cut each of the avocado wedges lengthwise into a thin fan, by keeping the slices attached at the end of each wedge.

On each of 6 dinner plates, place an avocado wedge on the bottom third, pressing gently on the slices to fan them out. Make a bed of lettuce in the center, then top with a portion of the seviche. Spoon the dressing onto the plate, and garnish with cilantro leaves, and niçoise olives.

Variations: Substitute striped bass or scallops for the snapper in this dish.

Tuna Tartare **with Herb Salad and Ginger Vinaigrette**

MAKES 6 SERVINGS

Thinking Ahead: The vinaigrette may be made up to 6 hours in advance and stored at room temperature. If you have enough space in your refrigerator, the cucumbers may be set up on the plates up to 2 hours before serving, wrapped in plastic, and refrigerated.

Special Equipment: $2^1/2$-inch round ($1^1/2$ inches deep) metal entremet ring mold (you'll need six of them if you are arranging individual plates ahead of serving so that the tartare discs hold their shape); citrus zester or channeling tool, for the cucumber; mandoline-type slicer

TUNA TARTARE

1 pound sushi-grade yellowfin tuna, well chilled

6 shiso leaves, cut into very fine chiffonade (page 44)

$1/3$ cup very thinly sliced scallions, white parts only

$1/2$ cup Ginger Vinaigrette (recipe follows)

Coarse salt and freshly ground white pepper to taste

To prepare the tuna, work quickly and think of slicing, not chopping, the delicate tuna. Using a sharp, thin-bladed knife and an impeccably clean cutting board, slice the tuna into $1/4$-inch dice. Cover and refrigerate until ready to use.

Just before serving (otherwise the vinaigrette will "cook" the tuna), mix the tuna, shiso leaves, scallions, and vinaigrette. Season with salt and pepper.

HERB SALAD

1 small head baby frisée, rinsed, dried, and torn into $1^1/2$- to 1-inch pieces

$1/2$ cup gently packed fresh chervil leaves

$1/3$ cup gently packed fresh flat-leaf parsley leaves

$1/3$ cup gently packed fresh cilantro leaves

TUNA TARTARE HAS experienced something of a renaissance in contemporary American restaurants; most destination establishments offer some version of this dish. Many of the recipes call for the tuna to be ground up or chopped with a heavy knife, which, I find, distorts the tuna's unique texture. In this recipe, we cut the fish into small dice, giving it a greater presence when combined with the highly seasoned vinaigrette. Shiso leaf gives this dish its distinct flavor, but it may be difficult to find. (See page 375 for seed source.) It may be grown easily in a window sill and will sprout in a few weeks. When combined with the herb salad and cool cucumber, ginger, and lime juice, the ingredients achieve a pleasing balance.

3 tablespoons Ginger Vinaigrette (recipe follows)

Coarse salt and freshly ground pepper to taste

Just before serving, toss the frisée and herbs with the vinaigrette, and season with salt and pepper.

ASSEMBLY

1 large seedless cucumber, unpeeled, elongated ends trimmed off

18 Croutons (see Sidebar, page 114), made from baguette slices cut on an extreme bias

Place the ring mold in the center of a chilled large dinner plate. Using the channel tool, remove strips of peel about ½ inch apart down the entire length of the cucumber, working around the circumference. Using a mandoline (or a very sharp knife and a steady hand), cut the cucumber into paper thin slices. Using the outside edge of the mold as a guide, make a ring of overlapping cucumber slices.

Spoon the tuna tartare into the mold, pressing it down lightly. Stand 3 croutons into the top of the tuna tartare. Pile the dressed salad into the center of the croutons. Carefully lift the ring mold up and off of the plate. Repeat with the remaining ingredients and plates.

Metal entremet ring molds are available at many kitchenware shops and by mail order (see Mail Order Sources, page 375). You can also make your own by removing the top and bottom from a 6-ounce can (such as a tuna can).

Everyday Presentation: This dramatic-looking dish is one of Gotham's most popular, so I am hesitant to change it too much. However, one could mound the tuna tartare on cucumber slices in the center of chilled plates, and arrange the salad and croutons alongside.

Variations: Shiso leaves are available at Japanese food stores and many produce markets. Their distinctive taste has a refreshing, citruslike flavor. If you can't find them, basil may be substituted.

At Gotham, we use chervil, chives, parsley, and cilantro in the Herb Salad. You may use any greens and herbs you prefer. For example, if you have trouble locating chervil, double the amounts of cilantro and parsley. Radish sprouts make an interesting addition.

Ginger Vinaigrette

MAKES ABOUT 1 ¼ CUPS

LIME JUICE AND GINGER lend this vinaigrette an Asian character.

¹⁄₃ cup fresh lime juice

3 tablespoons fresh ginger juice (see ingredients list, page 140)

¹⁄₈ teaspoon hot red pepper sauce, such as Tabasco

³⁄₄ cup plus 2 tablespoons grapeseed or canola oil

1 tablespoon finely minced shallot

1 garlic clove, minced and mashed to a paste with a sprinkle of salt

Coarse salt and freshly ground white pepper to taste

In a medium bowl, whisk together the lime juice, ginger juice, and hot pepper sauce. Gradually whisk in the oil until the vinaigrette has emulsified. Whisk in the shallot and garlic. Season with salt and pepper. Add additional lime juice or oil to balance the dressing, if needed.

Smoked Duck **Breast with**
Basmati Rice Salad and Apricot-Cherry Chutney

MAKES 8 SERVINGS

Thinking Ahead: The chutney may be prepared up to 1 week in
advance and refrigerated. The Basmati Rice Salad may be prepared
up to 1 hour in advance and stored at room temperature. The duck
may be prepared as much as a day in advance.

4 (12-ounce) boneless Moulard duck breasts or magrets

Coarse salt and freshly ground white pepper

1 cup applewood chips, soaked for 30 minutes in cold water to cover,
   drained, wrapped in foil, the foil pierced in several places (see Sidebar,
   page 60)

2 bunches arugula, tough stems removed, torn into 1-inch pieces

1 bunch baby red oak-leaf lettuce, washed, dried, and torn into separate
   leaves

2/3 cup Lemon Vinaigrette (page 60)

1 recipe Basmati Rice Salad (page 304)

1 cup Apricot-Cherry Chutney (recipe follows)

Using a sharp boning knife, trim away the skin and most of the fat
from each breast, leaving a 1/4-inch layer of fat. Score the fat lightly in
a crosshatch pattern, being careful not to cut into the meat. Season
with salt and pepper.

Build a charcoal fire banked on one side of an outdoor grill. Place
an empty disposable aluminum pan on the other side of the grill and
add enough water to come 1/2 inch up the sides of the pan. Let the
coals burn until they are covered with white ash and you can hold
your hand over them for 3 to 4 seconds (the coals should be medium-
hot). Place the wood-chip packet on the coals and let the wood begin to smolder. Lightly oil the grill grate.

Place the duck breasts on the grill over the pan. Cover and cook
until the duck is medium-rare, about 20 minutes. The heat inside the
grill should be 225° to 250° F. If your grill cover has a thermometer,
that's the most efficient way to gauge the heat, otherwise place an

YEARS AGO, LEAFING
through a used book of old
American recipes, I
discovered a pamphlet, left
behind by the original owner,
for the "Little Chief," a
combination cooker-smoker
sold at a staggeringly low
price. Though the pamphlet
was yellowed with age, I
dialed the telephone number
it offered . . . and was
pleasantly surprised when a
woman answered the phone.
I ordered one, and was
amazed to discover how well
it smoked duck breast. To
this day, we use the "Little
Chief" at the Gotham to
make this dish.

The Apricot-Cherry
Chutney unifies the elements
of this dish; its thick
sweetness underscores the
tart Basmati Rice Salad and
the rich, smokey duck
breast. By taking bites of
duck first with one, then the
other of these elements, this
starter achieves a unique
"rhythm."

oven thermometer next to the duck. Cool the duck completely. If cooking in advance, cover and refrigerate until ready to serve.

In a large bowl, toss the arugula and lettuce with the vinaigrette and season with salt and pepper.

Slice the duck on the bias into ⅛-inch-thick slices. On the bottom of each dinner plate, arrange overlapping slices of duck breast in a fan pattern. Garnish the plates with equal portions of rice salad, green salad, and some of the chutney.

Apricot-Cherry Chutney

MAKES ABOUT 2½ CUPS

⅓ cup distilled white vinegar

1 tablespoon chopped fresh ginger

1 large garlic clove, coarsely chopped

1½ cups (8 ounces) dried apricots, cut into ½-inch-thick slices

½ cup (3 ounces) dried sour cherries

½ cup (3 ounces) golden raisins

¾ cup plus 2 tablespoons sugar

⅛ teaspoon cayenne, or to taste

¼ teaspoon coarse salt

Approximately 2 cups water, or as needed

MANY CHUTNEYS ARE made with fresh or underripe fruits; by using dried fruits, this sweet and spicy condiment becomes viable year-round.

In a blender, combine the vinegar, ginger, and garlic and pulse until the solids are almost pureed. Pour into a nonreactive, heavy-bottomed medium saucepan. Add the remaining ingredients (except the water) and pour in enough water barely to cover. Stir well.

Bring to a simmer over medium-low heat, stirring often to dissolve the sugar. Cook slowly, stirring often to avoid scorching, until the chutney thickens and the liquid is syrupy, 45 minutes to 1 hour. Cool completely before serving.

Duck Salad with Beets, Endive, Arugula, and Walnut Vinaigrette

MAKES 4 SERVINGS

Special Equipment: mandoline

DUCK LEGS

4 duck leg-and-thigh quarters

Coarse salt and freshly ground white pepper

Season the duck quarters with salt and pepper. Place them, skin side down, in a 12-inch sauté pan. Put the sauté pan on the stove and turn the heat to medium-high. Cook, rendering the fat and crisping and browning the skin, 8 to 10 minutes. Turn and cook until medium (the duck is slightly pink when pierced at the bone), another 8 to 10 minutes.

Let the duck rest for 10 minutes. Discard the bones. Cut the meat into thin slices.

ASSEMBLY

4 small beets (about 12 ounces total)

1 head Belgian endive, cored and separated into individual leaves

1 bunch watercress, rinsed, dried, and tough stems removed

1 bunch arugula, rinsed, dried, and tough stems removed

1 small head radicchio, torn into 1-inch pieces

$1/4$ cup walnut pieces, toasted (see Sidebar, page 351)

$1/2$ cup Walnut Vinaigrette (recipe follows)

Coarse salt and freshly ground white pepper to taste

In a pot of boiling salted water, cook the beets over high heat until just tender, 10 to 15 minutes. Drain, and when cool enough to handle, peel. Using a mandoline-type slicer, cut the beets into $1/8$-inch rounds. Set aside.

IF YOU READ ENOUGH cookbooks, you'll no doubt notice that when a recipe calls for duck breast, the author will often instruct the reader to "set aside the rest of the duck for another use." Having read hundreds of cookbooks, and encountered very few uses for duck legs, it seemed my civic duty to include a recipe for them here. If you find cooking an entire duck to be a daunting prospect, you might be surprised to learn just how simple it is to sauté duck legs. I first made this dish for Julia Child's eightieth birthday party, as part of a collaborative meal designed by a group of chefs. Though the original was adorned with such touches as croutons spread with foie gras, this simpler version promises a shorter path to pleasure. The beets—which should be sliced paper-thin with a mandoline—provide a sweetness that serves as a counterpoint to the duck.

In a bowl, toss the greens and walnuts with the vinaigrette. Season with salt and pepper.

On 4 chilled dinner plates, arrange equal amounts of the beets, overlapping the rounds in a tight circle. Place the dressed greens in the center, and top with the sliced duck.

Variations: You may augment this salad with the use of thin or crisp croutons (see Sidebar, page 114) spread with Foie Gras Terrine (page 77) or a Roquefort cheese mixture (page 98). Also, while this dish was designed to be made with duck legs, breasts would be excellent as well. See cooking instructions on page 264.

Add Asian flavor to this salad by sprinkling the duck with 2 teaspoons five-spice powder before cooking. Substitute Curry Vinaigrette (page 87) for the Walnut Vinaigrette and toasted walnuts, and garnish with cilantro sprigs and thinly sliced scallion.

Try this salad with sliced lamb instead of the duck.

Walnut Vinaigrette

MAKES ABOUT 1 CUP

THIS VINAIGRETTE SHOULD be made with a high-quality French walnut oil. After opening the bottle, store it in the refrigerator.

3 tablespoons red wine vinegar

2 teaspoons Dijon mustard

3/4 cup plus 2 tablespoons imported walnut oil

Coarse salt and freshly ground white pepper to taste

In a medium bowl, whisk the vinegar and mustard until combined. Gradually whisk in the walnut oil until emulsified. Season with salt and pepper. Cover and refrigerate until ready to use. Whisk well before using.

Duck and Foie Gras Terrine with
Lentil Salad and Pickled Cipollini Onions

MAKES 16 SERVINGS

Thinking Ahead: At least 4 days before serving, marinate the forcemeat ingredients and season the foie gras. On the third day, prepare and cook the terrine. Refrigerate the cooked terrine at least 24 hours before serving. The lentil salad may be prepared as much as 4 hours before serving. The cipollini onions may be prepared as much as 2 weeks in advance and kept covered, in your refrigerator.

Special Equipment: large ($11^1/2$-x-$3^1/2$-x-$2^1/2$ inch) ceramic or enameled cast-iron terrine mold (do not use an uncoated metal mold); parchment paper; plastic wrap; large roasting pan to hold the terrine mold; an instant-read thermometer; 3 pieces of thick cardboard cut to fit the inside of the terrine, stacked, and wrapped together with a double thickness of plastic wrap; 3-pound weight, or its equivalent

TERRINE FORCEMEAT

8 ounces boneless, skinless duck meat (either breast or leg), cut into $1/4$-inch cubes

6 ounces boneless pork shoulder, cut into $1/4$ inch cubes

3 ounces pork fatback, cut into $1/4$-inch cubes

4 ounces chicken or duck (not foie gras) livers

$1^1/2$ teaspoons iodized (not coarse) salt

$1/2$ teaspoon ground white pepper

$1/4$ teaspoon sugar

1 tablespoon ruby port

1 tablespoon Cognac, Armagnac, or brandy

$1^1/2$ teaspoons minced shallot

1 small garlic clove, minced

In a small bowl, place half of the cubed duck. In a separate, medium bowl, combine the remaining duck with the pork and pork fat. In a third small bowl, place the chicken livers.

MOST PEOPLE DON'T MAKE terrine at home because a proper terrine is difficult to execute; there's a sensitivity to cooking and judging it correctly that isn't easily learned from a book, though entire books *have* been devoted to teaching this craft. During my early career, I picked up a lot of theory and practical experience that helped me come up with this terrine. Some of the more crucial rules to follow include keeping all of the ingredients cold during the preparation stage; otherwise, the texture will be lost. Also, the marination of the meats is of utmost importance—they should, in fact, be marinated for 36 hours.

This recipe makes a large terrine for up to 16 servings, but even if you are serving fewer, make the whole terrine (but adjust the lentil salad), since the recipe doesn't divide easily or well. The terrine keeps well and may be frozen.

You will need a large ceramic or enameled cast-iron terrine mold for this dish. These are available at specialty kitchenware stores.

(continued)

It is important to use a thick porcelain or enameled iron mold as these heavy materials will insulate the terrine, and foie gras needs gentle cooking. Also, an uncoated metal mold would react with the foie gras, and give it a metallic taste.

Like many foods, terrines have undergone an evolution. While they were originally made exclusively from spiced, ground meats, using the trim and by-products of more expensive cuts, chefs today have applied the concept to create a number of modern interpretations, such as seafood terrines, goat cheese terrines, vegetable terrines, and countless other varieties. I myself must have experimented with close to 20 different terrines.

The terrine offered here is unique—2 parts duck layered with 1 part foie gras. I hit on this structure after much experimentation and discovered that, although their consistencies and cooking times are different, the duck forcemeat moderates the heat that reaches the foie gras, cooking it perfectly. This one is accompanied by an earthy lentil salad and port-pickled cippolini that contribute sweetness and acidity to the plate. For a true indulgence, serve this with a glass of sauterne.

Combine the salt, pepper, and sugar. Season the ingredients in the 3 separate bowls evenly with the salt mixture, and then 1 teaspoon each port and Cognac. Combine the duck-pork mixture with the shallot and garlic. Gently toss the ingredients in each bowl, cover tightly with plastic wrap, and refrigerate overnight.

FOIE GRAS

$1\frac{1}{2}$ pounds Grade A foie gras, cleaned (see page 45)

1 teaspoon iodized (not coarse) salt

$\frac{1}{4}$ teaspoon ground white pepper

$\frac{1}{8}$ teaspoon sugar

1 tablespoon Cognac, Armagnac, or brandy

Place the foie gras in a glass or enameled dish (a glass loaf pan works well). Combine the salt, pepper, and sugar and season the foie gras all over with this mixture. Sprinkle with the Cognac, turning the foie gras to coat completely. Cover tightly with plastic wrap and refrigerate overnight.

ASSEMBLY

$\frac{1}{2}$ cup ($\frac{1}{2}$ ounce) dried black trumpet mushrooms (*trompettes de mort*)

$\frac{1}{2}$ cup hot water

1 large egg, beaten

$\frac{1}{3}$ cup shelled pistachios

1 tablespoon vegetable oil

2 teaspoons green peppercorns in brine, drained and rinsed

Softened unsalted butter, for the mold

Position a rack in the center of the oven and preheat to 400° F.

In a small bowl, soak the mushrooms in the hot water until they're softened, about 30 minutes. Lift the mushrooms out of the water and rinse them under cold water to be sure all grit is removed. Decant 1 tablespoon of the soaking liquid to a small bowl, being careful not to disturb the grit at the bottom. Add the egg and beat together.

Bring a small saucepan of water to a boil over high heat. Add the pistachios and boil for 3 minutes. Drain and rinse under cold water. Wrap the blanched pistachios in a clean kitchen towel and rub to remove the skins. Set the peeled pistachios aside.

In a medium saucepan, heat the oil over high heat. Add the marinated chicken livers and sauté quickly until seared on all sides, about 2 minutes. Transfer to the bowl with the duck and pork combination.

In a food processor fitted with the metal blade, process the duck/pork/liver combination one third at a time until finely chopped. Transfer the forcemeat to a bowl. Add the cubed duck, soaked mushrooms, pistachios, green peppercorns, and the egg mixture and mix well.

Lightly butter the terrine mold. (This will allow the parchment paper to stick to the mold.) Line the bottom and sides of the mold with strips of parchment paper cut to fit the mold, allowing about a 2-inch overhang on all sides.

Spread half the forcemeat in the prepared mold. Arrange the foie gras in the terrine, fitting and pressing it together to create a tight, even layer. (This is easiest to do by placing the large lobe, smooth side down, in the mold, and fitting the smaller lobe, smooth side up, over the large lobe. Fill in any gaps with smaller pieces of foie gras.) Spread the remaining forcemeat in the mold, smoothing the top. The terrine will fill the entire mold or maybe slightly higher, but don't be concerned. Fold the parchment paper over the top of the terrine to cover. Tightly wrap the entire terrine with a triple thickness of plastic wrap. Don't worry, the plastic wrap will not melt in the oven.

Place the terrine in the roasting pan and set it on the oven rack. Bake for 10 minutes. Pour enough hot water into the roasting pan to come about 1/2 inch up the sides of the mold. Reduce the oven temperature to 300° F. Bake until an instant-read thermometer inserted in the center of the terrine (go right through the plastic wrap) reads 126° F. This should take about 45 minutes.

Remove the mold from the roasting pan and pour out the water. Place the mold back in the roasting pan. Let stand at room temperature until slightly cooled, about 1 hour.

Remove plastic wrap from the terrine and place the terrine on a baking sheet. Place the wrapped cardboard over the top of the cooked terrine, and place the weight on top (you can use 3 or 4 cans of food) to evenly weigh down the terrine. Clear a space in the refrigerator to hold the weighted terrine and refrigerate overnight.

SERVING

2 heads red oak-leaf lettuce, washed and dried

2 heads lolla rossa (curly red-leaf) lettuce, washed and dried

2 heads frisée, washed and dried

Legume salads tend to soak up vinaigrettes as they stand. Always taste them before serving, and season with additional vinegar and oil (here, red wine vinegar and walnut oil), salt and pepper as needed.

Pickled Cipollini Onions with Port and Balsamic Vinegar: Combine in a medium saucepan 16 peeled cipollini or white boiling onions (about 1 pound), 1 cup balsamic vinegar, 2/3 cup ruby port, 1/3 cup distilled white vinegar, 1 1/2 teaspoons sugar, 1 teaspoon coarse salt, 1 teaspoon whole black peppercorns, and 2 whole allspice. Bring to a boil over high heat, and boil for 1 minute. Pour into a sterilized 1-quart canning jar and close tightly. Cool to room temperature. Refrigerate at least 1 day before serving.

¾ cup Walnut Vinaigrette (page 76), or as needed

Coarse salt and freshly ground white pepper to taste

Lentil Salad (recipe follows)

Pickled Cipollini Onions with Port and Balsamic Vinegar (see Sidebar, page 79)

Croutons (see Sidebar, page 114)

Scrape off any chilled yellow fat that has been pressed out of the terrine. Carefully run a sharp knife around the inside of the mold to release the terrine. Turn out the terrine onto a cutting board, and remove the parchment paper. Let stand at room temperature for 30 minutes before serving. To slice, use a thin-bladed sharp knife rinsed in hot water between slices.

In a large bowl, combine the greens, toss them with the vinaigrette, and season with salt and pepper.

To serve, place a slice of the terrine on a dinner plate. Add a spoonful of the lentil salad, a couple of the drained pickled onions, and some dressed greens. Pass the croutons on the side.

Lentil Salad

MAKES ABOUT 3½ CUPS

WHILE THIS SALAD works well with the foie gras terrine, it can stand on its own on a buffet table or at a picnic.

1 pound green lentils de Puy or small brown lentils

6 cups water

2 cups White Chicken Stock (page 33)

1 small onion, peeled and halved

4 small garlic cloves, peeled and crushed under a knife

1 medium carrot, finely chopped

1 medium celery rib, finely chopped

½ cup cornichons (small sour pickles) or tiny dill pickles, finely chopped

¼ cup finely chopped shallots

1½ cups Walnut Vinaigrette (page 76)

Coarse salt and freshly ground pepper to taste

2 tablespoons finely chopped fresh flat-leaf parsley

In a large bowl, soak the lentils in enough cold water to cover by 2 inches for 30 minutes. Drain well.

In a large saucepan, combine the lentils, measured water, stock, onion, and garlic, adding more water if needed to cover the lentils by 1 inch. Bring to a boil over high heat. Reduce the heat to low and simmer just until tender, about 30 minutes. Drain the lentils, discarding the onion halves and garlic cloves.

Transfer the lentils to a large bowl. Add the carrot, celery, cornichons, and shallots. Dress with the vinaigrette and season with salt and pepper. Let stand for 1 hour before serving. Taste, and check the seasonings—you may need to add a little more vinegar to lift the flavor. Just before serving, add the parsley.

Grilled Foie Gras **with**
Grilled Mango Salad and Balsamic Vinaigrette

MAKES 6 SERVINGS

Thinking Ahead: Make the balsamic vinegar glaze up to 1 day in advance and keep, covered, in the refrigerator.

³/₄ cup balsamic vinegar

3 ripe mangoes, peeled, halved, and pitted

2 teaspoons canola oil

Coarse salt and freshly ground white pepper

1¹/₂ pounds Grade A foie gras, cleaned (page 45), and cut crosswise into slices about ¹/₂ inch thick (keep refrigerated after slicing)

1 head baby red oak-leaf lettuce, washed, dried, and separated into leaves

1 head baby green-leaf lettuce, rinsed, dried, and torn into separate leaves

1 head baby frisée, rinsed, dried, and torn into separate leaves

¹/₂ small head radicchio, rinsed, dried, and torn into 1-inch pieces

Balsamic Vinaigrette (recipe follows)

To make the balsamic glaze, boil the balsamic vinegar in a small, nonreactive saucepan until thickened to a syrup, about 3 tablespoons. (This should take about 15 minutes.) Set aside at room temperature.

Build a charcoal fire banked on one side of an outdoor grill and let the coals burn until they are covered with white ash. Lightly oil the grill grate.

Brush the mangoes with the canola oil. Season lightly with salt and pepper. Grill, turning once, until lightly browned on both sides, about 3 minutes. Transfer to the other side of the grill, opposite the coals.

GRILLING FOIE GRAS CAN be a tricky business. Because of its high fat content, it will flare up almost at once, so you should only grill as many slices as you can comfortably handle at one time. After quickly searing them, move them to the side of the grill, away from the coals, to keep them warm.

Warm foie gras with grilled mango is a combination you must experience. The richness of the foie gras is tempered by the extreme sweetness of the fruit. I garnish this combination with a dramatic drizzle of balsamic vinegar glaze.

Season the foie gras slices with salt and pepper. Working quickly, sear the foie gras slices, a few at a time, directly over the coals for about 1 minute. (The fat will drip and cause flare-ups, so be careful. Have a spray bottle filled with water nearby to extinguish the flames, if necessary—but avoid spraying the foie gras.) Using a spatula, turn the foie gras, and cook on the other side until seared and the edges are browned, about 1 more minute. As they are cooked, move the foie gras slices to the other side of the grill, opposite the coals, where they will stay warm while you sear the remaining slices.

Remove the mangoes to a cutting board and cut lengthwise into thin slices.

Toss the lettuces, frisée, and radicchio with the balsamic vinaigrette, and season with salt and pepper to taste.

On each plate, fan out the mango slices, and top with 2 or 3 slices of grilled foie gras. Garnish with a bouquet of the dressed greens, and drizzle with a spoonful of the balsamic glaze.

Variations: Other seasonal fruits may be substituted for the mangoes. Use halved peaches, nectarines, or figs in the summer, or peeled, halved pears in the cooler months.

If you are fortunate enough to have a bottle of fine, aceto balsamico vinegar (I use a 50-year old vinegar, saved for special dishes like this), use it to drizzle each serving instead of the reduced balsamic vinegar glaze.

Balsamic Vinaigrette

MAKES ABOUT ³/₄ CUP

¼ cup high-quality balsamic vinegar

¼ teaspoon Dijon mustard

½ cup extra-virgin olive oil

Coarse salt and freshly ground white pepper to taste

In a small bowl, whisk together the vinegar and mustard. Gradually whisk in the oil until emulsified. Season with salt and pepper.

IF YOU ARE USING A modest balsamic vinegar that seems a bit sharp, you may have to adjust the amounts of the other ingredients to balance the vinaigrette.

Squab Salad **with**
Couscous, Currants, and Curry Vinaigrette

MAKES 4 SERVINGS

Thinking Ahead: The couscous may be prepared up to 2 hours in advance.

COUSCOUS

^{1}/$_3$ cup plus 1 tablespoon water

^{1}/$_3$ cup plus 1 tablespoon White Chicken Stock (page 33)

1 tablespoon unsalted butter

Coarse salt and freshly ground white pepper

1 cup quick-cooking couscous

^{1}/$_4$ cup dried currants

^{1}/$_4$ cup Curry Vinaigrette (recipe follows)

^{1}/$_8$ teaspoon harissa (see Sidebar, page 86)

2 scallions, finely cut on the bias

In a medium saucepan, bring the water, stock, butter, and 1 teaspoon salt to a boil over high heat. Place the couscous and currants in a medium bowl, add the hot stock and stir. Cover tightly with plastic wrap and let stand until the couscous absorbs the liquid, 7 to 10 minutes. Fluff the couscous with a fork.

In a medium bowl, combine the vinaigrette and harissa. Add to the couscous, along with the scallions. Toss well, and season with salt and pepper. Hold at room temperature.

SQUAB

2 tablespoons vegetable oil

2 (18-ounce) squab, backbones removed, each cut into breast and leg portions, breastbones removed

Coarse salt and freshly ground pepper

1 tablespoon unsalted butter

THIS DISH WAS CREATED in 1986, but it still feels new and different to Gotham customers today. Perhaps it's because squab remains all-too-rare an indulgence for American diners, or because Curry Vinaigrette isn't available many places outside of 12 East 12th Street. Or maybe it's because this plate offers an assortment of delights, such as spicy couscous and sweet currants. In a home setting, you will almost certainly find sautéing squab to be a more worry-free option than roasting it, which seems to be a daunting task for many people.

Harissa is a Moroccan hot chile paste. It is available in jars or tubes at major grocery stores and specialty food stores.

In a large nonstick sauté pan, heat the oil over high heat until very hot but not smoking. Season the squab with salt and pepper. Add the squab to the sauté pan, skin side down. Add the butter to the sauté pan. Cook, basting occasionally, until the squab skin is golden brown and crisp, about 5 minutes. Turn the squab and continue cooking and basting until the breasts are medium rare, about 2 minutes. Transfer the breasts to a plate and cover with foil to keep warm. Continue cooking the legs until they are medium, 3 to 4 minutes. Transfer to the plate and keep warm.

ASSEMBLY

1 head red oak-leaf or lolla rossa (curly red-leaf) lettuce, rinsed and dried

1 head frisée, rinsed and dried

³/₄ cup Curry Vinaigrette (recipe follows)

Coarse salt and freshly ground black pepper to taste

8 sprigs cilantro

In a bowl, toss the lettuce and frisée with 2 tablespoons of the curry vinaigrette. Season with salt and pepper.

Gotham Presentation: Using a slicing knife, cut the squab breasts on the diagonal into 5 or 6 slices. Transfer each breast to a warmed dinner plate, fanning out the slices on the plate. Place a mound of the couscous in the center of each plate. Rest the squab legs against the couscous. Add the dressed salad greens, and spoon the remaining curry vinaigrette around the plate. Garnish each plate with 2 cilantro sprigs.

Everyday Presentation: Place the couscous in the center of a large platter, and surround it with the squab. Garnish with the cilantro sprigs. Pour the remaining vinaigrette into a sauceboat, and serve it with the salad on the side.

Flavor Building: Serve this with a spoonful of the Apricot-Cherry Chutney (page 74).

Curry Vinaigrette

MAKES ABOUT ¾ CUP

3 tablespoons fresh lemon juice

1 garlic clove, peeled and crushed

1 teaspoon Dijon mustard

1 teaspoon Madras-style curry powder

¼ teaspoon ground fresh ginger

⅛ teaspoon harissa (see Sidebar, page 86)

⅓ cup vegetable oil

⅓ cup olive oil

Coarse salt and freshly ground white pepper to taste

THIS IS A VERY powerful vinaigrette due to the potent fragrance of curry. It's a quick way to put a Middle Eastern spin on fish, roast chicken, or even cooked vegetables.

In a blender (or in a medium bowl using an immersion hand blender), combine the lemon juice, garlic, mustard, curry powder, ginger, and harissa. With the machine running, gradually add the vegetable and olive oils until the vinaigrette emulsifies. Season with salt and pepper. Taste and balance the acidity with a little more lemon juice, if needed. Cover and refrigerate until ready to serve. (This vinaigrette may thicken upon standing, and can be thinned with up to 2 tablespoons hot water before serving.)

Autumn Salad of Pears, Gorgonzola, and Walnut Vinaigrette

MAKES 6 SERVINGS

AN UNEXPECTED presentation can make a simple, classic dish seem newly inspired, as it does in this recipe. This time-honored salad presents pears and cheese in perfect harmony, both of them offset by the warm crunchiness of the walnuts and the richness of the walnut oil vinaigrette. A slight tweak of the contents (apples, say, instead of pears) makes it a year-round option.

The presentation is not only striking, but it serves to isolate each ingredient, allowing each diner to set the "pace" of his or her own salad by varying bites of pears and greens with bites of cheese and greens.

Be sure you warm the walnuts in the oven just before plating them to unlock their full taste and "crisp" the nut.

While some classicists may deride the use of cheese in a first course, I find that the pleasures of this starter far outweigh this minor transgression.

Thinking Ahead: The Walnut Vinaigrette may be made up to a day in advance, covered, and refrigerated.

$\frac{1}{2}$ cup (about 2 ounces) fancy walnut halves

2 heads Belgian endive, trimmed, cut crosswise on a bias into $\frac{1}{2}$-inch-thick rounds, and separated into rings

1 medium head radicchio, torn into 1-inch pieces

2 bunches watercress, tough stems discarded

2 tablespoons chopped fresh flat-leaf parsley

Walnut Vinaigrette (page 76)

8 ounces Gorgonzola (preferably sweet or *dolce latte*), Stilton, or Roquefort cheese, either crumbled or cut into 18 pieces each about 1 inch square

2 ripe D'Anjou or Bartlett pears, halved, cored, and cut lengthwise into $\frac{1}{8}$-inch-thick slices

Coarse salt and freshly ground white pepper to taste

Preheat the oven to 350° F. Place the walnuts on a baking sheet. Bake, stirring occasionally, until lightly toasted, crisp, and fragrant, 10 to 12 minutes.

Gotham Presentation: Mound the dressed salad greens in the centers of 6 chilled dinner plates. On each plate, arrange 3 cheese cubes. Stand 2 or 3 of the pear slices up in each piece, fanning out the pear slices decoratively. Place a whole toasted walnut on top of each cheese wedge.

Everyday Presentation: Coarsely chop the walnuts and use the crumbled cheese. In a large bowl, combine the endive, radicchio, watercress, and parsley. Drizzle with the vinaigrette to lightly coat everything. Add the crumbled cheese, toasted walnuts, and pear slices, and season with salt and pepper. Toss well and serve immediately.

Variation: You may substitute Granny Smith apples for the pears to create a more tart, but no less enjoyable, salad.

Asparagus Salad with Beets, New Potatoes, and Mustard Vinaigrette

MAKES 4 SERVINGS

Thinking Ahead: The potato salad may be prepared as much as 6 hours in advance and stored at room temperature. The beets and asparagus may be prepared as much as 6 hours in advance, covered, and refrigerated. Bring to room temperature and dress just before serving.

POTATO SALAD

4 small new potatoes (9 ounces total), well scrubbed

¼ cup Mustard Vinaigrette (page 93)

2 teaspoons minced shallot

Coarse salt and freshly ground white pepper to taste

In a pot, cook the potatoes in boiling salted water over high heat until they are tender when pierced with the tip of a knife, about 15 minutes. Drain, and when cool enough to handle, cut the unpeeled potatoes into ¼-inch-thick rounds and place them in a bowl.

Add the vinaigrette and shallot and mix well. Season with salt and pepper.

BEET SALAD

3 medium beets (12 ounces total), tops trimmed to ½ inch

2 tablespoons Mustard Vinaigrette (page 93)

2 teaspoons minced shallot

Coarse salt and freshly ground white pepper to taste

In a pot, cook the beets in boiling, lightly salted water over medium-high heat until they are just tender when pierced with the tip of a sharp knife, 20 to 25 minutes. Drain, and when cool enough to handle, peel and cut into ¼-inch-thick rounds. Place the beets in a small bowl, and toss with the vinaigrette and shallot. Season with salt and pepper.

If making ahead, don't dress the beets until ready to serve.

ASPARAGUS ARE TRULY IN season for just a few months each year—mid-March through the end of June. But what a season! I prefer the fatter spears (known as "jumbo" or "colossal" asparagus), which can be as wide as 1 inch in diameter at their base. This is primarily a question of personal taste; I find the texture and "mouthfeel" of these stalks to be very sensuous, though there's really no correlation between size and sweetness or toughness. I recommend peeling the asparagus stalks, which improves the texture and renders more of the stalk usable. During the spring, you can find traces of asparagus all over my menu, sometimes as the center of attention, as it is here, and in other cases as seasonal punctuation in a risotto or a soup.

While I don't believe in combining ingredients for the sake of presentation, this happens to be a stunningly festive dish that unites disparate bright colors and shapes—sylvan green asparagus stalks, ivory

(continued)

potato rounds, and burgundy beet slices.

Beets should always be cooked unpeeled. When trimming them, you must take care not to cut off the top or the root, which keep the color (and flavor) from leeching out. A number of recipes in this book call for boiling beets, but steaming is a suitable alternative. If you're ever looking for a way to deepen or concentrate the flavor of a beet, then try roasting them. (See recipe for Duck Soup with Turnip and Roasted Parsnip Ravioli, page 108, for some guidance in roasting vegetables.)

The mustard vinaigrette dresses all three salads, providing a tangy consistency to these ingredients.

ASPARAGUS SALAD

2 pounds large asparagus spears (about 20 spears), ends trimmed, spears peeled with a vegetable peeler

$1/4$ cup Mustard Vinaigrette (page 93)

2 teaspoons minced shallot

Coarse salt and freshly ground white pepper to taste

Cook the asparagus in a large saucepan of boiling salted water over high heat until they are just tender, about 3 minutes. Drain and rinse under cold running water to set the color. Place on a kitchen towel, dry, and transfer to a large platter.

When ready to serve, whisk the mustard vinaigrette with the shallot, and pour just enough over the asparagus to coat evenly. Season with salt and pepper and carefully roll the asparagus in the vinaigrette to dress it.

ASSEMBLY

2 heads baby red oak-leaf lettuce, torn into separate leaves

2 tablespoons Mustard Vinaigrette (page 93)

Coarse salt and freshly ground white pepper to taste

Chopped fresh flat-leaf parsley, for garnish

In a large bowl, toss the lettuce with the vinaigrette and season with salt and pepper.

Divide the asparagus among 4 chilled dinner plates. Place a quarter of the potato salad and beet salad on each plate, then stand a bouquet of lettuce between these salads. Scatter the parsley over the plates.

Variations: Substitute 8 baby golden beets for the regular beets, and cook just until tender, about 10 minutes.

Garnish the salad with a scattering of 2 hard-boiled eggs, yolks and whites chopped separately.

Endive, Parsley, and Shallot Salad

MAKES 4 TO 6 SERVINGS

Thinking Ahead: The dressing may be prepared up to 1 day in advance, covered, and refrigerated.

5 heads Belgian endive (about 1¼ pounds)

3 tablespoons finely chopped shallot

¼ cup coarsely chopped fresh flat-leaf parsley

¾ cup Mustard Vinaigrette (recipe follows)

Coarse salt and freshly ground white pepper to taste

Cut the endive crosswise on the bias into 1½-inch pieces. Separate the endive into individual leaves and place it in a large bowl. Add the shallot and parsley, and drizzle with the vinaigrette to coat everything lightly. Toss well and season with salt and pepper. Serve the salad immediately.

> **Flavor Building:** To convert this light starter into a more substantial main course salad, add poached shrimp and/or sliced avocado. Both make delicious complements to the bite of the endive, and the touches of pink and green create a riot of primary colors.

THIS IS ONE OF THE simplest recipes in the book so it may be surprising that I learned it from a complex chef, Michel Guerard. Just after graduating from the Culinary Institute of America, I worked at Guerard's Comptoir Gourmand at Bloomingdale's, just a few blocks from where I now live in midtown Manhattan. Curiously, one of my most vivid taste memories of those days is this simple salad. In sharp contrast to the complex work in which we were engaged, we would prepare this dish for the "family meal" (staff lunch) every day, literally without exception. The mustard vinaigrette makes a lively everyday dressing for different salads.

Mustard Vinaigrette

MAKES ABOUT 1 CUP

3 tablespoons red wine vinegar

2 tablespoon Dijon mustard

¾ cup peanut or canola oil

Coarse salt and freshly ground white pepper to taste

In a medium bowl, whisk the vinegar and mustard. Gradually add the oil, whisking until emulsified. Season with salt and pepper.

Creamy Polenta, Chanterelle Mushrooms, and White Truffle Oil

MAKES 6 SERVINGS

THIS DISH IS INTENDED as an elegant starter to a formal, multicourse dinner, but can also accompany roast poultry or a game bird. It is uniquely rich and creamy because the polenta is made with heavy cream instead of water. Pay careful attention to how you cut each chanterelle, leaving the smaller ones whole and cutting the larger ones as needed into 1-inch pieces.

Thinking Ahead: The mushrooms may be prepared as much as 4 hours in advance, and reheated before serving. The polenta may be prepared as much as 1 hour in advance and kept warm by covering it with plastic wrap and holding it in an oven set at 180° F. or on top of the stove in a water bath.

MUSHROOMS

2 tablespoons unsalted butter

1/4 cup minced shallots

1 small garlic clove, finely minced

1 pound fresh chanterelle mushrooms, trimmed and cleaned

2 tablespoons White Chicken Stock (page 33), if needed

Coarse salt and freshly ground white pepper to taste

In a 12-inch sauté pan, heat the butter over medium heat. Add the shallots and cook them until softened, about 3 minutes, then add the garlic and cook for 1 minute. Add the mushrooms and cover. Cook until the mushrooms are tender and have released their juices, 7 to 10 minutes. If the mushrooms seem dry, add the chicken stock (some chanterelles are just naturally drier than others). Season with salt and pepper.

CREAMY POLENTA

2 cups milk

1 cup heavy cream

1 cup White Chicken Stock (page 33)

1 large garlic clove, peeled and crushed under a knife

2 sprigs thyme

1 cup quick-cooking polenta

Coarse salt and freshly ground white pepper to taste

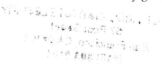

In a medium saucepan, bring the milk, cream, stock, garlic, and thyme to a simmer over medium heat. Be careful that it doesn't boil over. Remove from the heat and let stand for 10 minutes. Pick out the garlic and thyme. Return the liquid to a slow boil and whisk in the polenta. Cook over low heat, whisking constantly, until thick, about 5 minutes. Season with salt and pepper.

Mushrooms absorb water easily, which is why they should be wiped clean with a moist towel or brushed clean with a small pastry brush and rinsed quickly under water *only* if they are *very* dirty.

ASSEMBLY

1 tablespoon finely minced fresh chives

About 2 teaspoons White Truffle Oil (see note on page 31)

12 sprigs chervil, for garnish

Mix about one third of the mushrooms and the chives into the polenta. Divide the polenta evenly among 4 warmed deep soup bowls. Spoon the remaining mushrooms over the polenta, drizzle each serving with about 1/2 teaspoon of the white truffle oil and garnish with the chervil sprigs.

Variation: There's nothing like the taste of white truffle oil, but this dish will still be delicious without it.

Summer Tomato Salad **with**
Ricotta Salata and Creamy Garlic Vinaigrette

MAKES 4 SERVINGS

SOMETIMES RESTRAINT can make all the difference. This seasonal salad—which should be made only between July and September—features a thick, unctuous garlic dressing that is drizzled sparingly over the tomatoes and greens so that alternating bites contribute varying intensities of flavor. The interplay of robust garlic, ripe sweet tomato, and crunchy vegetables paces the experience. At the Gotham, we use as many different types of tomatoes as possible, each one contributing its own hue, sweetness, or acidity. Because we base our selection on the freshness of what's available, the salad changes every day. Green beans and fennel add an important texture and variety of flavor, while the olives and ricotta salata round out the dish with a Mediterranean boldness.

You should pay special attention to how you cut each tomato. Because tomatoes come in every conceivable shape and size, you should examine each one and make a thoughtful

Special Equipment: mandoline

1 small (8-ounce) head fennel, sliced paper thin on a mandoline

6 ounces haricots verts, ends pinched off (or substitute green beans)

2$\frac{1}{2}$ pounds ripe tomatoes, assorted according to what is in season

Coarse salt and freshly ground white pepper to taste

About 1 tablespoon extra-virgin olive oil

Creamy Garlic Vinaigrette (recipe follows)

$\frac{1}{4}$ cup gently packed fresh chervil leaves

1 tablespoon finely minced fresh chives

3 large basil leaves, cut into chiffonade (page 44)

4 ounces ricotta salata cheese, broken into chunks

$\frac{1}{2}$ cup black Mediterranean olives, such as niçoise, pitted

Soak the fennel in a large bowl of iced water until it crisps and curls, about 1 hour. Do not soak longer than 2 hours, or the fennel will wilt. Drain and spin dry in a salad spinner. Refrigerate until ready to use.

Cook the haricots verts in a pot of boiling salted water until crisp-tender, about 3 minutes. Drain, rinse under cold running water, and drain again. Transfer to a kitchen towel.

According to their size and shape, slice, quarter, or halve each tomato.

In the center of each chilled dinner plate, place a quarter of

Ricotta Salata: This salted, aged ricotta cheese boasts a firm texture and pungent flavor similar in some ways to a high-quality feta cheese.

the tomatoes, and season with salt and pepper. Separately coat the haricots verts and fennel with a little olive oil, and season with salt and pepper. Place the haricots verts on top of the tomatoes, and then the fennel. Drizzle with the vinaigrette. Garnish each with a scattering of herbs, the cheese, and a few of the olives.

Variations: Purists who object to drizzling perfect, ripe tomatoes with such a creamy dressing might prefer to use extra-virgin olive oil, coarse salt, and freshly ground pepper instead. Also, for a more pungent cheese, Roquefort or aged goat cheese make excellent substitutes for the ricotta salata.

decision about what makes the most sense—to cut them lengthwise, widthwise, to wedge them, or not to cut them at all. Each one should have its own distinct appearance.

Creamy Garlic Vinaigrette

MAKES ABOUT 1 ¼ CUPS

1 large egg yolk, at room temperature

2 tablespoons red wine vinegar

1 tablespoon fresh lemon juice

1 tablespoon Dijon mustard

1 small garlic clove, mashed to a paste with a sprinkling of coarse salt

1 cup extra-virgin olive oil

Coarse salt and freshly ground white pepper to taste

In a blender (or in a small bowl using a hand immersion blender), combine the egg yolk, vinegar, lemon juice, mustard, and garlic. With the machine running, slowly add the oil until the dressing is smooth and thick. Season with salt and pepper.

Frisée Salad with Roquefort Croutons and Caesar Vinaigrette

MAKES 6 SERVINGS

THIS SALAD RIFFS ON the classic Caesar, altering the type of lettuce and adding new complexity to the dressing. Because the frisée is very delicate, you must dress it gently with the Caesar vinaigrette, but don't worry about making an impact—this is a highly seasoned, garlicky dressing that packs a real punch. For a final flourish, we add another dimension by spreading croutons with a creamy Roquefort mixture and placing them around the perimeter of the salad.

The Caesar dressing offers a good example of an *emulsified* dressing, meaning that it is bound with an egg yolk, which holds the oil in suspension, yielding a creamy, thick consistency. (The same method is used to create mayonnaise.) It's very important to mix this dressing in a nonreactive bowl, such as a heavy, ceramic mixing bowl, or one made of stainless steel. This will keep the dressing from taking on a metallic taste.

Thinking Ahead: The vinaigrette should be made a couple of hours in advance so that the flavors have time to develop.

3 ounces cream cheese, at room temperature

2 ounces Roquefort cheese, at room temperature

2 tablespoons unsalted butter, at room temperature

2 teaspoons finely chopped fresh chives

1 teaspoon fresh lemon juice

Coarse salt and freshly ground white pepper to taste

3 medium heads frisée, rinsed, dried, and separated into leaves

Caesar Vinaigrette (recipe follows)

18 baguette slices, cut on the bias about 1/4 inch thick, lightly toasted

In a medium bowl, using a rubber spatula, mash together the cream and Roquefort cheeses, the butter, chives, and lemon juice. Season with pepper. Set aside at room temperature.

In a large bowl, lightly dress the frisée with the vinaigrette—overdressing will wilt the frisée. You may not need to use all of the vinaigrette. Season with salt and pepper. Divide the salad among 6 chilled dinner plates, piling the frisée into mounds. Garnish each plate with 3 baguette croutons spread with the Roquefort mixture.

Variations: If you like, you may incorporate as many of the traditional Caesar elements as you prefer, substituting romaine lettuce for the frisée, or omitting the cheese and tossing diced croutons into the salad.

Caesar Vinaigrette

MAKES ABOUT 1 1/3 CUPS VINAIGRETTE

1 large egg yolk, at room temperature

3 tablespoons fresh lemon juice

2 teaspoons Dijon mustard

2 whole salt-packed anchovies, soaked, filleted, and chopped to a paste (see page 64)

1 large garlic clove, mashed to a paste with a sprinkle of salt (page 30)

3/4 cup extra-virgin olive oil

1/3 cup freshly grated Parmigiano-Reggiano cheese

Coarse salt and freshly ground white pepper to taste

THE FLAVOR OF THIS dressing is bold, with lots of garlic and anchovy, but you can adjust the amounts to your taste.

In a blender (or in a small bowl using a hand immersion blender), combine the egg, lemon juice, mustard, anchovies, and garlic. With the machine running, slowly add the oil until the vinaigrette is smooth and thick. Transfer to a bowl and stir in the cheese. Season with salt and pepper.

5 Soups and Sandwiches

Chicken Soup with Asparagus, Black Forest Ham, and White Beans

Duck Soup with Turnip and Roasted Parsnip Ravioli

Roasted Corn Chowder with Grilled Shrimp and Cilantro Oil

Lobster Gazpacho with Cilantro and Cumin

Grilled Tuna Club Sandwich with Pancetta and Green Herb Mayonnaise

Grilled Soft-Shell Crab Sandwich with Arugula and Tartar Sauce

Grilled Ham, Smoked Mozzarella, and Red Onion Sandwich

Grilled Chicken Sandwich with Fontina and Aioli

Vegetable Sandwich with Goat Cheese and Charred Tomato Vinaigrette

Tomato, Basil, and Fresh Ricotta Sandwich with Tapenade

It seems that no matter how complex or sophisticated soups and sandwiches become, they always offer the charm of familiarity and retain some inexplicable ability to sooth our spirits. Perhaps this is because just about everyone seems to associate these foods with their childhood. Soups and sandwiches are popular dishes for parents to make their children, and for good reason: They're simple, economical, and nurturing.

Soups are one-pot meals that can be made on a Sunday and served all week. Once the initial preparation has been completed, they also allow for largely unattended cooking. They seem to understand the demands of busy times. I've provided a short range of soup recipes that offer a variety of flavors and forms. Chicken Soup with Asparagus, Black Forest Ham, and White Beans (page 105) is the most basic of these and is meant to offer a starting point for you to create a soup comprised of your own favorite ingredients.

The other three soups all take some well-thought-out

liberty with classic formulas. The Duck Soup with Turnip and Roasted Parsnip Ravioli (page 108) adapts the traditional French pairing of duck and turnips, reconfiguring them, along with the parsnip, to give the turnips more prominence while the duck bones and trimmings provide a foundation for the broth. Lobster Gazpacho with Cilantro and Cumin (page 113) adds an element of seafood to this spicy Spanish summer favorite, while offering a simple method for making Lobster Stock (page 113). Roasted Corn Chowder with Grilled Shrimp and Cilantro Oil (page 111) is designed to use an outdoor grill as the occasion for creating an exceptionally flavored soup.

I hope you'll find pleasure making these recipes, but they're truly intended to be representative of the possibilities of the medium. Soups offer a way to let your imagination run wild. By following a few simple rules, this is actually one of the safest arenas in which to attempt new ideas.

I've included sandwiches here for the same reason that I include them on the Gotham's lunch menu: While the restaurant aspires to a certain level of sophistication, I have always been careful not to make it a rarefied experience. We try to appeal to a broad range of tastes and keep the restaurant accessible to as wide a clientele as possible.

This is not to downplay my enthusiasm for sandwiches. On the contrary, they often serve as the main course when I'm cooking for myself at home. In addition to their utility as "mobile meals," sandwiches are useful teaching vehicles; the sandwiches in this book often demonstrate the importance of individual ingredients in a dish.

For example, the Grilled Tuna Club Sandwich with Pancetta and Green Herb Mayonnaise (page 115) is comprised of just a few simple elements, so it's essential that the tuna, bread, and the pancetta are all of high quality. The same may be said of the Grilled Ham, Smoked Mozzarella, and Red Onion

Sandwich (page 119), which is as satisfying and simple a pleasure as you are ever likely to find between two slices of bread.

Some of these sandwiches are intended for certain seasons, especially the summer. The Tomato, Basil, and Fresh Ricotta Sandwich with Tapenade (page 125), for example, was actually designed for a trip to the beach. The Grilled Soft-Shell Crab Sandwich with Arugula and Tartar Sauce (page 117) is confined to the year's warm months by the season of the crabs themselves. Be sure to try it next summer.

In selecting the bread for these sandwiches, you should make as careful a selection as you would for any of the other ingredients. American bread-making has really come into its own in the last few years, offering exceptional alternatives to mass-produced supermarket bread.

If you've never made your own sauces and condiments—such as mayonnaise and tartar sauce—I'd urge you to try it. I promise you that you will be stunned by the superior flavor. If you're not inclined, or do not have the time, take the shortcut of doctoring up a store-bought version with the ingredients suggested here, or with your own seasonings.

If there's one primary lesson to be gleaned from these sandwiches, it's the skill of proportion. When a sandwich is properly executed, there is a balance of flavors and textures in each bite. Too much "filling," or a bread that is too thick or too thin, can ruin a sandwich. Gauge your measurements carefully as you make these sandwiches, and others of your own design, and remember: Simplicity can be a sign of perfection.

Chicken Soup **with Asparagus, Black Forest Ham, and White Beans**

MAKES 8 SERVINGS

Thinking Ahead: The white beans must be soaked in advance.

1 cup dried white beans (cannellini), rinsed and sorted, soaked for at least 4 hours or overnight in cold water to cover, drained

Coarse salt and freshly ground white pepper to taste

12 asparagus spears, ends trimmed and spears peeled with a vegetable peeler

2 (12-ounce) chicken breast halves

6 cups White Chicken Stock (page 33), chilled

4 gently packed cups thinly sliced Swiss chard leaves

4 plum tomatoes, peeled, seeded, and cut into $1/4$-inch dice

2 ounces Black Forest ham, thinly sliced ($1/8$-inch thick) and cut into $1/4$-inch dice

Minced fresh chives, for garnish

Chopped fresh flat-leaf parsley leaves, for garnish

Place the beans in a pot and add enough cold water to cover them by 2 inches. Bring to a boil, reduce the heat to low, and simmer for 20 minutes. Add salt. Continue cooking until the beans are tender, about 20 more minutes, depending on the dryness of the beans. Drain and set aside.

Cook the asparagus in a large saucepan of boiling salted water over high heat until they're just tender, about 3 minutes. Drain, and rinse under cold running water to set the color. Cut crosswise on a slight bias into $1/2$-inch lengths. Drain and set aside.

Place the chicken breasts in a large saucepan and add the chicken stock. Slowly bring to a simmer. Cook, uncovered, skimming as needed, until the chicken breasts are cooked and show no sign of pink in the center, about 30 to 40 minutes from the time they began simmering.

Using kitchen tongs, transfer the breasts to a work surface and

THE FIRST TIME MY mother came to visit the Gotham, I was looking forward to making her something really special, to begin reciprocating for all the meals she'd cooked when I was growing up. There was just one problem—nothing on the restaurant menu appealed to her. Eager to please, I improvised this hearty soup—and I'm happy to report that she loved it. It's a fairly basic dish, but the recipe offers a few simple lessons: Beginning with the stock *cold* (rather than hot) keeps it from clouding up while poaching the chicken; and adding the meat, vegetables, and herbs at the last minute (instead of simmering them for hours) allows each one to keep its own flavor, texture, and color. This simple method also allows for easy ingredient adjustments to suit different seasons. While asparagus is ideal for spring, tomatoes, zucchini, escarole, and fava beans make a light summer option. Similarly, root vegetables or mushrooms reflect the bounty of the fall months. Used this way, chicken stock is one of the

(continued)

cool slightly. Discard the skin and bones and cut the meat into ½-inch dice.

Remove the stock from the heat and let stand for 5 minutes. Skim off any fat on the surface, and return to the boil. Add the garnishes: chicken breast, beans, asparagus, Swiss chard, tomatoes, and ham. Season with salt and pepper. Heat through, and ladle the soup into warmed soup bowls, sprinkling each serving with the chives and parsley.

true "blank canvases" of the kitchen, so you should feel free to experiment with your favorite flavors to create your own signature variation.

Variations: In addition to the options recommended in the headnote, cooked orzo pasta makes a fitting substitute for the white beans. Spoon as much orzo as you like into each serving.

In the spring, Braised Artichokes (page 312) work well in place of the asparagus.

Flavor Building: To add additional depth of flavor to this soup, drizzle each portion with extra-virgin olive oil and sprinkle with Parmesan cheese. You may also find that Basil Pesto (page 156) complements virtually any vegetable you choose to add. Put a teaspoonful in the bottom of each bowl before ladling the soup.

Duck Soup with Turnip and Roasted Parsnip Ravioli

MAKES 4 SERVINGS

THIS HEARTY SOUP IS based on the classic French paring of duck and turnips, but honoring this tradition in a soup was a fresh idea when we first did it at the Gotham. If your conscience finds it difficult to discard the remains of a Muscovy duck, this stock may offer some solace. (It uses the carcass, giblets, and trimmings of 2 ducks.) The soup's slightly gamey flavor and deep amber color are enhanced by an abundant use of root vegetables.

Roasting the parsnips serves 2 purposes—it releases their full flavor potential and dries them out to make a more suitable ravioli filling. At the Gotham, we make these ravioli in the standard way (see Goat Cheese Ravioli in Pancetta and Shallot Sauce, page 160), but I've supplied a less labor-intensive method here: Using round *gyoza* (won ton wrappers), it's easy to fashion ravioli by hand without having to make fresh dough. I resisted this technique for years; even though it originated in France, my conservative

Thinking Ahead: The duck stock may be prepared up to 3 days in advance and stored, covered, in the refrigerator. The beans, turnips, and the ravioli may be prepared up to 6 hours in advance and stored in the refrigerator.

DUCK STOCK

2 tablespoons vegetable oil

About 3 pounds carcasses, necks, wing tips, giblets (no livers), and trimmings from 2 Muscovy ducks, chopped into large pieces with a heavy knife or cleaver

1 medium onion, cut into $1/4$-inch dice

1 small carrot, cut into $1/4$-inch dice

1 small celery rib, cut into $1/4$-inch dice

8 garlic cloves, peeled and crushed

$1/2$ teaspoon whole black peppercorns

1 sprig thyme

1 sprig flat-leaf parsley

$1^1/2$ quarts cold water, or as needed

In a large pot, heat the oil over medium heat. Add the duck bones, giblets, and trimmings and cook, stirring often, until browned, 10 to 15 minutes. Add the onion, carrot, and celery and cook until they're browned, about 8 minutes. Add the garlic, peppercorns, thyme, and parsley and stir for 1 minute.

Add enough water to cover by 2 inches and bring to a boil over high heat, skimming off any foam that rises to the surface. Reduce the heat to low and simmer uncovered until well flavored, 4 to 6 hours.

Strain the stock into a large bowl, pressing hard on the solids to extract as much flavor as possible, and discard the solids. Let the stock stand for 5 minutes. Skim off any fat that rises to the surface.

You should have 4 cups. If necessary, return the stock to the pot and boil gently until reduced to 4 cups.

ROASTED PARSNIP RAVIOLI

Coarse salt and freshly ground white pepper

2 medium parsnips (8 ounces total)

16 round gyoza (round won ton) wrappers, available at Asian grocers and many supermarkets); or use square wrappers and cut out 3-inch rounds with a cookie cutter

1 large egg yolk beaten with 1 teaspoon water, for sealing the ravioli

training made me skeptical. Truth be told, it's a great alternative to the traditional method. Be sure to buy fresh gyoza, from a reputable grocer. Keep them covered at all times, because they can dry out in a matter of minutes.

Position a rack in the center of the oven and preheat to 400° F. Pour a ¼-inch-deep layer of coarse salt into a small baking dish just large enough to hold the parsnips. Roast the parsnips, turning occasionally, until tender when pierced with the tip of a sharp knife, about 45 minutes. Brush off any salt. When cool enough to handle, peel the parsnips, then transfer them to a small bowl and mash with a fork. Season with salt and pepper.

Work with 4 of the wrappers at a time, keeping the remaining wrappers covered with plastic wrap. Place a heaping teaspoon of mashed parsnip in the center of each wrapper. Brush the edges with some of the beaten yolk. Place a plain wrapper on top of each, pressing the edges together to seal. Transfer the ravioli to a large baking sheet. Repeat the procedure with the remaining ingredients. Cover and refrigerate until ready to use.

WHITE BEANS AND TURNIP

1 cup dried white beans (cannellini), rinsed and sorted, soaked in cold water for at least 4 hours, and drained

1 small onion, halved

2 garlic cloves, crushed

1 sprig thyme

Coarse salt, to taste

1 large turnip, peeled and cut into ½-inch dice

Place the beans, onion, garlic, and thyme in a medium saucepan and add enough cold water to cover by 2 inches. Bring to a boil over high heat. Reduce the heat to low and simmer for 20 minutes. Add the salt. Continue cooking until the beans are just tender, about 20 additional minutes, depending on the dryness of the beans. Let the beans cool in their cooking liquid.

Bring a medium saucepan of lightly salted water to a boil over high heat. Add the turnip and cook until barely tender, about 7 minutes. Drain well and set aside.

ASSEMBLY

2 tablespoons vegetable oil

8 ounces cremini or white button mushrooms, thinly sliced

Coarse salt and freshly ground white pepper to taste

Finely chopped fresh flat-leaf parsley and chives, for garnish

In a large pot, heat the oil over medium heat. Add the mushrooms and cook, stirring often, until they release their juice, it evaporates, and the mushrooms brown lightly, about 8 minutes.

Add the duck stock and bring to a boil over high heat. Add the turnips and white beans and reduce the heat to low. Season the soup with salt and pepper, and keep the soup warm while cooking the ravioli.

Bring a large pot of lightly salted water to a boil and cook the ravioli until just tender, about 3 minutes. Drain well.

Divide the ravioli among 4 warmed soup bowls. Ladle in the soup. Garnish with the chopped herbs.

Foie Gras Ravioli: Use 6 ounces foie gras terrine (preferably the one on page 77, or use store-bought terrine or mousse), cut into 16 pieces, and $1/4$ cup mashed cooked white beans. Place a piece of foie gras and about 1 teaspoon of the white beans in the center of each wrapper and seal with the egg wash.

Variations: Create a variation on the French *garbure* (a kind of vegetable-based stew) by adding potato and Cooked Savoy Cabbage (page 198).

Pumpkin ravioli are an interesting variation, or try foie gras if you desire a richer ravioli filling (see Sidebar). Or, you may omit the ravioli. Add asparagus and increase the mushrooms (porcini, chanterelle, or cremini) in the soup.

Roasted Corn Chowder with Grilled Shrimp and Cilantro Oil

MAKES 4 SERVINGS

Thinking Ahead: The soup (without the shrimp) and cilantro oil may be prepared up to 1 day in advance, covered, and refrigerated. Reheat the soup before serving (or allow it to warm to room temperature). Grill the shrimp just before serving.

4 ears corn, unhusked, silks removed (see Sidebar, page 112)

3 tablespoons vegetable oil

2 ounces slab bacon, cut into $1/2$-inch cubes

1 medium onion, cut into $1/4$-inch dice

1 medium carrot, cut into $1/4$-inch dice

1 medium celery rib, cut into $1/4$-inch dice

2 garlic cloves, minced

1 medium red bell pepper, seeded and cut into $1/4$-inch dice

1 quart White Chicken Stock (page 33)

Coarse salt and freshly ground white pepper to taste

1 cup fresh cilantro leaves

$1/4$ cup olive oil

12 jumbo shrimp, peeled, deveined, and butterflied (see Sidebar, page 112)

THIS RECIPE IS DESIGNED to be enjoyed on a summer afternoon, when the cook can grill the corn, and then the shrimp, in the company of friends or family. While you could cook these ingredients indoors, the smoky flavor of the grill adds a new, distinct element to the chowder. The other factor that distinguishes this dish is the cilantro oil. Almost a pesto, it packs the soup with bold flavor.

This soup may be served hot or cool—if the summer sun is really sweltering. The yellow corn, pink shrimp, red peppers, and green cilantro lend each bowl a visual energy. Note the versatility of shrimp and how comfortably it adapts to this southwestern setting.

Build a charcoal fire in an outdoor grill and let the coals burn until they are covered with white ash. Lightly oil the grill grate. Grill the corn, turning occasionally, until the husks are charred and the corn is tender, 15 to 20 minutes. (The corn, husks removed, can also be roasted in a preheated 500° F. oven, turning occasionally, until golden brown, about 30 minutes.) When cool enough to handle, husk and then cut the corn kernels off the cob in wide sections.

In a medium saucepan, heat 2 tablespoons of the vegetable oil over medium heat and cook the bacon until crisp and lightly browned, about 5 minutes. Using a slotted spoon, transfer it to paper towels.

Add the onion, carrot, celery, and garlic to the saucepan. Reduce

To butterfly shrimp, slice it lengthwise starting at the head and stopping just short of the tail. This will create a "butterfly" effect formed by the 2 halves with the tail intact.

To remove the corn silks, peel back the husk, leaving it attached at the base. Pull out the silk and "rewrap" the corn.

the heat to medium-low and cook gently until the vegetables soften, about 5 minutes. Add the red pepper and cook for 5 minutes. Add the corn and cook for 10 minutes.

Add the stock and bring to a boil over high heat. Reduce the heat to low and simmer for 10 minutes. Season with salt and pepper. Stir in the reserved bacon.

While the stock simmers, make the cilantro oil. Bring a small saucepan of water to a boil over high heat. Add the cilantro leaves and blanch for 10 seconds. Drain, and rinse under cold water. Gently squeeze out the excess moisture, and transfer the cilantro to a blender. Add the olive oil, and process until smooth. Season with salt and pepper. Pour into a small bowl and set aside.

Add fresh charcoal to the grill and let it burn until covered with white ash. Toss the shrimp with the remaining tablespoon of vegetable oil, and season with salt and pepper. Grill, turning once, until firm and pink, about 4 minutes. Transfer to a plate.

To serve, ladle the soup into deep bowls. Arrange 3 shrimp in a mound in the center of each bowl. Drizzle a little of the cilantro oil into each serving.

Lobster Gazpacho
with Cilantro and Cumin

MAKES 8 SERVINGS

Thinking Ahead: The gazpacho and croutons may be prepared as much as 8 hours in advance and stored at room temperature in an airtight container.

LOBSTER AND STOCK

¼ cup distilled white vinegar

6 quarts water, or as needed

Coarse salt

2 (1½-pound) lobsters

2 tablespoons olive oil

½ cup (¼-inch) diced onion

¼ cup (¼-inch) diced carrot

¼ cup (¼-inch) diced celery

¼ cup seeded and (¼-inch) diced/ripe plum tomato

2 cups White Chicken Stock (page 33)

THE SUCCESS OF THIS recipe depends on using ripe summer vegetables and dicing them (rather than mincing them in a processor or blender) so that they retain their flavor and color. My version uses a lobster stock, and is garnished with chunks of lobster and toasted croutons, both of which add levels of flavor and texture to the traditional Spanish recipe. Cumin is not a classic gazpacho ingredient but it works perfectly in this setting.

In a large stockpot, bring at least 5 quarts of water to a boil over high heat. Add the vinegar and some salt. Plunge the lobsters, head first, into the boiling water and cover. Cook until the lobster shells are red, 6 to 7 minutes. Remove the lobsters and, when cool enough to handle, working over a bowl to catch the juices, twist the lobster heads from the tails. Coarsely chop the lobster heads and put them in the bowl along with any juices. Set aside. Remove the lobster meat from the claws and tails. Cut into ¼-inch cubes, cover, and refrigerate.

In a large pot, heat the oil over medium heat. Add the lobster heads (reserve the juices) and cook, stirring occasionally, for 5 minutes. Add the onion, carrot, and celery, and cook gently without browning until the vegetables are soft, about 10 minutes. Add the tomato and cook for 10 minutes. Add the chicken stock, reserved lobster juices, and enough cold water to barely cover the ingredients, about 1 quart. Bring to a gentle boil, skimming as needed, and reduce the heat to a simmer. Cook until the stock is well flavored, about 45 minutes. Remove from the heat and let stand for 10 minutes. Strain into a large bowl, pressing hard on the solids. Reserve 2 cups of the stock and freeze the rest for another use.

GAZPACHO

2 pounds ripe beefsteak tomatoes, peeled, seeded, and cut into $1/4$-inch dice

1 large red bell pepper, seeded and cut into $1/4$-inch dice

1 large green bell pepper, seeded and cut into $1/4$-inch dice

2 medium Kirby cucumbers, peeled, seeded, and cut into $1/4$-inch dice

1 medium onion, cut into $1/4$-inch dice

1 medium celery rib, cut into $1/4$-inch dice

1 fresh hot green or red chile pepper, such as serrano, peeled, seeded, and chopped

1 medium garlic clove, mashed to a paste with a sprinkle of coarse salt

3 tablespoons extra-virgin olive oil

2 tablespoons aged sherry vinegar, plus more as needed

1 teaspoon toasted ground cuminseed (see Sidebar)

Coarse salt and freshly ground white pepper to taste

Hot red pepper sauce to taste

16 homemade croutons (see Sidebar)

Cilantro sprigs, for garnish

Combine the vegetables, oil, vinegar, and cumin in a large bowl, along with the 2 cups reserved lobster stock. Taste and add more vinegar if desired. Season carefully with salt, pepper, and hot pepper sauce. Cover and refrigerate until chilled, at least 2 hours or up to 8 hours.

Ladle the soup into 8 shallow bowls. Place equal amounts of the lobster meat into the center of each bowl. Stand 2 croutons up in the lobster meat, leaning them towards the center to meet and support each other. Garnish with cilantro sprigs.

To toast and grind cuminseed, place 2 teaspoons cuminseed in an empty sauté pan. Cook over medium heat, stirring almost constantly, until the cumin is fragrant and toasted, 2 to 3 minutes. Turn it out onto a plate and cool completely. Grind with a mortar and pestle, an electric coffee grinder, or a mini–food processor.

Croutons: Cut a baguette of French bread on the bias into $1/8$-inch slices. Place on a baking sheet. Bake in a preheated 375° F. oven until golden brown, 5 to 10 minutes. When cool, brush with extra-virgin olive oil, a total of about 2 tablespoons for 16 croutons.

Variations: Substitute 1 pound large unpeeled shrimp for the lobster. Cook the shrimp in a large saucepan of salted water until pink and firm, about 3 minutes. Drain and cool. Peel and devein the shrimp. Cut the shrimp in half lengthwise, cover, and refrigerate. Make the soup, substituting 2 cups chicken stock for the lobster stock.

Grilled Tuna Club Sandwich with Pancetta and Green Herb Mayonnaise

MAKES 4 SANDWICHES

Thinking Ahead: The mayonnaise may be prepared as much as 1 day in advance, covered, and refrigerated. The pancetta may be prepared several hours before serving and kept covered at room temperature. The tuna should be grilled and the bread toasted immediately before serving.

1 cup Basic Mayonnaise (page 140)

2 tablespoons finely chopped fresh chives

2 teaspoons finely chopped fresh tarragon

1 teaspoon anchovy paste

Freshly ground white pepper to taste

12 slices pancetta

1½ pounds tuna steak, cut about 1 inch thick

2 tablespoons extra-virgin olive oil

Coarse salt to taste

12 slices firm, white sandwich bread, lightly toasted

2 ripe medium tomatoes, thinly sliced

Red-oak lettuce leaves

In a small bowl, mix the mayonnaise with the chives, tarragon, and anchovy paste. Season with the pepper. Cover and refrigerate.

Lay out the pancetta slices in a large sauté pan, and place over medium-high heat. Cook, turning the pancetta once, until lightly browned, about 5 minutes on each side. Transfer to paper towels.

Build a charcoal fire in a grill, letting the coals burn until covered with white ash. (Or, position a broiler rack about 6 inches from the source of heat and preheat.) Lightly oil the grill.

Brush the tuna steaks with the oil and season with salt and pepper. Grill (or broil), turning once, until medium-rare, 2 to 3 minutes on each side. Cut the tuna into ½-inch-thick slices.

To build the sandwiches: Divide a third of the herbed mayonnaise

THIS SANDWICH OFFERS A complete range of flavors and textures that fully satisfies the palate: rare yellowfin tuna; crisp pancetta; and the creamy, herbacious mayonnaise, all in blissful proportion to one another. No less spectacular is a version of this sandwich using poached chicken breast and avocado (see Sidebar, page 116).

By starting the pancetta in a cold sauté pan and raising the heat gradually, it cooks evenly, without shriveling up. (This is also a good method for cooking bacon.)

If you make the mayonnaise just before serving, it will retain its brilliant green color. You may also make it in advance and refrigerate it, allowing the flavors to develop, but the acid in the mixture will turn the herbs to a "khaki" color. (An alternative method would be to make the mayonnaise in advance and refrigerate, adding the herbs just before assembly.)

Chicken and Avocado Club Sandwich: In a large saucepan, bring 4 chicken breast halves and 4 cups White Chicken Stock (page 33) to a simmer over medium heat. Reduce the heat to low and simmer for 20 minutes. Remove from the heat and cover. Cool completely (the chicken will continue to cook in the stock). Remove the skin and bones from each breast. (The chicken breasts may be prepared up to 1 day in advance, covered, and refrigerated.) To make the sandwich, slice each chicken breast on the bias into $1/4$-inch-thick slices. Halve, pit, peel, and thinly slice 2 ripe avocados. Prepare the sandwiches as in the main recipe, but substitute the chicken slices for the tuna, and top with avocado slices.

among 4 slices of the toasted bread. Divide the sliced tuna among the sandwiches, then add another slice of bread. Spread with half the remaining mayonnaise, and arrange the pancetta, lettuce, and tomatoes on top. Spread the rest of the mayonnaise on the last 4 slices of bread and cover the stacks. Secure each sandwich with 2 toothpicks, press firmly, and cut into halves.

Variations: Avocado mingles well with these ingredients, but slice it thin so it doesn't compete with the tuna steaks. Swordfish and lobster make fine substitutes for the tuna— if you prefer one of these fish, the sandwich will lose nothing in translation. You might also use bacon instead of pancetta.

Grilled Soft-Shell Crab Sandwich
with Arugula and Tartar Sauce

MAKES 4 SANDWICHES

Thinking Ahead: The mayonnaise for the tartar sauce may be prepared several days in advance, covered, and refrigerated.

8 thick slices smoked bacon (optional)

4 large (6-ounce) soft-shell crabs

1 small red onion, cut into $1/4$-inch-thick rounds

3 tablespoons canola oil

Coarse salt and freshly ground white pepper to taste

4 soft sandwich rolls, toasted

$1/2$ cup Gotham Tartar Sauce (recipe follows)

1 medium tomato, sliced

1 bunch arugula, tough stems discarded, washed, and dried

If using the bacon, arrange the slices in a large, cold sauté pan. Place over medium-high heat and cook until the bacon is lightly browned, about 5 minutes. Drain on paper towels.

Build a charcoal fire in a grill, letting the coals burn until covered with white ash. Lightly oil the grill.

Brush the crabs and onion rounds with the oil and season with salt and pepper. Grill the crabs and onion, turning once, until the onion is tender, about 6 minutes, and the crabs are red, lightly browned, and firm to the touch, 8 to 10 minutes.

Spread each roll with 2 tablespoons of tartar sauce. Build the sandwiches with the crab, bacon (if using it), tomato, arugula, and red onion.

Variations: If you don't have a grill, you can sauté the crabs. Heat 2 tablespoons of olive oil in a 12-inch sauté pan over medium-high heat. Season the crabs with salt and pepper and sauté them, turning once after the crabs are nicely browned and crisp, about 10 to 12 minutes.

THIS RECIPE IS USEFUL not just to create a memorable summer sandwich, but because it demonstrates a method for grilling soft-shell crabs, slow-cooking them over medium heat to elicit a wonderful smoky flavor and crisp exterior.

This sandwich is also noteworthy for the Gotham Tartar Sauce, which stays more or less faithful to the traditional tartar sauce preparation. If you've never made your own sauce, try it at least once; you'll be stunned by how superior it is to store-bought varieties.

Gotham Tartar Sauce

MAKES ABOUT 1 ⅓ CUPS

OUR TARTAR SAUCE HAS punch, thanks to healthy quantities of shallots and capers.

1 cup Basic Mayonnaise (page 140)

3 tablespoons finely chopped fresh flat-leaf parsley

1 tablespoon chopped fresh tarragon

2 tablespoons finely chopped shallot

6 cornichons, rinsed and finely chopped (about 2 tablespoons)

3 tablespoons capers, rinsed and finely chopped

2 teaspoons fresh lemon juice

Coarse salt and freshly ground white pepper to taste

In a small bowl, combine all the ingredients. Cover and refrigerate for at least 1 hour before serving.

Grilled Ham, **Smoked Mozzarella, and Red Onion Sandwich**

MAKES 4 SANDWICHES

$^1/_2$ cup mayonnaise, preferably homemade (page 140)

5 teaspoons prepared ketchup

$^1/_4$ teaspoon Cognac or brandy

8 slices crusty Italian bread, cut from a large round loaf with a close crumb

12 ounces smoked mozzarella, sliced

12 ounces smoked ham, sliced off the bone

1 small red onion, thinly sliced

4 tablespoons unsalted butter

In a small bowl, combine the mayonnaise, ketchup, and Cognac. Spread onto the bread slices. Build the sandwiches using the mozzarella, ham, and red onion.

In a large sauté pan, melt the butter over medium heat. Sauté the sandwiches, turning once, until both sides are golden brown and the cheese melts, about 5 minutes. Lower the heat if necessary to keep the bread from burning. Cut the sandwiches in half and serve.

THIS SANDWICH CAN elevate a pickles, chips, and beer occasion into something casually sublime. To give credit where it's due, I adapted this recipe from the second restaurant that ever saw fit to give me a job. One of the first people to hire me was the great Buffalo restaurateur Michael Delmont. While his restaurant served accomplished and sophisticated food, one of the most popular lunch dishes on the menu was this sandwich, which was consumed every day by the proprietor of the Chevy dealership next door. I've included it here because it points out just how important ingredients themselves are: homemade mayonnaise; warm, smoked mozzarella; and a high-quality bread (at the Gotham we use one from the Tom Cat Bakery in Long Island City) can lead to something unexpectedly special. It doesn't sound like much, but I still get hungry just thinking about it.

Grilled Chicken Sandwich
with Fontina and Aioli

MAKES 4 SANDWICHES

IN THIS RECIPE, I recommend marinating the chicken before grilling. Even a simple marinade—here, a basic mix of oil, lemon juice, and pepper—is worth using because it will heighten the flavor of the poultry. The chicken should be grilled slowly over medium or indirect heat to keep it from drying out.

Thinking Ahead: The basil aioli may be prepared as much as 1 day in advance, covered, and refrigerated. The chicken breasts should be marinated for 4 hours.

2 tablespoons extra-virgin olive oil

3 tablespoons fresh lemon juice

4 (6-ounce) boneless, skinless white chicken breasts, lightly pounded to even thickness

Freshly ground pepper to taste

1 cup Aioli (page 226)

$1/4$ cup finely chopped fresh basil

Coarse salt to taste

8 slices crusty Italian bread, cut from a large round loaf with a close crumb

6 ounces Fontina d'Aosta cheese, rind removed, thinly sliced

2 ripe medium tomatoes, thinly sliced

1 bunch arugula, thick stems discarded, washed and dried

In a small bowl, combine the extra-virgin olive oil and lemon juice. Add the chicken breasts and season with the pepper. Turn to coat, cover, and refrigerate for 4 hours. In a small bowl, combine the aioli and basil, and set aside.

Build a charcoal fire in an outdoor grill, letting the coals burn until covered with white ash. (Or, position a broiler rack about 6 inches from the source of heat and preheat the broiler.) Lightly oil the grill.

Season the chicken breasts with coarse salt. Grill or broil the breasts, turning once, until the breasts feel firm when pressed in the center, about 8 minutes. When the chicken breasts are almost done, toast the bread slices over the coals.

Spread the basil aioli on all of the toast slices and build the sandwiches with the chicken, Fontina cheese, tomatoes, and arugula. Season with salt and pepper, and cover with the remaining toasts. Cut each sandwich in half and serve.

Vegetable Sandwich with Goat Cheese and Charred Tomato Vinaigrette

MAKES 4 SANDWICHES

Thinking Ahead: Every item in this dish may be made 2 hours in advance and kept covered at room temperature.

MARINATED GOAT CHEESE

6 ounces fresh goat cheese,
  at room temperature

$1/2$ cup extra-virgin olive oil

2 tablespoons thinly sliced shallot

1 tablespoon chopped fresh rosemary

1 sprig thyme, roughly chopped

1 medium garlic clove, sliced

$1/2$ teaspoon coarsely crushed black peppercorns

Place the goat cheese on a 12-inch square of plastic wrap. Knead the cheese into a cylinder about 8 inches long. Wrap it tightly in the plastic wrap and refrigerate until firm. Unwrap and cut into twelve $3/4$-inch-thick rounds.

Place the cheese in a small dish and add the remaining ingredients. Cover tightly and let stand at room temperature for at least 2 hours or up to 8 hours, or refrigerate for up to 3 days. If refrigerated, let the cheese come back to room temperature before using.

BASIL OIL

8 large basil leaves

$1/4$ cup extra-virgin olive oil

Bring a small saucepan of salted water to a boil over high heat. Add the basil leaves and blanch for 10 seconds. Drain and rinse under cold running water to set the color. Gently squeeze the excess moisture from the leaves.

THIS LABOR-INTENSIVE open-faced sandwich (in some ways more of a salad) takes a few hours to produce, but there's ample reason to go to the trouble. You might consider this sandwich an opportunity to add 5 highly versatile elements to your cooking repertoire: charred tomato vinaigrette, basil oil, lemon vinaigrette, aioli, and marinated goat cheese. It also offers a crash course in grilling a variety of vegetables. After you're done, you'll not only have learned these simple techniques, but you'll have a sandwich that's ideal as a first course for dinner, or as a lunchtime entrée. For parties, create a buffet of the vegetables, bread, vinaigrettes, and goat cheese, and let everyone make their own sandwiches.

In a blender, combine the basil and oil and process until the basil is pureed, about 1½ minutes. Scrape into a small bowl and let stand for 2 hours.

The basil oil can be used as is, or it can be refined by straining it through a fine sieve into a small bowl.

VEGETABLES

6 ounces haricots verts or green beans, trimmed

2 medium red bell peppers

1 medium eggplant, trimmed, cut lengthwise into 12 slices

2 small zucchini, trimmed, cut lengthwise into 12 slices

1 medium fennel bulb, feathery tops discarded, cut in half lengthwise, and then into ¼-inch-thick wedges

3 tablespoons extra-virgin olive oil, plus more as needed

Coarse salt and freshly ground white pepper to taste

Bring a medium saucepan of salted water to a boil over high heat. Add the haricots verts and cook until just tender, about 3 minutes. Drain and rinse under cold running water.

Build a charcoal fire in a grill, letting the coals burn until covered with white ash. (Or, position a broiler rack about 6 inches from the source of heat and preheat.) Lightly oil the grill.

Grill or broil the peppers, turning occasionally, until the skins are charred, about 20 minutes. (See Roasted Peppers, page 48, for additional instruction on cooking peppers.) When cool enough to handle, remove the charred skin, seeds, and stem from the peppers. Cut lengthwise into quarters and place on a platter.

Brush the eggplant, zucchini, and fennel with the olive oil and season with salt and pepper. Grill or broil the vegetables, turning once, until tender, about 5 minutes for the zucchini, and about 10 minutes for the eggplant and fennel. As they are cooked, remove the vegetables to the platter with the peppers. If you wish, drizzle the vegetables with 1 or 2 tablespoons of olive oil, and season again with salt and pepper.

ASSEMBLY

8 large slices sourdough bread

½ cup Aioli (page 226)

Charred Tomato Vinaigrette (recipe follows)

Whole basil leaves and flat-leaf parsley leaves, for garnish

Toast the bread lightly on the grill. Spread the toasted bread with the aioli. On each of 4 dinner plates, place 2 slices of bread side by side. Arrange the vegetables on top of the bread. Remove the goat cheese from the marinade and place 3 rounds on each plate. Drizzle with the vinaigrette and a few drops of the basil oil. Garnish with a scattering of basil and parsley leaves.

Variation: Many goat cheese companies make small "button" cheeses that are just the right size for this sandwich and don't need to be formed. They are often coated with fresh herbs or peppercorns, which will save you the step of marinating the cheese.

Charred Tomato Vinaigrette

MAKES ABOUT 1 ⅓ CUPS

2 large plum tomatoes, halved crosswise

5 tablespoons extra-virgin olive oil

Coarse salt and freshly ground white pepper to taste

¼ cup red wine vinegar

1 tablespoon minced shallot

1 small clove garlic, minced

MORE A SAUCE THAN A vinaigrette, this enhances grilled fish very well.

Build a charcoal fire in a grill, letting the coals burn until covered with white ash. (Or, position a broiler rack about 6 inches from the source of heat and preheat the broiler.) Lightly oil the grill grate.

Brush the tomatoes with 1 tablespoon of the oil and season with salt and pepper. Grill or broil the tomatoes, turning once, until they soften and are lightly charred, 6 to 8 minutes.

Transfer to a bowl and cover tightly with plastic wrap. Let stand until cool enough to handle. Peel and chop fine. Return to the bowl. Add the vinegar, shallot, and garlic. Whisk in the remaining 4 tablespoons of oil. Season with salt and pepper. Taste and balance the acidity with more vinegar, or, if needed thin the vinaigrette by adding up to 2 tablespoons chicken or vegetable stock, or water.

Tomato, Basil, and Fresh Ricotta Sandwich with Tapenade

MAKES 4 SANDWICHES

8 large slices crusty sourdough or Italian bread, lightly toasted

1/2 cup Tapenade (page 64)

2 large ripe beefsteak tomatoes, thickly sliced

2 tablespoons extra-virgin olive oil

Coarse salt and freshly ground white pepper to taste

1/2 cup fresh ricotta cheese

12 large basil leaves

To make each sandwich, spread 1 toasted bread slice with 2 tablespoons of tapenade. Cover with a few overlapping tomato slices, drizzle with olive oil, then season with salt and pepper. Spread with 2 tablespoons of the fresh ricotta, season again with salt and pepper, then top with 3 basil leaves. Top with another slice of toasted bread, then cut in half with a serrated knife.

Variations: Make this into an open-faced sandwich, and serve it with a bouquet of dressed salad greens.

Substitute Roquefort cheese for the ricotta, and leave out the tapenade.

THIS SANDWICH illustrates how much pleasure can be created with just a few drastically different ingredients. Juicy beefsteak tomatoes and fragrant basil leaves set against the bracing taste of tapenade and cool ricotta cheese—all within the confines of toasted bread. Each bite teases the tastebuds for a long, expectant moment before all the ingredients begin to register. Don't even think about making this sandwich outside of August or September, when tomatoes are at their juiciest, plumpest peak. This sandwich is a great indulgence to bring to the beach, especially since it actually gets better after the flavors have had some time to blend.

# 6 Pasta and Risotto

Pappardelle with Lamb Sausage, Broccoli Rabe, and Parmigiano

Penne with Manila Clams and Chorizo Sauce

Fettuccine, Braised Veal Shanks, and Herbed Ricotta

Cool Lobster, Caviar, and Penne Salad with Ginger and Chervil

Farfalle with Prosciutto di Parma, Pea Leaves, and Parmigiano

Linguine with Clams

Fettuccine with Lobster Bolognese Sauce

Pappardelle, Sea Scallops, Salmon Roe, and Parsley Pesto

Linguine and Prawns in a Tarragon-Coriander Broth

Mussel Risotto, Tomatoes, Saffron, and Tarragon

Farfalle, White Beans, Cherry Tomatoes, Pesto, and Ricotta Salata

Butternut Squash Risotto, Maple-Smoked Bacon, and Sage

Goat Cheese Ravioli in Pancetta and Shallot Sauce

Lemon Basil Pasta

Bucatini with Wild Mushroom Sauce

Asparagus and Morel Mushroom Risotto with Pea Leaves and Chervil Butter

Ratatouille Risotto

Semolina Pasta Dough

Since I was raised by parents of 100 percent Sicilian heritage, it should come as no surprise that my mother prepared pasta dishes several nights a week. We'd enjoy portions from seemingly bottomless pots of tomato sauce with meatballs, braciola, pork, and so on. On Friday, observing religious guidelines, we ate pasta with a variety of seafood—squid, baby clams, and even tuna. And on special occasions, we'd have more involved dishes, such as lasagne or ravioli, which were a big treat. In fact, my earliest memory of chefdom was of helping my mother make ravioli by standing on a chair at our family's kitchen counter sealing the edges of the dough with a fork. But best of all were the tomatoes. . . .

Every August there came a day when we would hear my father's car pull up in the driveway and he would begin unloading bushels of ripe tomatoes. He purchased them from a local farm at the end of each summer, when local tomatoes were at their best, and my sister and I would help bring them into the house. There, my mother and I would work for hours, peeling the tomatoes by the score and packing them, with basil leaves and garlic cloves, into large glass containers with clasp-fasteners. The smell of the tomatoes, an olfactory preview of months of home-cooked meals to come, was intoxicating. These jars were stored in a dark corner of our basement next to my mother's preserved peaches and plums and bottles of my grandfather's homemade wine.

Today, I serve a pasta at the Gotham every day, and we're one of the few three-star restaurants in New York to do this. The menu indicates that these dishes are "composed daily" which for me re-creates some of the anticipation my family would feel as we sat down to my mother's cooking every night.

Appropriately enough, the recipes I've selected for this book vary from simple, family favorites like Linguine with Clams (page 144), to dishes *adapted* from family recipes, like Farfalle with Prosciutto di Parma, Pea Leaves, and Parmigiano (page 141), to more contemporary American expressions such as Fettuccine with Lobster Bolognese Sauce (page 146) and Goat Cheese Ravioli in Pancetta and Shallot Sauce (page 160).

I've included a cold pasta (Cool Lobster, Caviar, and Penne Salad with Ginger and Chervil, page 138) to show you how to make a pasta salad, and a variety of sauces to show the range of flavors that work in this versatile medium. Consider the vast difference, for example, between the texture and flavors in Fettuccine, Braised Veal Shanks, and Herbed Ricotta (page 136), and the Linguine and Prawns in a Tarragon-Coriander Broth (page 150), which places the pasta in a light, clear, and spicy shellfish broth.

Because pastas may be an appetizer or a main course, I have provided serving quantities for both size portions in the recipes. The portion size varies from person to person, but a safe measurement on which to rely is four ounces of dry pasta per person for a main course and between two and three ounces for an appetizer. Double these measurements if using fresh pasta.

Having cooked pasta my entire life, I have developed several strong biases. Among these is my absolute preference for imported dried Italian pasta. While prepackaged "fresh" pasta might seem the more logical choice, the extruded shapes in which it comes produce an unappealing gummy texture. Fresh flat noodles such as fettuccine and pappardelle are perfectly acceptable, but for pasta shapes such as penne and farfalle, dry Italian pasta will produce the proper, firm bite.

Pasta should always be cooked in a large pot of rapidly boiling, heavily salted water. (One exception: Ravioli should be cooked at a more gentle boil to keep the noodle from rupturing.) Contrary to popular belief, olive oil does not keep pasta from sticking during cooking. Just be sure to have enough water at a heavy boil and stir the pot often. If you lose your boil after adding the pasta, cover the pot to regain the boil, and then remove the cover to avoid bubbling over. *After* thoroughly draining the pasta, add a tablespoon of good olive oil.

Doneness is a matter of preference, but I prefer it very al dente with a firm bite.

Use real, imported Parmigiano-Reggiano cheese on your pasta. Don't use prepackaged supermarket varieties, which won't work with many of the recipes in this book.

When making ravioli, use one or two egg yolks per pound of filling to bind the filling.

I've tried to explain why a particular noodle is used in a particular dish, to give you a sense of how you might approach this decision yourself. The choice of pasta shape is subjective, but you might consider the shape and size of the noodle in relation to the size of the other ingredients or the thickness of the sauce. For example, I selected far-falle to accompany peas, pea leaves, and torn-up prosciutto (page 141) so that each bite would contain pieces of all the ingredients. In strong contrast, the broad surface of the fettuccine carries the big flavors of Braised Veal Shanks and Herbed Ricotta (page 136).

Risotto

If pasta was the first dish I ever felt comfortable with, risotto was one of the last. Because of the rigors of risotto preparation—it requires a lot of careful attention and much stirring—I was timid about making it in a restaurant setting. I knew I didn't want a menu item that said "please allow 30 to 40 minutes." (This is in addition to the mystery and controversy that surrounds this dish, with chefs arguing over the type of rice, the type of spoon, and even whether it should be stirred clockwise or counterclockwise, for God's sake.)

One day, an Italian chef/friend of mine taught me how to make risotto in a restaurant setting, and I'm passing along the method here because you could use it at home to do a lot of advance work if you're entertaining: At the Gotham, we cook enough for thirty orders, stopping after the rice has absorbed the second-to-last addition of stock. Then, we spread it out on a sheet pan lined with parchment paper so it will cool quickly. Finally, we transfer it to a container and wrap it tightly to ensure that the rice does not absorb any moisture.

When we're ready to serve the pasta, we return the rice to a hot pot, add the final addition of hot stock and the other ingredients, and cook it for five minutes, stirring continually. Will this method produce the same results as the classic cooking method? You tell me.

Risotto is made from short-grain rice, which people generically refer to as arborio rice. Truth be told, there are many different varieties, the finest being *vialone nano,* then *carnaroli.* The most widely used rice in Italy and the United States is arborio. If you see the appellation *superfino,* it refers to the size of the individual rice grain; the term is meaningless because all of these varieties are *superfino.*

There are a few things to remember when cooking risotto: The pot must be heavy-bottomed; the rice must be of a high quality; and the cooking process merits special attention. After softening the onions in oil—the *soffritto,* as it's known in Italian cooking—add the rice. You must cook the rice slowly, stirring often until it begins to clump up, feel heavy on the spoon, and stick to the bottom of the pot. This process of activating the starches in the rice is extremely important. The heat should be medium-high, enough so that when the wine is added it will reduce in a matter of minutes.

Finally, risotto can only be as good as the stock, which doesn't reduce but is actually absorbed into the rice. For this reason, I recommend Double Turkey Stock (page 37) for a number of these recipes.

Pappardelle with Lamb Sausage, Broccoli Rabe, and Parmigiano

MAKES 6 APPETIZER OR 4 MAIN-COURSE SERVINGS

IN THE COURSE OF MY career, I have learned quite a bit about making sausages, which is great because it gives me total control over the ingredients that go into them. I've included this pasta recipe here to provide a forum for including sausage-making in the book. The lamb sausage in this pasta isn't stuffed into casings, so you won't need any special equipment. As with terrines, sausages should be made with all the ingredients ice cold at all times to prevent a dry, crumbly texture from resulting. It's also absolutely essential that the blade on the grinder or processor you use be razor sharp; otherwise, you will mash the meat and not achieve the proper texture.

Broccoli rabe can be found in Italian produce markets and is often cooked with sausage because its slightly bitter taste offsets the spiciness of the meat.

This particular dish is a variation on the classic Italian combination of orrechiette ("ear-shaped" pasta), sausage, and broccoli

Thinking Ahead: Marinate the meat overnight (at least) in the refrigerator before preparing the sauce. The sauce may be prepared up to 3 days in advance, cooled, covered, and refrigerated.

LAMB SAUSAGE

$^1/_2$ cup dry red wine

$^1/_2$ small carrot, roughly chopped

$^1/_2$ small celery rib, roughly chopped

1 large shallot, roughly chopped

2 large garlic cloves, sliced, plus 3 large garlic cloves, minced and crushed into a paste with a sprinkle of coarse salt

2 sprigs thyme

8 ounces lamb shoulder, trimmed, cut into 1-inch cubes

8 ounces pork butt, trimmed, cut into 1-inch cubes

2 teaspoons finely chopped fresh rosemary leaves

$^1/_2$ teaspoon ground fennel seed

$1^1/_2$ teaspoons coarse salt

$^1/_2$ teaspoon freshly ground black pepper

In a medium nonreactive bowl, combine the red wine, carrot, celery, shallot, sliced garlic, and thyme. Add the lamb and pork and mix well. Cover and refrigerate for at least 8 hours or up to 24 hours.

Remove the meat from the marinade. Discard the carrot, celery, garlic, and thyme. Using a meat grinder fitted with a $^1/_4$-inch die, or a food processor with the metal blade, coarsely chop the meat and shallot. Add the garlic paste, rosemary, fennel, salt, and pepper and mix.

PASTA SAUCE

4 tablespoons olive oil

1 pound Lamb Sausage (see above) or high-quality sweet Italian pork sausage

1 medium onion, cut into ¼-inch dice

1 medium carrot, cut into ¼-inch dice

1 medium celery rib, cut into ¼-inch dice

3 cups White Chicken Stock (page 33)

1 cup heavy cream

Coarse salt and freshly ground black pepper to taste

Crushed hot red pepper flakes to taste

rabe. For a change, I recommend using pappardelle to accompany these ingredients, making their seasoning seem almost understated. You'll want to serve this pasta with a soup spoon—the brothy sauce left behind after the pasta has been eaten will be brimming with the flavors of the lamb and the seasonings.

In a large saucepan, heat 2 tablespoons of the oil over medium-high heat. Add the chopped meat and cook, stirring occasionally, until the meat is seared, about 6 minutes. Drain in a colander.

Add the remaining 2 tablespoons of oil to the saucepan and heat over medium heat. Add the onion, carrot, and celery. Cover and cook until the vegetables soften, about 4 minutes. Add the drained meat and the stock and bring to a boil. Reduce the heat to medium-low and simmer until the sauce reduces to approximately 2¼ cups, about 15 minutes.

In a medium saucepan, bring the cream to a boil over high heat and reduce it by half, 12 to 15 minutes. Add to the simmering sauce. Taste, and season with salt and pepper and hot red pepper flakes. Keep warm.

ASSEMBLY

1 large bunch broccoli rabe, thick stems removed

1 pound fresh pappardelle or fettuccine

1 cup freshly grated Parmigiano-Reggiano cheese

2 tablespoons chopped fresh basil, chives, and flat-leaf parsley, in any combination

Bring a medium pot of lightly salted water to a boil over high heat. Add the broccoli rabe and cook until just tender, about 6 minutes. Drain and cover to keep warm.

Bring a large pot of lightly salted water to a boil over high heat. Add the pappardelle and cook until barely tender, about 3 minutes. Drain well.

Transfer the pasta to 4 warmed deep pasta bowls. Stir ½ cup of the cheese and all of the herbs into the sauce, then ladle over the pasta. Garnish with the broccoli rabe and the remaining cheese.

Penne with Manila Clams and Chorizo Sauce

MAKES 6 APPETIZER OR 4 MAIN-COURSE SERVINGS

ONE OF THE MOST exciting developments in American cuisine has been the incorporation of international influences into our nation's culinary consciousness—a fitting reflection of our melting-pot heritage. This recipe is a good example of a Portuguese–influenced dish (a departure for me), as well as an illustration of how to turn a culinary experience into the inspiration for a new dish of your own.

In the mid-1980s, I spent time vacationing in the Algarve, the coastal fishing region in the south of Portugal. Just about every night, we sat down to eat at a dockside restaurant on the pier that served simple grilled fish and an immensely satisfying native dish called *cataplana,* a garlicky pork and clam stew served in a hinged copper cooking vessel. The wait staff would deliver this sealed to the table and open it like a giant clam shell, releasing a burst of steam emanating the rich aromas of seafood and spices.

It occurred to me that this

Thinking Ahead: The sauce may be made the morning before the day of final preparation, covered, and refrigerated.

CLAMS

1 tablespoon olive oil

1 small onion, chopped

$1/3$ cup finely chopped celery

3 garlic cloves, peeled and crushed

4 sprigs flat-leaf parsley

2 cups dry white wine

$1/2$ teaspoon whole black peppercorns

5 dozen Manila or 3 dozen littleneck clams, well scrubbed

In a large pot, heat the oil over medium heat. Add the onion, celery, garlic, and parsley. Cook, stirring often, until the onion is softened, about 3 minutes. Add the wine and peppercorns. Bring to a boil over high heat and cook until the wine is reduced by approximately one third, about 10 minutes. Add the clams and cover. Cook until the clams open, 3 to 5 minutes.

Using a slotted spoon, transfer the clams to a small bowl. When cool enough to handle, remove the meat, discarding the shells, and set the meat aside. Let the clam broth stand for 10 minutes, then decant it through a wire strainer into another bowl, leaving any sand behind. Set the clam broth aside.

CHORIZO SAUCE

2 tablespoons olive oil

4 ounces chorizo or other spicy smoked sausage, sliced into $1/4$-inch-thick rounds

1 small onion, chopped

1 medium carrot, cut into ¼-inch dice

1 medium celery rib, cut into ¼-inch dice

3 garlic cloves, finely minced

1 (28-ounce) can imported Italian plum tomatoes, chopped, with their juice

2 ounces smoked ham, cut into ¼-inch dice

1 sprig thyme

1 dried bay leaf

½ teaspoon crushed hot red pepper flakes, or to taste

Coarse salt and freshly ground white pepper to taste

ingenious combination of pork and clams, brimming with spicy, bold flavors, would make a fun and unconventional pasta sauce. To accompany it, I settled on penne; with its ridged surface and short length, it makes an ideal vehicle for the sauce and its size complements the pieces of chorizo and seafood, allowing each mouthful to include morsels of all three.

In a large saucepan, heat the oil over medium heat. Add the chorizo and cook, stirring often, until the sausage is lightly browned, about 5 minutes. Add the onion, carrot, and celery and reduce the heat to medium-low. Cook, stirring often, until the vegetables are softened but not browned, 3 to 5 minutes. Add the garlic and stir for 1 minute. Add the reserved clam broth, the tomatoes with their juice, the ham, thyme, bay leaf, and crushed red pepper; bring to a simmer. Reduce the heat to low and simmer until reduced by about one fourth, approximately 40 minutes. Taste and season with salt and pepper.

ASSEMBLY

1 pound dried penne

3 tablespoons chopped fresh flat-leaf parsley

2 tablespoons chopped fresh basil

In a large pot of boiling salted water, cook the pasta until al dente, about 9 minutes. Drain well and transfer to a warmed serving bowl.

If necessary, reheat the sauce. Just before serving, add the clams. Pour the sauce over the pasta, add the parsley and basil, and toss well. Serve in individual soup bowls.

Fettuccine, Braised Veal Shanks, and Herbed Ricotta

MAKES 6 APPETIZER SERVINGS OR 4 MAIN-COURSE SERVINGS

ANYONE PRESENTED WITH this dish—based on the classic osso bucco—will be amazed at the transformation that occurs on the plate after the dish is served. The herbed ricotta cheese offers a refreshing counterpoint to the heavy, gelatinous quality of the shanks. The dollop you place on top of the dish at serving time will gradually melt and meld into the osso buco sauce, blending into a creamy, hearty mixture.

Pay careful attention to how you braise the veal shanks. Successfully braising veal (or any meat) depends on achieving the slowest, most imperceptible bubble you can. Be sure you season the meat well before braising because you will not be able to effectively correct the seasoning afterward. The liquid in which you braised the veal is later used to make a pasta sauce by reducing and carefully seasoning it.

Thinking Ahead: The sauce may be prepared up to 3 days in advance, cooled, covered, and refrigerated. The ricotta may be prepared up to 8 hours in advance, covered, and refrigerated. Bring it back to room temperature before serving.

BRAISED VEAL SHANKS

3 tablespoons olive oil

3 pounds veal shanks (osso buco), sawed into 1-inch-thick rounds

Coarse salt and freshly ground pepper

1 large onion, coarsely chopped

10 garlic cloves, peeled and crushed

1 cup dry white wine

2 cups White Chicken Stock (page 33)

1½ cups peeled, seeded, and chopped plum tomatoes (substitute canned if ripe tomatoes are unavailable)

1 teaspoon finely chopped fresh rosemary leaves

1 teaspoon finely chopped fresh sage leaves

Preheat the oven to 275° F. In a heavy roasting pan, heat the oil over medium-high heat. Season the veal shanks generously with salt and pepper. Cook, uncovered, turning occasionally, until well browned, about 10 minutes. Transfer to a plate and set aside.

Add the onion and garlic to the pan. Cook over medium-low heat, stirring occasionally, until the onion is golden, about 5 minutes. Add the wine and reduce slightly, about 2 minutes. Add the chicken stock, tomatoes, rosemary, and sage and bring to a boil. Return the veal to the pan and cover. Place in the oven and braise until the veal is very tender and falling off the bone, about 1¾ hours. Turn occasionally and check that the veal is simmering gently, not boiling. Reduce the oven temperature if necessary.

Remove the veal from the sauce, and when it is cool enough to work with, remove the meat from the bones and chop coarsely. Push the marrow out of the bones and discard the bones. Return sauce to stove and skim any fat from the surface. If necessary, reduce slightly to thicken and concentrate flavors. Return the veal and marrow to the sauce. Taste and season with salt and a generous amount of pepper.

HERBED RICOTTA

$^3/_4$ cup fresh ricotta cheese

3 tablespoons heavy cream (if using packaged ricotta)

2 tablespoons freshly grated Parmesan cheese

1 tablespoon chopped fresh basil

1 tablespoon finely chopped fresh flat-leaf parsley

1 small garlic clove, minced and mashed to a paste with a sprinkle of coarse salt

Freshly ground black pepper to taste

In a small bowl, combine all the ingredients, including the cream if using packaged ricotta. Cover and refrigerate until ready to serve. Bring to room temperature before serving.

ASSEMBLY

1 cup fresh peas (from 1 pound unshelled peas) or frozen petit pois

1 pound fresh or dried fettuccine

Chopped fresh flat-leaf parsley, for garnish

In a pot of boiling salted water, cook the peas over high heat until tender, 3 to 5 minutes. Drain well and add to the veal.

Bring a large pot of lightly salted water to a boil over high heat. Add the fettuccine and cook until al dente, 2 to 3 minutes for fresh, 8 to 10 minutes for dried. Drain well.

Transfer the fettuccine to warmed deep pasta bowls. Spoon the sauce over the pasta, then add a spoonful of herbed ricotta and a scattering of chopped parsley to each serving.

Variations: For Braised Lamb Shanks, substitute 3 (1-pound) lamb shanks for the veal shanks. They can be left whole, but they may take slightly longer than the veal shanks to cook until tender. Use red wine instead of white.

Typically this dish is served with a broad noodle, but rigatoni works exceptionally well.

Flavor Building: Since this recipe is based on osso buco, you might enjoy this recipe for *gremolata*. Omit the parsley garnish and combine $^1/_4$ cup chopped parsley, 1 minced garlic clove, and the grated zest of 1 lemon and $^1/_2$ orange. Sprinkle some of this over each serving to cut the richness of the sauce.

Cool Lobster, Caviar, and Penne Salad with Ginger and Chervil

MAKES 6 APPETIZER OR 4 MAIN-COURSE SERVINGS

ONE OF THE BEST sources of inspiration for a chef can be the inspiration of another chef, and this recipe offers one of the best examples from my own experience. While traveling several summers ago, I had lunch at L'Auberge de Père Bise, on Lake Annecy. For a first course, I was presented with a deceptively simple looking lobster salad dressed with an ivory-colored sauce. Expecting an herbed mayonnaise of some sort, I was surprised to taste the tang of lemon and ginger, which infused the lush lobster meat with extraordinary success. I was so eager to find a way to use this combination myself that I was mentally transported from this pastoral setting to the Gotham kitchen, twenty feet underground on East 12th Street in Manhattan. As soon as I returned from vacation, I set about designing this dish.

The caviar adds an extra dimension of texture and salinity here, and the ginger mayonnaise unites these components seamlessly with the penne. As for the chervil,

Thinking Ahead: The ginger mayonnaise and lobster meat may be prepared up to 1 day in advance, and stored, covered, in the refrigerator.

LOBSTER

5 quarts water

$^1/_4$ cup white wine vinegar

1 (2-pound) live lobster

Coarse sea salt and freshly ground white pepper to taste

In a large stockpot, bring the salted water and the vinegar to a boil over high heat. Add the lobster head-first and cover. Return to the boil and cook until the lobster shell is bright red, about 10 minutes. Remove, and when easy to handle, crack the lobster shell and remove the meat. Cut the meat into $^1/_2$-inch pieces. You should have about $2^1/_2$ cups. Cover and refrigerate. (If desired, save the lobster head and shell for another use, such as the Lobster Stock on page 113.)

VEGETABLES

1 large leek, white part only, halved lengthwise and cut into $^1/_8$-inch julienne

1 small red bell pepper, seeded and cut into $^1/_8$-inch julienne (page 43)

1 small yellow bell pepper, seeded and cut into $^1/_8$-inch julienne (page 43)

1 large tomato, peeled, seeded, and cut into $^1/_4$-inch dice

In a pot, cook the leek in boiling salted water until tender, about 2 minutes. Drain and rinse under cold water. Drain well again.

Set some of the julienned red and yellow pepper aside to use as a garnish. In a large bowl, toss the leek with the tomato and the remaining julienned peppers.

ASSEMBLY

$1/3$ cup plus $1/2$ cup Ginger Mayonnaise (recipe follows)

1 pound dried penne

Approximately 2 tablespoons fresh lemon juice

$1/4$ cup chopped fresh chives

Coarse salt and freshly ground white pepper to taste

2 tablespoons or more sevruga caviar, for garnish

Chervil sprigs, for garnish

In a small bowl, dress the lobster with about $1/3$ cup of the ginger mayonnaise. Season with salt and pepper. Cover and set aside.

Cook the pasta in a large pot of boiling salted water over high heat until al dente, about 9 minutes. Drain and rinse under cold water to stop the cooking. Drain well again. Transfer to the bowl of vegetables. Add the remaining $1/2$ cup of ginger mayonnaise and toss and taste, adding enough lemon juice to give the pasta a citrusy edge. Add the chives and season with salt and pepper.

Spoon the pasta into individual bowls. Arrange equal amounts of the lobster on top of each serving, along with a spoonful of sevruga. Arrange a few of the reserved julienned red and yellow peppers over the top of the lobster to set off the color and texture, and garnish with the chervil sprigs.

it's one of my favorite aromatics, and I was delighted to discover how well it rounded out this refreshing summer stunner.

A note about using vinaigrette on pasta: After you have cooked the pasta, cool it under cold water before adding the vinaigrette. Otherwise the vinaigrette will curdle or thin out. Also, this dish depends on a delicate balance of flavors that might require some extra work. You must taste the dish carefully. If it seems flat, but you're confident it has enough salt and pepper, add some lemon juice to bring up the flavors. All of this should be done before adding the fresh herbs, so that they stay green.

Variations: You might find a different but comparable pleasure in using lump crabmeat or cooked shrimp instead of lobster. Try using $2^{1}/2$ cups of either and see what you think.

Flavor Building: You may add additional caviar for more special or elegant occasions.

Ginger Mayonnaise

MAKES ABOUT 2 CUPS

8 ounces fresh ginger (the fresher the ginger, the more juice)

2 large egg yolks, at room temperature

2 tablespoons fresh lemon juice

1 tablespoon Dijon mustard

Coarse salt and freshly ground white pepper to taste

Cayenne to taste

1 cup olive oil

1 cup canola oil

1 garlic clove, minced and mashed to a paste with a sprinkle of coarse salt

THIS VERSATILE SAUCE may be used with grilled fish or chicken or as a dip for vegetables.

Using the medium-fine holes of a cheese grater, grate the ginger. In batches, wrap the ginger in the corner of a piece of cheesecloth or a clean kitchen towel and squeeze to extract the juice into a small bowl. You should have 1/4 cup of juice.

Whisk the egg yolks in a medium bowl, along with the lemon juice, mustard, salt, and the white and cayenne peppers. Place the bowl inside of a medium saucepan. (This will keep the bowl from moving on the counter while you add the oil.) Using a whisk or a hand blender set on low speed, add the oils, drop by drop, to the egg mixture. After the mayonnaise begins to thicken, add the oils a bit faster. When all the oil has been absorbed, beat in the ginger juice and garlic. Taste carefully—the mayonnaise should have a little heat to its flavor, with a bright citrusy edge. Add more lemon juice, salt, and white and cayenne peppers as needed. The mayonnaise will keep, covered and refrigerated, for up to 2 days.

Variation: To make a Ginger Aioli, increase the amount of garlic to 3 cloves. To make a Basic Mayonnaise, delete the ginger juice and garlic.

Farfalle with Prosciutto di Parma, Pea Leaves, and Parmigiano

MAKES 6 APPETIZER OR 4 MAIN-COURSE SERVINGS

Thinking Ahead: The garlic butter may be prepared as much as 1 week in advance and kept in the freezer.

1$\frac{1}{2}$ cups fresh peas (from 1$\frac{1}{2}$ pounds unshelled peas)

1 pound imported Italian bow-tie pasta (farfalle)

Herbed Garlic Butter (page 231)

1$\frac{1}{2}$ cups (3 ounces) loosely packed pea leaves, or substitute an equal amount of arugula

4 ounces prosciutto di Parma, torn into bite-size pieces

$\frac{3}{4}$ cup (3 ounces) freshly grated Parmigiano-Reggiano cheese, plus additional for grating at the table

4 ripe plum tomatoes, peeled, seeded, and cut into $\frac{1}{2}$-inch dice

3 tablespoons finely minced fresh chives

Coarse salt and freshly ground white pepper to taste

Bring a medium saucepan of salted water to a boil over high heat. Add the peas and cook until just tender, about 2 minutes. Drain the peas and rinse in cold water to set the color.

Bring a large pot of salted water to a boil over high heat. Add the pasta and cook until al dente, about 8 minutes. Scoop out 1 cup of the pasta water and set it aside. Drain the pasta and transfer it to a warmed serving bowl.

While the pasta is still hot, immediately add the herbed garlic butter, peas leaves, peas, prosciutto, grated cheese, and tomatoes. Tossing constantly, gradually add 2 to 3 tablespoons of the reserved pasta water as the butter and cheese melt and emulsify into a rich and creamy sauce. Add the chives and toss again. Season with salt and pepper.

Spoon the pasta into individual warmed bowls, and serve it with extra Parmigiano for grating at the table.

THIS RECIPE OFFERS AN ideal illustration of a simple concept—a few basic ingredients tossed while piping hot with garlic butter and cheese. The sauce is just a rich, creamy emulsion that intensifies the flavors of the other ingredients. I learned this lesson early in life from my mother's pasta with peas, which was one of my favorite boyhood dishes.

A few years ago, when produce purveyors began selling pea leaves, I had a taste "flashback" to this old family favorite. Almost immediately, the rest of the ingredients fell into place in my mind: prosciutto, diced tomatoes, and a handful of fresh chopped herbs to round out the ensemble. While my mother made it with linguine, I began using farfalle (bow-tie pasta) because its shape is in better proportion to the other components of the dish. Virtually each mouthful delivers a quietly potent combination of flavors and textures.

Variations: Substitute $1/3$ cup extra-virgin olive oil for the butter.

Substitute defrosted frozen tiny peas (*petit pois*) for the fresh peas. There is no need to cook the thawed peas.

Substitute arugula for the pea leaves.

Flavor Building: Mushrooms and asparagus may be used to add greater depth and complexity to this dish, loading it with a pleasing variety of vegetables.

Cook 8 ounces of fresh, quartered morel or cremini mushrooms in 2 tablespoons unsalted butter over medium heat until the mushrooms give off their liquid, about 4 minutes. Set aside. Cook 4 ounces asparagus tips in boiling salted water until just tender, about 3 minutes. Drain. Add the cooked mushrooms and asparagus to the pasta while it's still hot, and immediately add the garlic butter and the remaining ingredients. Just before serving, drizzle with White Truffle Oil (page 31) to taste.

Pea Leaves are the young tender sprouts of snow-pea vines.

Prosciutto di Parma: This is the finest Italian ham, rosy pink, with a delicate flavor and texture. Regardless of how you vary the peas and greens, be sure to use this prosciutto. It's far less salty than its American counterparts.

A Vegetarian Option: This may be converted to a vegetarian dish simply by omitting the prosciutto.

Linguine **with Clams**

MAKES 6 APPETIZER OR 4 MAIN-COURSE SERVINGS

THIS IS A FUN AND deceptively simple dish to make for parties because the actual cooking offers a sensory experience in its own right. When the clams and garlic hit the pan, the resulting sizzle and aroma are unforgettable. It uses no wine (the clams are delicious on their own), 2 types of pepper to balance the heat, and just enough butter to smooth out the sauce. We make it with littlenecks because they have more juice than delicate Manila clams. Time the linguine so it is finished at the same time as the clams, which will take about 10 minutes.

Thinking Ahead: You can make the garlic, parsley, olive oil mixture 4 hours in advance.

A generous $1/2$ cup extra-virgin olive oil

A generous $1/3$ cup chopped fresh flat-leaf parsley

4 large garlic cloves, mashed to a paste with a sprinkle of coarse salt

$1/2$ teaspoon coarsely cracked black peppercorns

$1/4$ teaspoon crushed hot red pepper flakes

3 tablespoons vegetable oil

3 dozen littleneck clams, well scrubbed

3 tablespoons unsalted butter

1 pound dried linguine

In a small bowl, mix the olive oil, parsley, garlic, black and red peppers. Set aside.

In a large saucepan, heat the vegetable oil over high heat until very hot but not smoking. Add the clams and cover. Cook for 3 minutes, until some of the clams have opened and released their juices. Add the oil mixture and butter. Cover and cook until all the clams open, about 4 minutes. Discard any clams that don't open.

Meanwhile, cook the linguine in a large pot of salted water over high heat until al dente, 8 to 10 minutes. Drain, and use tongs to transfer the pasta and clams to individual bowls. Then spoon the clam broth over all.

Fettuccine **with**
Lobster Bolognese Sauce

MAKES 6 TO 8 APPETIZER OR 4 MAIN-COURSE SERVINGS

WHEN I BEGAN MY career at the Gotham in 1985, I became one of the first young American chefs who were riffing on time-honored dishes, revamping them in ways that people had never imagined. This dish was one such departure that I've always felt played a part in our earning the first of four three-star reviews from *The New York Times.* Before we introduced this dish, bolognese sauce had always been made with ground meats like veal, pork, and chicken livers, and finished with cream. This was never altered. When designing the Gotham's menu, I wanted to be sure to include a number of pastas. Maybe it's just my Italian heritage, but at the time I felt American restaurants never made enough room on their rosters for this pasta.

Using some creative license, I put a spin on the concept of bolognese and devised this decadent sauce, loaded with lobster, cream, and herbs. It's thick enough to coat a flat noodle like fettuccine. It also offers a *small* economy as three lobsters will feed four hungry adults.

Thinking Ahead: The sauce may be prepared as much as 8 hours in advance, cooled, covered, and refrigerated.

LOBSTER BOLOGNESE SAUCE

10 quarts water

$^3/_4$ cup white wine

3 (1- to $1^1/_4$-pound) live lobsters

2 tablespoons olive oil

1 medium onion, chopped

$^1/_2$ medium carrot, chopped

$^1/_2$ small celery rib, chopped

4 garlic cloves, sliced

5 sprigs flat-leaf parsley

1 dried bay leaf

3 tablespoons tomato paste

$^1/_4$ cup Cognac or brandy

6 cups White Chicken Stock (page 33), or as needed

1 cup heavy cream

Coarse salt and cayenne to taste

Using a large stockpot, bring the salted water and $^1/_4$ cup of the wine to a boil over high heat. In batches, if necessary, add the lobsters and cover. Cook for 5 minutes. (The lobsters will be only partially cooked.) Drain the lobsters, place them in a bowl, and set aside until cool enough to handle.

Working over a bowl to catch the juices, twist the lobster bodies away from the tails; reserve the bodies. Saving as much of the juice as possible while working, crack the lobster tails and claws. Remove the meat and cut it into $^3/_4$-inch dice. Transfer the meat to a bowl, cover with plastic wrap, and refrigerate. Coarsely chop the lobster shells.

In a large stockpot, heat the oil over medium heat. Add the onion, carrot, celery, garlic, parsley sprigs, and bay leaf. Cover and cook, stirring occasionally, until the vegetables soften, about 10 minutes. Stir in the tomato paste. Add the lobster shells and bodies and cook, stirring often, for 2 minutes. Add the Cognac and reduce by half, about 2 minutes. Add the remaining wine and reduce by half, about 3 minutes. Add the reserved lobster juices and enough stock to barely cover the ingredients. Bring to a boil over high heat, skimming off any foam that rises to the surface. Reduce the heat to low and simmer until well flavored, about 45 minutes. Strain into a large bowl, pressing hard on the solids to extract as much flavor as possible, then discard the solids. (If making in advance, cool, cover, and refrigerate.)

In a large saucepan, bring the lobster stock to a boil over high heat and reduce it to 1 cup, about 30 minutes. Add the cream, return to a boil, and cook until the sauce thickens slightly, about 5 minutes. Taste and season carefully with salt and cayenne.

ASSEMBLY

1 pound fresh or dried fettuccine

2 tablespoons unsalted butter, cut into eight pieces

1 tablespoon finely chopped fresh flat-leaf parsley

2 teaspoons finely chopped fresh tarragon

10 basil leaves, cut into chiffonade (page 44)

10 sprigs chervil

Bring a large pot of salted water to a boil over high heat. Add the fettuccine and cook until al dente, 2 to 3 minutes for fresh, 8 to 10 minutes for dried. Drain and return the pasta to the pot.

If necessary, reheat the lobster sauce over low heat and stir in the butter a piece at a time. Add the lobster meat and cook just to heat through, about 2 minutes. Stir in the parsley, tarragon, and basil. Add the warm lobster sauce to the pasta and toss well.

Serve in warmed pasta bowls, garnishing each serving with the chervil sprigs.

Variations: Just about any flat noodle will work in this dish. If you have a preference for tagliarini, pappardelle, or another pasta, you should experiment and determine which works best for you.

Pappardelle, Sea Scallops, Salmon Roe, and Parsley Pesto

MAKES 6 TO 8 APPETIZER OR 4 MAIN-COURSE SERVINGS

IF YOU GROW PARSLEY in your garden (or on your window sill), the recipe for Parsley Pesto used in this dish will allow you to enjoy your bounty year-round. (You can make a more conventional pesto in the summertime using fresh basil and storing it in jars. A thin film of oil at the top of the jar should keep the pesto fresh in your refrigerator for months.) This pesto has a visual vibrancy because the parsley is blanched and shocked, locking in its brilliant green color. As good as it is with scallops, it works equally well with a lot of foods, such as littleneck clams and shiny black mussels, and can turn something as simple as fresh tomatoes into a delicious and satisfying small meal.

Thinking Ahead: The Parsley Pesto may be prepared as much as 4 hours in advance.

1 small yellow bell pepper, cut into very thin julienne (page 43)

1 small red bell pepper, cut into very thin julienne (page 43)

$1/2$ cup heavy cream

$1/2$ cup Clam Broth (page 40)

2 tablespoons unsalted butter, cut into 8 pieces

Coarse salt, freshly ground white pepper, and cayenne to taste

2 tablespoons canola oil

$1^1/2$ pounds fresh sea scallops, preferably diver scallops

1 pound fresh or dried pappardelle

Parsley Pesto (recipe follows)

4 ounces salmon roe

Flat-leaf parsley sprigs, for garnish

About 1 hour before serving, place the julienned yellow and red peppers into a medium bowl of iced water. Refrigerate until the peppers have curled, about 1 hour.

In a small saucepan, bring the cream and clam broth to a boil over high heat. Cook until reduced to about $2/3$ cup, 8 to 12 minutes. One piece at a time, whisk in the butter, or use a handheld immersion blender. Remove the sauce from the heat and let the sauce stand in a warm place to keep warm. Taste carefully (the clam broth may already be salty) and season with salt, white pepper, and cayenne.

In a 12-inch sauté pan, heat the oil over high heat until very hot but not smoking. Season the scallops with salt and white pepper. Place in the sauté pan and cook until the undersides are golden brown, about 2 minutes. Turn and cook until the scallops are warm in the center, but still rare, about 1 minute. (If you wish, the scallops can be cooked for an additional 2 minutes or so, until cooked through, but I prefer them cooked rare.)

Meanwhile, bring a large pot of salted water to a boil over high heat. Add the pappardelle and cook until al dente, 2 to 3 minutes for fresh, 8 to 10 minutes for dried. Drain well and return to the pot. Add the parsley pesto and warm clam sauce to coat the pasta.

Drain the peppers well. Transfer the pasta to warmed deep pasta bowls. Place the scallops on top, then the salmon roe, and garnish with the pepper curls and parsley.

Parsley Pesto

MAKES ABOUT ½ CUP

1 cup packed fresh flat-leaf parsley

6 tablespoon extra-virgin olive oil

6 tablespoons Roasted Garlic Puree (see Sidebar, page 47)

Coarse salt and freshly ground white pepper to taste

In a blender or food processor fitted with the metal blade, combine half the parsley and the oil. Process, stopping to scrape down the pesto as needed, until smooth. Add the remaining parsley and the roasted garlic and process until combined. Season with salt and pepper. Transfer to a bowl and cover with plastic wrap, pressing the plastic directly onto the surface of the pesto. Refrigerate until ready to use. Return to room temperature and stir well before using.

PESTO IS USUALLY thought of as a summer pleasure when basil is at its peak. In the other seasons, parsley combined with roasted garlic makes an excellent pesto as well. The slow roasted garlic lends it a mellow depth of flavor.

Linguine **and Prawns in a**
Tarragon-Coriander Broth

MAKES 6 APPETIZER OR 4 MAIN-COURSE SERVINGS

THIS RECIPE EVOLVED while looking for a new way to use fresh, head-on spot prawns to maximize their potent flavor. After a period of experimentation, I came up with the broth used in this dish—the prawn heads and shells lend the broth an intense flavor that coexists nicely with the powerful taste of coriander. At the Gotham, we also reduce champagne in the broth, but this may be impractical in a home setting. Here, I've supplied a recipe that uses white wine instead. I recommend serving the fragrant broth in a large bowl with the pasta and prawns perched on top.

Thinking Ahead: The prawns and prawn stock may be prepared 1 day in advance, covered, and refrigerated.

PRAWN STOCK

2$^{1}/_{4}$ pounds prawns, preferably spot prawns with heads on (if headless, purchase 8 additional prawns)

2 tablespoons vegetable oil

1 small onion, cut into $^{1}/_{2}$-inch dice

$^{1}/_{4}$ cup finely chopped carrot

$^{1}/_{4}$ cup finely chopped celery

3 garlic cloves, sliced

1 cup peeled, seeded, and chopped ripe plum tomatoes

1 tablespoon tomato paste

1 teaspoon coriander seed

$^{1}/_{2}$ cup white wine

4 cups White Chicken Stock (page 33)

Coarse salt, freshly ground white pepper, and cayenne to taste

If using head-on prawns, twist off and reserve the heads. If using headless prawns, coarsely chop 8 unpeeled prawns to substitute for the heads, and set aside. In both cases, peel and devein the remaining prawns. Cover and refrigerate the prawn meat. Reserve the shells.

In a large sauté pan, heat the oil over medium-high heat. Add the prawn shells (or chopped prawns) and heads. Cook until bright red, about 3 minutes. Add the onion, carrot, celery, and garlic and reduce the heat to medium-low. Cook until the vegetables soften, 8 to 10 minutes. Add the tomatoes, tomato paste, and coriander seed and cook for 3 minutes. Add the wine and reduce slightly, about 2 minutes. Add the stock and bring to a boil. Reduce the heat to very low and simmer until reduced to about 2 cups, 30 to 40 minutes.

Strain into a large bowl, pressing hard on the solids; discard the solids. Transfer the prawn stock to a medium saucepan and bring to a boil over high heat. Boil gently until reduced to 1 cup, about 15 minutes. Season with salt, white pepper, and cayenne, and set aside.

ASSEMBLY

    1 pound dried linguine

    2 tablespoons vegetable oil

    3 tablespoons unsalted butter

    Coarse salt and freshly ground white pepper

    1 tablespoon finely minced fresh chives

    1 tablespoon finely chopped fresh tarragon

Bring a large pot of salted water to a boil over high heat. Add the linguine and cook until al dente, about 9 minutes. Drain well.

Meanwhile, in a large sauté pan, heat the oil over medium-high heat. Season the reserved prawn meat with salt and pepper. Add to the pan and cook, turning once, until the meat is firm and pink, about 3 minutes.

Bring the prawn sauce back to the boil. Reduce the heat to very low. Whisk in the butter, a tablespoon at a time. Keep the sauce warm, but not simmering.

Divide the pasta evenly among heated deep soup bowls. Stir the herbs into the sauce, then ladle over the pasta perching the prawns precariously on top.

Mussel Risotto, Tomatoes, Saffron, and Tarragon

MAKES 6 APPETIZER OR 4 MAIN-COURSE SERVINGS

TRADITIONAL ITALIAN seafood risottos are often comprised of 3 or 4 types of shellfish. While this can be very satisfying, the flavors of the various fish can also drown each other out. I began looking for just one shellfish to use—shrimp, lobster, even clams—so that its flavor could really be focused. For this book, I settled on mussels, and, to add unexpected, non-Italian accents to the recipe, I borrowed a little from Provence, inserting tarragon, orange peel, fennel, and saffron. Visually, this dish is a knockout, the mussels, orange peel, and herbs dotting the risotto with pinpoints of color.

Thinking Ahead: The mussels and stock may be prepared up to 8 hours in advance, cooled, covered, and refrigerated.

MUSSELS AND STOCK

3 tablespoons olive oil

$1/3$ cup chopped onion

$1/4$ cup chopped celery

$1/4$ cup chopped leek, white part only

4 garlic cloves, peeled and crushed

1 cup dry white wine

36 mussels, preferably cultivated, washed, beards removed if necessary

Herb Sachet: 1 teaspoon whole black peppercorns, 2 sprigs flat-leaf parsley, and 1 sprig thyme, wrapped in cheesecloth and tied

In a large pot, heat the oil over medium heat. Add the onion, celery, leek, and garlic. Cover and cook until the vegetables soften, about 5 minutes. Add the white wine, bring to a boil over high heat, and cook until the wine is reduced by half, about 5 minutes. Add the mussels and the herb sachet. Cook until the mussels open, about 5 minutes. Strain the stock into a large bowl, discarding the herb sachet. Remove the mussels and decant the stock through a fine wire sieve into a bowl, leaving any sand behind. Reserve the stock. Let the mussels cool, discard the shells, and reserve the meat.

RISOTTO

About $4^{1}/2$ cups White Chicken Stock (page 33)

3 tablespoons unsalted butter

$1/2$ cup thinly sliced shallots

$1/2$ cup ($1/4$-inch) diced fennel

1 large ripe beefsteak tomato, peeled, seeded, and chopped into $1/4$-inch dice

1 (14-inch) strip of orange peel, removed from orange with a vegetable peeler

$^1/_8$ teaspoon crumbled saffron

1 sprig thyme

2 garlic cloves, minced

$^1/_2$ cup dry white wine

1 pound Italian rice, preferably Vialone Nano, if available, or arborio

4 tablespoons Herbed Garlic Butter (page 231)

2 tablespoons finely chopped fresh flat-leaf parsley

2 tablespoons chopped fresh tarragon

Coarse salt and freshly ground white pepper to taste

Combine the reserved mussel stock with enough chicken stock to measure 7 cups. Bring the stock to a boil in a large saucepan over high heat. Reduce the heat to very low, so the stock is barely simmering.

In a large heavy-bottomed saucepan, heat the butter over medium-low heat. Add the shallots, fennel, and garlic and cook, stirring occasionally, until the vegetables soften, about 5 minutes. Stir in the rice, tomato, orange peel, saffron, and thyme. Cook, stirring constantly with a wooden spoon, until the rice is coated, turns a milky opaque white, and begins to stick to the bottom of the pan, 7 to 10 minutes. Add the wine and cook until it is almost completely absorbed by the rice, about 2 minutes. Ladle about 1 cup of the simmering stock into the rice. Cook, stirring often, until the stock is almost completely absorbed, about 2 minutes. Continue cooking and stirring, adding another cup of stock only when the previous addition has been absorbed. After 15 minutes, begin tasting the rice. At this point, add stock judiciously. The rice should be firm, yet cooked through in 18 to 20 minutes total cooking time. Remove the orange peel and thyme sprig. During the last 2 minutes of cooking, stir in the reserved mussels to heat them through.

Stir in the garlic butter, parsley, and tarragon. Season with salt and pepper. Transfer the risotto to warmed serving bowls and serve immediately.

Variations: You may substitute 5 dozen Manila clams, or 3 dozen littleneck clams for the mussels. If you elect to do this, leave out the tarragon, orange peel, and saffron—they don't work as well with the clams.

There is enough information contained in the recipes for Fettuccine with Lobster Bolognese Sauce (page 146) and Linguine and Prawns in a Tarragon-Coriander Broth (page 150), including the stock recipes, for you to experiment with other shellfish risottos.

Farfalle, White Beans, Cherry Tomatoes, Pesto, and Ricotta Salata

MAKES 6 TO 8 APPETIZER OR 4 MAIN-COURSE SERVINGS

THIS IS ONE OF THE FEW dishes in the book that may be packed up and taken on a picnic. It uses a lot of very small, super sweet, red and yellow tomatoes to create a summery aura. It's also very simple to prepare—tomatoes tossed with pasta and pesto to create a colorful, portable delight.

Thinking Ahead: Soak the dried beans for at least 4 hours or overnight. The basil pesto may be prepared 1 day in advance, covered, and refrigerated. The bean and tomato salads may be made up to 2 hours in advance, covered, and refrigerated.

CHERRY TOMATO SALAD

1 pound cherry tomatoes, rinsed and halved

1 tablespoon minced shallot

2 medium garlic cloves, mashed to a paste with a sprinkle of coarse salt

$1/4$ cup red wine vinegar

$1/4$ cup extra-virgin olive oil

Salt and freshly ground white pepper to taste

In a medium bowl, combine all of the ingredients. Cover and set aside at room temperature.

ASSEMBLY

1 pound dried farfalle (bow-tie pasta)

$3/4$ cup Basil Pesto (recipe follows)

2 ounces ricotta salata cheese (see Sidebar, page 96), crumbled, or substitute an equal amount of Roquefort

Basil leaves, cut into chiffonade (page 44), for garnish

Bring a large pot of salted water to a boil over high heat. Add the pasta and cook until al dente, about 9 minutes. Drain well. Return the pasta to the empty pot. Add enough pesto to coat the pasta.

Transfer to individual deep pasta bowls. Top with the beans and the cherry tomato salad. Garnish with the crumbled cheese and basil leaves.

Variations: Use aged goat cheese or fresh mozzarella instead of the ricotta salata.

When they are in season, use cooked fresh cranberry or fava beans instead of the white beans.

Substitute ripe beefsteak tomatoes, cut into 1-inch chunks, for the cherry tomatoes.

Flavor Building: To create a more substantial dish, top each serving with grilled prawns or grilled tuna.

WHITE BEAN SALAD

3/4 cup dried cannellini (white kidney) beans, rinsed

1 small onion, halved

1 small carrot, halved

1 small celery rib, halved

2 cups White Chicken Stock (page 33)

2 cups water, or as needed

Coarse salt and freshly ground white pepper to taste

1/4 cup red wine vinegar

1 tablespoon minced shallot

1 medium garlic clove, mashed to a paste with a sprinkle of coarse salt

1/4 cup extra-virgin olive oil

Place the beans in a large container and add enough cold water to cover. Let stand at least 4 hours or overnight. Drain well.

In a medium saucepan, combine the beans, onion, carrot, and celery. Add the stock and 2 cups of cold water, enough to cover. Bring to a boil, reduce the heat to low, and simmer for 20 minutes. Add salt and cook until the beans are barely tender, about 20 minutes, depending on the dryness of the beans. Drain well, discarding the vegetables.

In a medium bowl, combine the warm beans, vinegar, shallot, garlic, and olive oil. Season with salt and pepper. Cover and set aside at room temperature. Just before serving, taste the beans and reseason with more vinegar or oil, salt, and pepper, if needed.

> To flavor dried beans, I often cook them in equal amounts of chicken stock and water, with onion, carrot, and celery.

Basil Pesto

MAKES ABOUT 1 ¼ CUPS

THIS IS A CLASSIC PESTO mixture that may be stored in the refrigerator, covered with a thin film of oil, for up to 2 weeks, or frozen for up to 2 months.

2 tablespoons pine nuts

2 cups packed basil leaves, rinsed and completely dried in a salad spinner

½ cup extra-virgin olive oil

¼ cup freshly grated Parmigiano-Reggiano cheese

1 large garlic clove, minced

Coarse salt and freshly ground white pepper to taste

In a small sauté pan over medium heat, heat the pine nuts, stirring often, until lightly toasted, about 3 minutes. Transfer to a plate to cool.

In a blender or food processor fitted with the metal blade, combine half the basil with the pine nuts, oil, cheese, and garlic. Process, stopping to scrape down the pesto as needed, until smooth. Add the remaining basil and process until combined. Season with salt and pepper. Transfer to a bowl and cover with plastic wrap, pressing the plastic directly onto the surface of the pesto. Refrigerate until ready to use. (Return to room temperature and stir well before using.)

Butternut Squash Risotto, Maple-Smoked Bacon, and Sage

MAKES 6 APPETIZER OR 4 MAIN-COURSE SERVINGS

Thinking Ahead: The spiced butter may be prepared up to 8 hours in advance, covered, and refrigerated. The caramelized squash may be prepared as much as 1 hour in advance, covered, and held at room temperature.

SPICED BUTTER

8 tablespoons (1 stick) unsalted butter, at room temperature

4 tablespoons Roasted Garlic Puree (page 47)

2 teaspoons finely chopped fresh chervil

1 teaspoon finely chopped fresh marjoram

$1/2$ teaspoon ground cinnamon

$1/4$ teaspoon ground ginger

Coarse salt and freshly ground white pepper to taste

In a small bowl, combine all the ingredients. Cover and set aside at room temperature.

CARAMELIZED SQUASH

3 tablespoons unsalted butter

1 large (2-pound) butternut squash, peeled, seeded, and cut into $3/4$-inch cubes

Coarse salt and freshly ground white pepper to taste

2 teaspoons light brown sugar

In a large sauté pan, melt the butter over medium heat. Season the squash with salt and pepper, add it to the pan, and cook, stirring occasionally, until nicely browned, about 6 minutes. Cover and cook until tender, about 5 minutes. Add the brown sugar and cook until the squash is caramelized, but still holding its shape, about 2 minutes. Set aside.

WHEN SUMMER HAS LONG since turned to fall and the bitter cold of winter is just weeks away, I suggest preparing this dish to offer reassuring warmth to a small circle of family or friends. Based on a Venetian holiday recipe, this risotto boasts a rare and invigorating combination of ingredients both to welcome and combat the chill of the season. Part of the recipe's impact derives from the spiced butter that finishes it with a powerful dose of garlic, chervil, marjoram, cinnamon, and ginger. But there's an equally important step that's worth noting here: Many risotto recipes cook all the ingredients into the rice, but the success of this dish depends on *not* doing this, but adding the squash at the end to keep its flavor isolated and allow each bite to bring a different sensation to the palate. To achieve this effect, it's absolutely essential that the delicate, caramelized squash cubes be stirred in as gently as possible just prior to serving. Not only does this preserve the integrity of the squash's

(continued)

RISOTTO ASSEMBLY

About 2 quarts Double Turkey Stock (page 37)

2 tablespoons olive oil

2 ounces slab bacon, preferably maple-smoked, cut into 1/2-inch dice

1 cup minced shallots or onions

1 pound Italian rice, preferably Vialone Nano, if available,
  or arborio

1 teaspoon chopped fresh sage

1/4 teaspoon fresh thyme leaves

1/2 cup dry white wine

2 tablespoons chopped fresh flat-leaf parsley

Coarse salt and freshly ground white pepper to taste

flavor, but the orange cubes will punctuate the risotto with dazzling bursts of color.

You might also break with the convention of serving risotto as either an appetizer or an entrée, and use this one as a side dish with roast pork (squash, cinnamon, and marjoram are commonly used to season pork) or simple roast chicken. Also, the bacon in this risotto will provide an understated continuity to the plate.

In a large saucepan, bring the stock to a boil over high heat. Reduce the heat and keep hot on a very low flame.

In a large heavy-bottomed saucepan, heat the oil over medium heat. Add the bacon and cook until lightly browned, about 5 minutes. Add the shallots and cook, stirring often, until softened, about 3 minutes.

Reduce the heat to medium-low. Stir in the rice, sage, and thyme. Cook, stirring with a wooden spoon, until the rice is coated, has released its starch, turns a milky opaque white, and begins to stick to the bottom of the pan, 7 to 10 minutes. Add the wine and boil until completely reduced, 2 to 3 minutes. Ladle about 1 cup of the simmering stock into the rice. Cook, stirring often, until the stock is almost completely absorbed by the rice. Continue cooking and stirring, adding another cup of stock only when the previous addition has been absorbed. After 15 minutes, begin tasting the rice. At this point, add the remaining stock judiciously. The rice should be firm, yet cooked through in 18 to 20 minutes total cooking time.

Stir in the spiced butter and the parsley, and season with salt and pepper, then gently fold in the squash cubes, keeping them as intact as possible. Transfer the risotto to warmed bowls and serve immediately.

Variations: You may substitute another winter squash for the butternut. I recommend Hubbard, acorn, or buttercup. To expand your knowledge of the varieties of squash, try a different one each time you prepare this dish to determine which you like best and how each one plays in this context.

Goat Cheese Ravioli
in Pancetta and Shallot Sauce

MAKES ABOUT 100 RAVIOLI; 8 TO 10 APPETIZER
OR 6 MAIN-COURSE SERVINGS

IN 1985, I WAS INVITED to interview for the chef's position at Gotham. The process involved the review of sample menus and a tasting. As I've mentioned, I was determined to find a place for pasta on the menu, and I was haunted by two formative pasta experiences in my life. The first was during my childhood, when I would stand on a chair beside my mother and help her make ravioli, sealing their edges with a fork.

Twenty years later, as a young, post-graduate line cook in France, I found myself marveling at black truffle ravioli, impressed at how an Italian standard had found a home in a three-star French kitchen. When I was agonizing over what dishes to include on my "application" menu for the Gotham, goat cheese was just beginning to appear in restaurants all over the United States, and my girl friend made a crazy suggestion—"Why not try goat cheese ravioli?" The rest of the recipe came to me fairly quickly.

Making ravioli by hand is hard work, but it can be a

(continued)

Thinking Ahead: The ravioli may be prepared up to 1 day in advance, covered, and refrigerated. They may also be frozen for up to 2 months. Freeze the raviolis on flour- or cornmeal-dusted baking sheets just until hard, then transfer them to plastic freezer bags. The pancetta and shallot sauce may be prepared up to 8 hours before serving, covered, and refrigerated.

Special Equipment: manual pasta machine; pastry bag fitted with a number 5 plain tip; fluted pastry wheel or ravioli cutter

GOAT CHEESE RAVIOLI

12 ounces fresh goat cheese

1 large egg plus 1 egg yolk

Coarse salt and freshly ground white pepper

Semolina Pasta Dough (page 174)

1 large egg beaten with 1 tablespoon water

$1/2$ cup unbleached flour to cover work surface

In a bowl, beat the cheese, egg, and egg yolk until smooth. Season with salt and pepper. Transfer to a pastry bag fitted with a number 5 plain tip.

Roll out a quarter of the dough at a time. Place the pasta dough sheet on a lightly floured work surface. Brush off excess flour from the dough. Cut off any irregularly shaped ends, making a long rectangle, then cut the sheet in half to make two equal-size rectangles.

About 1 inch from the top of one sheet of dough, pipe out mounds of the filling about $1 1/2$ inches apart. The mounds should be about $3/4$ inch wide. Pipe out another row of mounds parallel to the first, about 1 inch from the bottom of the dough. Brush the second sheet lightly with the egg wash.

Place the egg washed sheet, brushed side down, over the piped sheet. Using your fingers, gently press around each mound of cheese to seal. Using a fluted pastry wheel, cut out ravioli about 1¹/₂ inches square, trimming away the excess dough as necessary. Place the ravioli on a semolina-dusted baking sheet. Repeat the procedure with the remaining dough and filling, placing the ravioli on more baking sheets as needed. Refrigerate until ready to use.

PANCETTA AND SHALLOT SAUCE

1 quart White Chicken Stock (page 33)

2 teaspoons olive oil

8 ounces pancetta, ¹/₈ inch thick, cut into ¹/₂-inch squares

1 cup thinly sliced shallots

Coarse salt and freshly ground white pepper to taste

In a medium saucepan, bring the stock to a boil over high heat. Cook until the stock has reduced to 3 cups and the flavor concentrates, 10 to 15 minutes.

Heat a large sauté pan over medium-low heat. Add the oil, then the pancetta. Cook, stirring occasionally, until the pancetta begins to release some of its fat, about 3 minutes. Add the shallots and cook without browning, stirring often, until softened, about 3 minutes. Stir the pancetta mixture into the reduced stock. Season with salt and pepper. Set aside.

ASSEMBLY

3 tablespoons Herbed Garlic Butter (page 231), cut into 3 pieces

3 ripe plum tomatoes, peeled, seeded, and cut into ¼-inch dice

2 teaspoons finely minced fresh chives

4 large basil leaves, cut into chiffonade (page 44)

fun project with a child or a friend. The extra pair of hands will make the work go quickly.

Bring the pancetta and shallot sauce to a boil over high heat. Reduce the temperature to low and whisk in the herbed garlic butter, one piece at a time. Stir in the diced tomatoes. Keep the sauce warm.

Meanwhile, bring a large pot of salted water to a boil over high heat. Add the prepared ravioli and cook until tender, about 3 minutes. Carefully drain the ravioli in a colander.

Place the ravioli in warmed soup plates. Ladle the sauce over the them, then garnish with the chives and basil.

Variation: As a vegetarian option, you can omit the Pancetta and Shallot Sauce and drizzle the ravioli with extra-virgin olive oil and a healthy dash of freshly ground pepper. Sprinkle this dish with chives, basil, and Parmigiano-Reggiano cheese.

Lemon Basil Pasta

MAKES 6 TO 8 SIDE-DISH OR APPETIZER SERVINGS
OR 4 MAIN-COURSE SERVINGS

THIS DISH WAS INSPIRED by lemon pasta, which is popular in Italy. I sampled it for the first time in Rome, and I knew right away it would make a clever accompaniment to seafood, offering an unexpected variation on the lemon wedges that are often served on the plate.

To create my interpretation of this pasta, I based a recipe on a French *beurre monter* (mounted butter): An inch of water is brought to a boil in a pot and butter is whisked into the hot liquid, yielding a creamy, yellow butter sauce. Seasoned with salt and pepper, this serves as a very useful sauce in the professional kitchen.

This dish uses herbs and cream to add richness and additional levels of taste. Linguine or tagliarini are ideal here—their strands provide a suitable surface for the sauce. The basil adds a subtle counterpoint, matching the lemon and complementing its tang with an herbal fragrance. In addition to making a terrific side dish to fish, this pasta can be served as an appetizer or as an entrée on its own.

$^1/_2$ cup heavy cream

8 tablespoons (1 stick) unsalted butter, cut into pieces

2 tablespoons fresh lemon juice, plus more if needed

1 small garlic clove, finely minced

Coarse salt, freshly ground white pepper, and cayenne to taste

1 pound fresh or dried linguine or tagliarini

3 tablespoons chopped fresh basil, plus whole fresh leaves, for garnish

2 tablespoons finely minced fresh chives

In a medium saucepan, bring the cream to a boil over medium-high heat. Cook until slightly thickened, about 5 minutes. Remove from the heat and whisk in the butter, 1 tablespoon at a time, to make a creamy sauce. Whisk in the lemon juice and garlic. Taste, and season with salt, white pepper, and cayenne.

Meanwhile, bring a large pot of salted water to a boil over high heat. Add the linguine and cook until al dente, 2 to 3 minutes for fresh, 8 to 10 minutes for dried. Drain well. Return to the warm pot.

Add the warm sauce, chopped basil, and chives. Toss well. Taste to check the sauce for an authoritative tang—season with more lemon juice, salt, white pepper, and cayenne as needed.

Using a carving fork with 2 long, straight tines, spear a serving of pasta onto the bottom tine. Twirl the fork, wrapping the pasta around both tines. Place the pasta-entwined fork over a plate, and invert the fork, letting the pasta slide off into a neat stack. Repeat with the remaining pasta. Garnish with the whole basil leaves and serve immediately.

Variation: For a variation on the basil, use 1 tablespoon of chopped fresh tarragon and garnish with whole tarragon sprigs.

Flavor Building: To make this dish more substantial, perhaps in order to serve it as a small meal on its own, toss in 2 cups of cooked lobster meat or shrimp. You might also finish the dish with 2 cups of delicate, lump crab meat. All 3 of these options will mingle well with the lemon and basil.

If you like a stronger lemon flavor, add the zest of 1 lemon (julienned, blanched in boiling water for 1 minute, and drained) to the pasta along with the lemon juice.

I often serve this to accompany simple grilled fish such as swordfish or tuna steaks.

For an outrageous appetizer, omit the basil and chives and top each portion with an ounce of sevruga caviar. Serve with champagne.

Bucatini **with Wild Mushroom Sauce**

MAKES 6 APPETIZER OR 4 MAIN-COURSE SERVINGS

Thinking Ahead: The morel sauce and mushroom garnish may be prepared up to 3 hours in advance, covered, and refrigerated.

MOREL SAUCE

$1^{1}/_{2}$ ounces dried morels ($1^{1}/_{2}$ loosely packed cups)

$1^{1}/_{2}$ cups hot water

2 tablespoons unsalted butter

1 medium onion, chopped

1 medium carrot, cut into $^{1}/_{4}$-inch dice

1 medium celery rib, cut into $^{1}/_{4}$-inch dice

1 large leek, trimmed, well washed to remove grit, and cut into $^{1}/_{4}$-inch dice

2 garlic cloves, minced

3 cups White Chicken Stock (page 33)

Bouquet Garni: 5 thyme sprigs, 5 parsley sprigs, and 1 dried bay leaf, tied together with kitchen string

3 cups heavy cream

Coarse salt and freshly ground white pepper to taste

In a medium bowl, combine the dried morels with the hot water. Let stand until the morels are softened, about 20 minutes. Lift the morels out of the soaking liquid, rinse well, and set aside.

In a large saucepan, heat the butter over medium heat. Add the onion, carrot, celery, and leek. Cook, stirring often, until softened, but not browned, about 5 minutes. Add the garlic and stir for 1 minute. Then, add the soaked morels and cook for another minute.

Add the chicken stock and bouquet garni and bring to a boil over high heat. Cook until the liquid has reduced to about $^{1}/_{2}$ cup, 20 to 30 minutes. Add the heavy cream and bring to a boil. Reduce the heat to medium-low and simmer until the sauce is thick enough to coat a metal spoon, about 15 minutes. The sauce should be on the thick

IF YOU LOVE MUSHROOMS, cook this dish, in which the flavor of the stock is enhanced by using mushrooms to make it and then adding a handful of freshly sautéed mushrooms at the end.

Depending on when you make this dish, the sauce may include chanterelles, hedgehogs, pluerotte, or black trumpets. When foraged mushrooms are scarce, use exotic cultivated mushrooms such as cremini or shiitake. When preparing the mushrooms, consider the size and shape and cut them accordingly. I like to use dried morels in the sauce because they give it a tremendous depth of flavor.

Additional levels of flavor are layered in with the abundant use of fresh herbs, which balance the woody quality of the sauce. The toasted pine nuts add yet another—and unexpected—note of flavor, texture, and aroma.

If you use fresh morels as part of the mushroom garnish mix, clean them carefully. Wash well without soaking, then cut them in half to reveal any hidden stones. Other mushrooms can be wiped clean with a damp towel or rinsed briefly under cold water and dried immediately.

Toast pine nuts in a dry skillet over medium heat, stirring almost constantly, until lightly browned about 3 minutes. Turn out onto a plate to cool.

side, as it will thin out when the wild mushroom garnish and its liquid are added. Season with salt and pepper.

WILD MUSHROOM GARNISH

2 tablespoons unsalted butter

$1^{1}/_{2}$ pounds fresh wild mushrooms (see headnote), trimmed

2 tablespoons minced shallot

Coarse salt and freshly ground white pepper to taste

In a 12-inch sauté pan, heat the butter over medium-high heat. Add the mushrooms and cook, stirring often, just until the mushrooms give off their liquid, about 5 minutes. Then add the shallot and cook until softened, about 1 minute. Season with salt and pepper.

ASSEMBLY

1 pound dried bucatini

3 tablespoons chopped fresh basil

3 tablespoons minced fresh chives

3 tablespoons chopped fresh flat-leaf parsley

Coarse salt and freshly ground white pepper to taste

1 large tomato, peeled, seeded, and cut into $^{1}/_{4}$-inch cubes (optional)

$^{1}/_{3}$ cup pine nuts, toasted (see Sidebar)

Reheat the morel sauce and mushroom garnish, if necessary.

In a large pot of salted water, cook the bucatini at a boil until al dente, about 10 minutes. Drain well and transfer to a heated serving bowl.

Meanwhile, add the basil, chives, and parsley to the morel sauce. Taste, and season with salt and pepper.

Toss the bucatini with half the sauce and place in heated soup bowls. Spoon the remaining sauce and the mushroom garnish over the pasta, and sprinkle with the chopped tomatoes and toasted pine nuts.

Variations: Other dried mushrooms, such as porcini or chanterelles, may be substituted for the morels, but morels give the best flavor. An interesting and tasty version may be made with inexpensive Chinese dried black mushrooms.

Flavor Building: Drizzle each serving with white truffle oil.

Asparagus and Morel Mushroom Risotto with Pea Leaves and Chervil Butter

Thinking Ahead: The asparagus, peas, and mushrooms may be prepared as much as 4 hours in advance and stored at room temperature.

ASPARAGUS AND MUSHROOMS

8 ounces medium asparagus, ends trimmed, spears peeled with a vegetable peeler

1/4 cup fresh peas

2 tablespoons unsalted butter

1 garlic clove, thinly sliced

6 ounces fresh morel mushrooms, halved lengthwise if large

In a large saucepan of boiling salted water, cook the asparagus over high heat until just tender, about 3 minutes. Using a large skimmer, remove the asparagus and plunge them into a bowl of iced water to cool and set the color. Drain, cut into 1/2-inch-long pieces, and set aside.

Add the peas to the boiling water and cook until just tender, about 3 minutes. Drain and plunge them into a bowl of iced water to cool, and drain again. Add to the asparagus.

In a 12-inch sauté pan, heat the butter over medium heat. Add the garlic and cook for 1 minute. Add the mushrooms and cook, stirring occasionally, until the mushrooms are tender, about 7 minutes. Set aside in a separate bowl.

RISOTTO

About 2 quarts Double Turkey Stock (page 37)

4 tablespoons unsalted butter

1 tablespoon olive oil

1/2 cup finely chopped shallots

THIS DISH UNITES 3 vegetables closely associated with spring—peas, asparagus, and morel mushrooms—in the context of a hearty risotto. As flavorful as this dish is, the interplay of textures is equally pleasing. The tender, emerald green asparagus stalks contrast the rice itself, while the plump morels echo the chewy texture of the risotto.

A generous amount of chervil and sweet butter stirred in at the end gives this dish a soft, herbaceous flourish of flavor.

1 pound Italian rice, preferably Vialone Nano or arborio

¹/₂ cup dry white wine

1 cup (2 ounces) loosely packed pea leaves (see Sidebar, page 142) or an equal amount of arugula

2 tablespoons chopped fresh chervil; plus 12 sprigs, for garnish

Coarse salt and freshly ground white pepper to taste

In a large saucepan, bring the stock to a boil over high heat. Reduce the heat to a low simmer.

In a large heavy-bottomed saucepan, heat 2 tablespoons of the butter with the olive oil over medium heat. Add the shallots and cook, stirring often, until they're softened, about 3 minutes.

Reduce the heat to medium-low. Add the rice and cook, stirring almost constantly, until the rice is glistening and has turned milky opaque white, 7 to 10 minutes. Add the wine and cook until almost completely absorbed by the rice. Ladle 1 cup of the simmering stock into the rice. Cook, stirring often, until the stock has been almost completely absorbed, about 2 minutes. Add another cup of the simmering stock to the rice. Continue cooking and stirring, adding more stock only when the previous addition has been completely absorbed. After 15 minutes, begin tasting the rice. At this point, add the remaining stock judiciously. The rice should be firm, yet cooked through, in about 18 minutes total cooking time. During the last 2 minutes, add the pea leaves, and the reserved asparagus, peas, and mushrooms.

Remove from the heat and stir in the remaining 2 tablespoons of butter and the chopped chervil. Spoon the risotto into 4 large warmed soup bowls, and garnish with the chervil sprigs.

Variation: Substitute trimmed, blanched fiddleheads for the asparagus.

Flavor Building: Drizzle each serving with white truffle oil.

Ratatouille **Risotto**

MAKES 6 APPETIZER OR 4 MAIN-COURSE SERVINGS

IN MOST RATATOUILLE recipes, the vegetables are slow-cooked together for a long time, creating a stew in which the components melt together and become virtually indistinguishable. What a shame, especially when these vegetables are in season. I recommend a shorter, more segmented cooking process that retains the color, texture, and taste of each vegetable. The virtues of this technique are amplified in the context of a risotto. The flavor of each vegetable becomes even more pronounced, much the way different colors stand out when placed against a white background.

Incidentally, I came up with this recipe when my East Hampton garden left me with too many zucchini at the end of a summer a few years ago. Feel free to experiment with your own favorite vegetable combinations, using the techniques below. I recommend trying this risotto by itself, or as a flavorful side dish for grilled lamb or chicken.

Thinking Ahead: The ratatouille may be prepared up to 1 day in advance, covered, and refrigerated. Reheat gently over medium-low heat before using.

RATATOUILLE

About 5 tablespoons extra-virgin olive oil

1 medium onion, thinly sliced

1 medium eggplant, cut into $1/4$-inch dice

1 medium zucchini, cut into $1/4$-inch dice

1 medium yellow squash, cut into $1/4$-inch dice

1 medium red bell pepper, seeded, cut into $1/4$-inch dice

2 garlic cloves, finely minced

2 ripe plum tomatoes, peeled, seeded, and cut into $1/4$-inch dice

1 teaspoon fresh whole thyme leaves

Salt and freshly ground white pepper to taste

Preheat the oven to 425° F. In a large ovenproof sauté pan, heat 1 tablespoon of the oil over medium-low heat. Add the onion and cook, stirring often, until the onion is soft but not browned, about 8 minutes. Transfer to a large bowl and set aside. Heat another tablespoon of the oil in the sauté pan and cook the zucchini and yellow squash, stirring occasionally, until they're lightly browned, about 8 minutes, and add to the bowl with the onion. Using 2 more tablespoons of oil, cook the eggplant over medium heat until lightly browned, about 8 minutes, and transfer to the bowl of vegetables.

Heat the remaining oil and cook the red pepper until lightly browned, about 6 minutes. Add the garlic and cook for 1 minute. Add to the bowl, along with the tomatoes and thyme. Season with salt and pepper.

Return the ratatouille to the sauté pan. Place it in the oven and roast, stirring often, until the vegetables are just cooked through and the flavors marry, about 8–10 minutes.

RISOTTO ASSEMBLY

    About 2 quarts White Chicken or Vegetable Stock (pages 33 or 42)

    2 tablespoons olive oil

    1 pound imported Italian rice, preferably Vialone Nano or arborio

    3 tablespoons unsalted butter

    2 tablespoons chopped fresh flat-leafed parsley

    Coarse salt and freshly ground white pepper to taste

    Whole basil leaves, for garnish

In a large pot, bring the stock to a boil over high heat. Reduce the heat to very low, so the stock is barely simmering.

In a large heavy-bottomed saucepan, heat the oil over medium-low heat. Add the rice. Cook, stirring often, until the rice is coated, turns a milky opaque white, and begins to stick to the bottom of the pan, 7 to 10 minutes. Ladle about 1 cup of the simmering stock into the rice and cook, stirring often, until the stock is almost completely absorbed, about 2 minutes. Add another cup of the simmering stock to the rice. Continue cooking and stirring, adding another cup of stock only when the previous addition is absorbed. After 15 minutes, begin tasting the rice. At this point, add the remaining stock judiciously. The rice should be firm, yet cooked through, in about 15 to 18 minutes total cooking time.

Stir in the butter. Fold in the ratatouille and parsley. Taste and season with salt and pepper. Transfer the risotto to warmed serving bowls, garnish with the whole basil leaves, and serve immediately.

Flavor Building: For a Mediterranean variation, stir $1/2$ cup pitted, chopped black Mediterranean olives, such as kalamata, into the risotto just before serving.

    You can also mix a touch of pesto into the risotto to round out its flavor and underscore the vegetables in the ratatouille.

Semolina Pasta Dough

MAKES 1¼ POUNDS

ALTHOUGH I PREFER imported dried pasta shapes such as farfalle, penne, or rigatoni to the fresh variety, fresh fettuccine, pappardelle, and other flat noodles are somehow different, and there's something irresistible about making pasta from scratch. In addition to the tactile pleasure of kneading the amorphous mounds of dough, there are few culinary transformations as fun to watch as that of flour, eggs, olive oil, and water becoming wonderfully ordered sheets and wide ribbon shapes. If you have the time and the equipment, you should try this at least once, just for the satisfaction of the creation. This is an especially fun thing to do with your children.

Thinking Ahead: The pasta can be made up to 8 hours in advance and stored at room temperature, although it will begin to dry out and take slightly longer to cook.

Special Equipment: pasta machine

1¼ cups unbleached flour, plus additional for dusting the pasta dough

1¼ cups durum semolina (also called pasta flour)

4 large eggs, at room temperature

½ teaspoon olive oil

2 tablespoons water, or as needed

In a food processor fitted with the metal blade, pulse the flour and semolina about 40 seconds to combine. In a small measuring cup, mix the eggs and olive oil. With the machine running, pour the egg mixture through the feed tube, then add water just until the dough comes together into a mass, about 1 minute. Check the consistency of the dough. If it feels too soft and sticky, add a tablespoon or so of flour. If it is dry and crumbly, add a tablespoon or so of water. Process the dough for 30 seconds and check again. Remove the dough and knead it on a lightly floured surface until smooth and resilient, 5 to 10 minutes. Wrap the dough in plastic wrap.

Attach the pasta machine to a work surface. Set the rollers to the widest setting. Place a bowl of flour near the machine.

Cut the dough into 4 equal portions and work with one portion at a time. Pat the dough to form a thick oblong, and run it through the machine, turning the crank with one hand while supporting the rolled dough with the other. Fold the dough into thirds and repeat until the dough has straight, even sides approximately the width of the rollers. Dust with flour as needed. Continue to roll and adjust the width of the rollers until the dough has passed through the second-to-last setting and is about ¹⁄₁₆th inch thick. Lay the pasta sheets on a lightly floured work surface. Repeat the procedure with the remaining dough.

Let the pasta sheets dry, turning occasionally, until they are slightly leathery but still pliable. Depending on the temperature and humidity, this will take anywhere from 15 to 60 minutes. **To make fettuccine,** roll each pasta sheet through the wide cutters on the pasta machine. **To make linguine,** roll through the narrow cutters. **To make pappardelle,** cut each pasta sheet into 15-inch lengths and roll them into cylinders. Using a sharp knife, cut each cylinder into 1/2-inch (or wider) strips. Unravel each portion, twist it into a spiral, and place it on a lightly floured baking sheet. Cover loosely with plastic wrap and let stand at room temperature until ready to cook.

What is *semolina?*:

Semolina is *not* a wheat variety. It describes the grainy, gritty texture of the flour itself. Semolina flour is ground from durum wheat, a hard grain with stronger gluten than the average white wheat.

7 Fish and Shellfish

Grilled Marinated Octopus with Chick-peas and Charred Tomatoes

Grilled Prawns with Lime, Cilantro, and Chiles

Scallops with Potatoes, Leeks, Sea Urchin, and Sevruga Caviar

For many reasons, fish and shellfish are my favorite foods to cook. I wasn't introduced to truly great seafood until after culinary school, when I spent a year in France. While working the *poissonier* station at the Troisgros brothers' restaurant, I became intimately familiar with the many varieties of fish and seafood, and developed a profound respect for fresh fish. Local mongers would actually deliver fresh catches to our door twice a day. We had access to the finest lobsters in the world from Brittany; fresh, immaculate crayfish and sea urchin (I actually had blisters from cleaning so many of these); and peerless salmon, which we used in the restaurant's Salmon with Sorrel Sauce, a famously popular dish.

In addition to my six months at this restaurant, I traveled around Europe, spending a lot of time in Brittany in particular, visiting fishing villages with some extraordinary markets where the catch was just hours old.

I also find that fish and seafood offer a greater flexibility than any other type of food. There is a much greater variety of fish and shellfish than, say, meat. A steak, to oversimplify a bit, is always a steak. Game and poultry offer more variety and creative possibilities, but not to the extent that fresh seafood does.

In order to secure the highest quality, freshest fish available for the Gotham, I use several purveyors. I buy tuna and certain other items from a Japanese fish purveyor. When I first started looking for a source, I couldn't match the quality I found at sushi bars around town. Finally, a sushi chef I knew referred me to his purveyor. Back then, I would go down to his shop myself and bring sushi-grade tuna back to the restaurant on my lap in the back seat of a taxi cab. Fortunately, after a while, they began to deliver.

Because New York is so close to the Atlantic, we're very fortunate to have access to some of the best seafood in the country, much of which we purchase for the restaurant direct from the Fulton Fish Market. Also, we buy our fin fish and shellfish from Maine, using a couple of highly specialized purveyors that deal directly with fishermen and boat captains, so they get catches before they reach the general market.

You should be comparably selective with the seafood you purchase for home use. The key to using the best seafood available is to be very flexible. Go to the market and see what the best selection is that day. Don't plan your seafood cooking in advance if it will lock you into just one fish option. For this book, I've chosen dishes calling for fish that I believe will be very obtainable and accessible. For the most part, I deliberately stayed away from using very exotic, esoteric fish. Many of the recipes should also allow you to make a change at the last minute, if that's what the market dictates.

Seafood is also distinct from meats and poultry because much of it is seasonal. For example, domestic red snapper has a very short season, usually February, March, and April. The rest of the year, it's imported, so you should only prepare snapper dishes in those months. (The recipe I've included for Red Snapper with Baby Clams, Merguez Sausage, and Romesco, page 211, is a personal favorite.)

Because of this seasonality, I find myself grilling lots of fish steaks at my Long Island weekend home in the summertime. I have come up with a lot of very quick and delicious sauces for fish, such as stock-based vinaigrettes, or a dollop of flavored aioli, which is all you need to bring out the flavor of, say, a piece of grilled swordfish.

Other fish, such as salmon, are very reliable year-round. Most salmon is farmed in Maine, where the water's cold temperature produces very consistent salmon, rich in fat and wonderfully flavorful. In Maine the fish are iced, packed in Styrofoam, and arrive in New York (or another destination) within about twenty-four hours. This is a remarkable resource.

I've also included several recipes for fish that I feel are a little less well-known, such as monkfish. Because of its meaty texture, monkfish can stand up to a variety of treatments, seasonings, and sauces without being overwhelmed. For this reason, chefs like to use it in ways that mirror meat preparations, such as cooking it *au poivre* or in a bordelaise sauce.

Monkfish is also very "user friendly." It has very few bones—just a cartilage backbone, really—so deboning it is relatively easy. It's also an economical fish.

A few notes on selecting, purchasing, and storing fish:

✳ It's important to know how to judge the quality of fish and shellfish. Most fishmongers won't let you touch the fish, so it's important to know what to *look* for.

* Whole fish should look firm, without wrinkled skin or loose scales, and should have a glistening sheen. Clear eyes are not always a sign of freshness, since the eyes of some varieties of fish cloud up immediately after they are caught. If the merchant will allow it, lift up the gill flap and check that the gills are bright red.

* Steaks or fillets should appear slightly translucent without any "rainbows." There should be no gaps in the flesh.

* Fresh fish should have a slightly sweet smell, or no smell at all. It should definitely *not* smell fishy.

* When I go shopping for fish, I head for Chinatown, which happens to be the best source in New York. But every city has its own good markets. By asking friends (or accommodating restaurateurs) you should be able to locate a reliable local source.

Here are some thoughts on the fish and shellfish used in this book:

Bass

There are two types of striped bass—wild bass and farmed bass. Farmed striped bass are always available, while wild has a short season and is hard to find outside of the East Coast. Wild striped bass can be anywhere from eight to twelve pounds, or even larger; fillets can be up to one inch thick, and require longer cooking time than farm-raised. Wild striped bass is a superior fish with a fine, sweet taste and large flake. Farmed striped bass are rarely over five pounds, so the filets generally require half the cooking time of wild bass.

Caviar

Buy it from a caviar dealer. If there's not one in town, you can order by mail. (See source on page 376.) Because of its reputation as an ingredient of excess, you might be tempted to select the most expensive beluga available for *any* occasion, but this isn't necessary for use in the context of a dish—beluga is probably enjoyed best on its own, or with an accompaniment of iced vodka. Sevruga will do just fine when mingled with several ingredients. Most good dealers will let you taste caviar before buying to check its flavor and texture, which is always a good idea.

Clams

For the recipes in this book, large chowder clams (sometimes called "quahogs") are used to make the clam stock that I prefer over stocks made with fish bones. Chowder clams are too tough to eat, although some cooks will tell you to grind them up in a food processor and use them in a chowder. For cooking, I often use small, sweet Pacific coast Manila clams, with their distinctive brown and beige–striped shells. You can substitute Atlantic littlenecks, but use slightly fewer because they are a little bigger.

Halibut

Halibut can be purchased in steaks or fillets. Atlantic halibut has the best flavor, and I love its firm white texture and large flake.

Lobsters

When purchasing lobster, be sure it is lively—it should flap its tail and wave its claws. Lobster, if not cooked the day it is bought, can be stored for a day or two in its own paper (not plastic) bag. The best way to keep lobsters is in the crisper drawer of your refrigerator. Put them in with damp newspaper strips and keep them alive in there. When buying lobsters in the summertime, watch out for soft-shell lobsters; they have less meat in their tails and an inferior flavor and texture.

If your fish store does a brisk lobster business or sells wholesale, they may carry "culls," which are one-clawed lobsters. Culls are less expensive and, if you feel you can sacrifice the amount of meat found in that one claw, a perfectly suitable alternative.

I recommend you cook lobsters in salted water with a little vinegar, which works very well. An even better way is to make a court bouillon of onions, celery, carrots, bay leaf, thyme, and peppercorns, simmered for fifteen to twenty minutes before cooking the lobsters in it.

Another method is to steam the lobsters in 4 inches of boiling, salted water.

Mackerel

I developed a fondness for mackerel in France, and for the last ten years, I've served it in a variety of ways. The recipe I selected for this book would work just as well with sardines, blue fish, or any number of other fish, but it happens to be one of my favorite mackerel dishes.

I prefer Spanish mackerel, which has gorgeous, flashy markings and a finer flavor than the Atlantic (Boston) mackerel. Mackerel has a very thin, transparent film covering the skin, which I prefer to remove before cooking. If you don't remove the film, the fish will curl. Use a very sharp, thin-bladed knife to make an incision on the skin, look carefully to locate the film, then pull it off.

Monkfish

Monkfish, often called "loins," is cut from the large, meaty tail of this fish. There's no need to worry about small bones, because there aren't any. The meat is white, firm, and sweet in flavor.

Mussels

Cultivated mussels are a good thing for home cooks because they have good flavor and are easier to clean than wild mussels. Another advantage of cultivated mussels is that the eater doesn't have to be concerned about the water safety of the mussels' hatching grounds. If you live near the seashore, and are using local mussels, buy them from a reliable dealer.

Octopus

Even though an Italian fish market may be the best place to find octopus (they may call it *pulpo),* it is usually from Japanese or Portuguese waters. It is almost always frozen, but there is no loss of quality as long as it has been defrosted properly. Octopus is supposed to retain its resilient texture, but it shouldn't be tough or chewy. My method for marinating and braising (see Grilled Marinated Octopus with Chick-peas and Charred Tomatoes, page 235) yields the proper bite. (The recipe also features instructions on cleaning octopus.)

Tako or Japanese octopus can be purchased in Japanese fish markets. It's this variety that I use in the Gotham Seafood Salad (page 55).

Salmon

Virtually all the salmon available on the New York market is farm-raised. If a fish purveyor offers me line-caught, wild Pacific or Alaskan salmon, I buy all I can get, but farm-raised salmon is excellent, constantly fresh, and the flavor is consistent.

Scallops

We use diver-harvested sea scallops at Gotham. The main advantage to these first-rate scallops is that they are not soaked in a phosphate solution on the fishing boats. (If you've bought them from a fish store and they're in a milky liquid, that is *not* the natural fluid.) While this chemical bath preserves the scallops, it also makes them unnaturally plump and full of water that runs out as soon as they hit the skillet. The other advantage of diver scallops, not secondary at all, is that they have an exceptionally firm texture and sweet flavor. Ask your fish store to get you "dry" (or unprocessed) scallops. Diver sea scallops are large, but don't overcook them or they will toughen.

The Japanese eat scallops raw, as sashimi. Similarly, I sear them, leaving the inside uncooked.

Sea Urchin

If you have access to a Japanese fish store, you can buy *uni,* which comes in small wooden trays. This is fresh sea urchin, which has been dipped for a few seconds in a saline solution, which rinses off any bits of shell and firms up the meat. If you can get whole urchins, by all means do so. Judge the quality by the color of the pockets of roe inside. The color will range from pale yellow to bright orange. There is a huge difference in taste. The bright orange is cleaner, richer, and downright sweet.

Skate

Skate has a mild, slightly sweet flavor and interesting texture. I prefer to fillet the skate wings and quickly sauté them until golden brown and crisp. This method is quicker and easier than the more traditional method of poaching.

Soft-Shell Crab

If you're buying these and not cooking them right away, you must buy them live and be prepared to clean them yourself. If you're going to cook them right away, have the market clean them. I prefer the smaller, or "hotel size" crabs—allowing 3–4 per person—to the larger crabs, only because, when cooked, there is a greater ratio of crispy surface to creamy center.

Tuna

We use forty pounds of sushi-grade yellowfin tuna every day at the Gotham, so it's amazing to think that just a few years ago Americans ate tuna only out of cans. When purchasing tuna, buy thick steaks and trim off any dark colored meat or "chiai," the mid-lateral strip of dark meat, which is bitter when cooked. With a little experience you can easily judge freshness by seeking out a bright red color, shiny, brilliant surface, and a clear fresh smell. Avoid dull or opaque-looking tuna and brownish coloring.

Striped Bass with Sweet Corn Custard and Champagne Vinaigrette

MAKES 4 SERVINGS

THIS SUMMER-THEMED dish features fresh striped bass, fava beans, and new potatoes. The remarkably concentrated, sweet corn flavor packed into the custards is underscored by corn kernels on the plate.

In the stock-based vinaigrette, champagne vinegar provides the acidic element. Combined with diced tomato and fresh herbs, it's a simple sauce for the bass. I use this recipe frequently when I want to serve a simple grilled fish for friends or family.

Thinking Ahead: The corn custards may be prepared up to 8 hours in advance, covered, and refrigerated. The vinaigrette may be prepared up to 1 day in advance, covered, and refrigerated. The vegetables may be prepared up to 1 hour ahead, and kept at room temperature. Reheat the potatoes and Swiss chard, if necessary.

Special Equipment: 4 (6-ounce) ramekins

SWEET CORN CUSTARD

$1^1/2$ cups fresh corn kernels (from about 3 large ears of corn)

1 cup heavy cream

2 large eggs

$^1/4$ teaspoon coarse salt

$^1/8$ teaspoon freshly ground white pepper

Preheat the oven to 300° F. Lightly butter the ramekins. In a medium saucepan, bring the corn and cream to a boil over medium heat. Reduce the heat to very low and simmer slowly until the corn is very tender, about 15 minutes. (Do not simmer too quickly or the cream will reduce too much.) Set the pan into a larger bowl of iced water and stir often until cooled.

In a blender (or directly in the saucepan using a hand immersion blender), puree the corn and cream. Add the eggs, salt, and pepper and process until smooth. Strain through a wire sieve.

Place the ramekins in a large baking dish. Pour the corn mixture into the prepared ramekins and put the baking dish in the oven. Carefully pour enough hot water in the dish to come about $^1/2$ inch up the sides of the ramekins. Cover the pan with aluminum foil.

Bake until the custards are set, $1^1/4$ to $1^1/2$ hours. (The centers will still seem a little loose.) Remove from the water bath. If not serving immediately, cool completely, cover with plastic wrap, and refrigerate

until ready to reheat. To reheat the custards, place the unwrapped ramekins in a large sauté pan and add enough water to come $1/2$ inch up the sides. Bring to a simmer over low heat. Heat until the custards are warmed through, about 30 minutes. Off the heat, the custards will keep warm in the water bath for up to 30 minutes.

VEGETABLES

4 medium fingerling or new potatoes, unpeeled

12 pearl onions, peeled (see Sidebar, page 274)

$1/2$ teaspoon sugar

$1^1/2$ cups fresh fava beans (from about $1^1/2$ pounds of unshelled beans)

$1/2$ cup fresh corn kernels

In a pot of boiling salted water, cook the potatoes until tender, 15 to 20 minutes. Remove with a slotted spoon, halve each lengthwise, and return to the cooking liquid to keep warm.

Cook the pearl onions in a small saucepan of boiling salted water with the sugar over medium heat until just tender, 10 to 12 minutes. Drain and set aside.

Cook the fava beans in a medium saucepan of boiling salted water over high heat until barely tender, 2 to 3 minutes. Using a large skimmer or slotted spoon, transfer the fava beans to a bowl of iced water. Drain, peel off the tough skins from the beans, and set the peeled beans aside.

Return the bean water to a boil, add the corn, and cook for 2 minutes. Drain and set aside.

ASSEMBLY

2 cups water

2 tablespoons unsalted butter

$1^1/2$ pounds Swiss chard, stems discarded, washed

Coarse salt and freshly ground white pepper to taste

4 (6-ounce) striped bass fillets

3 tablespoons canola oil

1 cup Champagne Vinaigrette (recipe follows)

1 scallion, cut on a severe bias into very thin slices

8 sprigs chervil

In a medium saucepan, bring the water and butter to a boil over high heat. Add the chard and season with salt and pepper. Cook just until the chard is wilted, about 3 minutes. Drain, cover, and keep warm.

Season the fish on both sides with salt and pepper. In a 12-inch sauté pan, heat the oil over medium-high heat. Add the fish, skin side down. Cook until lightly browned, about 2 minutes. Turn, reduce the heat to medium, and cook until the fish is opaque in the center and the other side is browned, 3 to 4 minutes.

Meanwhile, in a small saucepan, combine the pearl onions, corn, and fava beans. Add about $1/3$ cup of the vinaigrette and warm gently over low heat.

On each of 4 warmed dinner plates heap a spoonful of chard. Place the halved potatoes on top, and then a sea bass fillet. Run a knife around the inside of a ramekin, and unmold it onto the plate. Add a spoonful of the dressed vegetables. Garnish with the scallion and chervil. Pour the remaining vinaigrette into a sauceboat and stir before serving.

Champagne Vinaigrette

MAKES ABOUT 1 CUP

$1/2$ cup Clam Broth (page 40) or bottled clam juice

$1/4$ cup champagne vinegar

1 teaspoon Dijon mustard

2 teaspoons finely minced shallot

$1/4$ teaspoon finely minced garlic

$1/4$ cup extra-virgin olive oil

Coarse salt and freshly ground white pepper to taste

2 ripe plum tomatoes, cut in half, seeded, and cut into $1/4$-inch dice

2 tablespoons finely minced fresh chives or flat-leaf parsley

STOCK ADDS ANOTHER dimension to this vinaigrette, also allowing the cook to use less oil. Neutral yet flavorful chicken or vegetable stock also will work especially well.

In a medium bowl, whisk together all the ingredients except the tomatoes and chives, seasoning with salt and pepper. This vinaigrette does not have to emulsify, and will form pools when spooned onto the plate. Just before serving, stir in the tomatoes and chives.

Striped Bass, Leeks, Shiitake Mushrooms, and a Vintage Port Sauce

MAKES 4 SERVINGS

THIS DISH WAS FEATURED on my first Gotham menu in 1985, and I've presented it here as we first served it. The recipe calls for shiitake mushrooms. Although sometimes we use more costly chanterelles. The vintage port sauce uses plenty of garlic, which gives the sauce a heady undercurrent of flavor. Similarly, the reduction of the port concentrates its notes of sugar and fruit, giving the sauce a surprising balance. This sauce is a variation on a *beurre blanc,* the classic French butter sauce, in which butter is whisked, one piece at a time, into a reduction of wine and vinegar to which a few tablespoons of cream are added. While *beurre blancs* are used more sparingly in today's calorie-conscious society, it's a classic sauce and an important technique to understand.

   In this dish, the bass is cooked over high heat to crisp its skin, adding yet another texture and a pleasing "mouthfeel."

Thinking Ahead: The leeks and mushrooms may be prepared as much as 4 hours in advance. The sauce may be prepared as much as 1 hour in advance. Both should be kept at room temperature.

LEEKS

4 medium leeks, trimmed

2 cups water

3 tablespoons unsalted butter

Coarse salt and freshly ground white pepper to taste

Cut the leeks crosswise on a bias into $1/2$-inch slices, including 1 inch of the light green tops. Rinse the leeks well, separating them into individual rings. In a large saucepan, combine the leeks, water, and butter. Season with salt and pepper. Bring to a boil over high heat. Reduce the heat to medium-low and simmer until the leeks are barely tender, about 7 minutes. Remove from the heat and set aside. If necessary, reheat the leeks in their cooking liquid. Drain just before serving.

SHIITAKE MUSHROOMS

3 tablespoons unsalted butter

14 medium shiitake mushrooms, stems discarded, caps sliced into $1/4$-inch-thick strips

Coarse salt and freshly ground white pepper to taste

In a medium sauté pan, heat the butter over medium heat. Cook the mushrooms, stirring occasionally, until lightly browned, about 6 minutes. Season with salt and pepper and set aside.

ASSEMBLY

3 tablespoons vegetable oil

4 (7-ounce) striped bass fillets

Coarse salt and freshly ground white pepper to taste

Vintage Port Sauce (recipe follows)

In a 12-inch nonstick sauté pan, heat the oil over medium-high heat until it's very hot but not smoking. Season the bass on both sides with salt and pepper. Place the bass, skin side down, in the sauté pan. Cook until nicely browned, about 3 minutes. Turn and cook until the fish is barely opaque in the center, about 1 minute. Remove from the heat.

In the center of 4 warmed dinner plates, place mounds of leeks and mushrooms, then a bass fillet and spoon the port sauce around the fish.

Flavor Building: Serve this dish with Garlic Flan (page 295) or Gotham Mashed Potatoes (page 206).

Vintage Port Sauce

MAKES ABOUT ³/₄ CUP

9 tablespoons (1 stick plus 1 tablespoon) unsalted butter, chilled, cut into tablespoons

2 tablespoons finely chopped shallots

1 large garlic clove, finely chopped

¹/₂ cup imported ruby port wine

¹/₄ cup plus 2 tablespoons red wine vinegar, plus more if needed

¹/₂ cup heavy cream

Coarse salt and freshly ground white pepper to taste

A generous 2 tablespoons chopped fresh chives

In a medium nonreactive saucepan, heat 1 tablespoon of the butter over medium heat. Add the shallots and garlic and cook without coloring, stirring often, until softened, about 2 minutes. Add the port wine and vinegar. Bring to a boil over high heat and reduce to about 2 tablespoons, 10 to 12 minutes. Add the heavy cream and cook until slightly thickened, about 3 minutes. Reduce the heat to very low. Whisk in a piece of butter at a time, whisking until the butter is incorporated into the sauce before adding more. Strain. Taste, season with salt and pepper, and balance the acidity with more vinegar if necessary. Keep the sauce warm. Wait until just before serving to stir in the chives.

Butter-based sauces can be kept warm for up to 1 hour by placing the saucepan in a skillet filled with hot tap water. Keep the water hot, but not simmering, over very low heat. Or, pour the sauce into a large-mouthed vacuum jar (warm the jar first by rinsing it out with hot water), and close tightly.

Sautéed Halibut, Roast Fennel, Swiss Chard, and Warm Coriander Seed Vinaigrette

MAKES 6 SERVINGS

IF YOU HAVE A SPECIAL fondness for the anise flavor of fennel, this is a recipe that uses it in 3 ways to create a complex and deep range of related flavors and textures. I improvised an early version of this dish during a friendly chefs' competition for *New York* magazine in which six of us were presented with a "Mystery Box"—a supply of ingredients, not announced in advance, from which to fashion a dish . . . in under an hour. Faced with this challenge, I began looking for a way to derive complementary flavors from the limited offerings and found myself drawn to a bulb of fennel, wondering how many ways I could use it in one dish . . . essentially varying one ingredient so that it could complement itself. This worked surprisingly well and, after some tweaking, I added the resulting entrée to the restaurant's menu.

The first treatment of the fennel here involves braising it in an aromatic stock, creating an infused broth that allows the essence of

(continued)

Thinking Ahead: The pan-roasted fennel may be prepared up to 2 hours in advance. The fennel curls should be prepared no longer than 2 hours prior to serving and stored in the refrigerator. The vinaigrette and Swiss chard may be prepared up to 2 hours in advance, as well. All should be kept covered at room temperature.

Special Equipment: mandoline-type slicer

PAN-ROASTED FENNEL

1 large (1½-pound) fennel bulb, trimmed, feathery tops discarded

5 tablespoons extra-virgin olive oil

1 medium onion, chopped

2 garlic cloves, sliced

2 ripe plum tomatoes, chopped

⅓ cup dry white wine

Herb Sachet: 1 tablespoon coarsely crushed coriander seeds, 2 sprigs thyme, and 1 dried bay leaf, tied in cheesecloth

2½ cups White Chicken Stock (page 33), or more as needed

Coarse salt and freshly ground white pepper to taste

Trim the end of the fennel bulb, making sure not to cut too deeply—the fennel's layers must remain connected at the bottom or the wedges won't hold together. Using a large, sharp knife, cut the fennel bulb lengthwise into 4 wedges.

In a 12-inch nonstick sauté pan, heat 3 tablespoons of the olive oil over medium heat. Add the onion and garlic and cook, covered, without browning, until soft, about 5 minutes. Stir in the tomatoes, wine, and herb sachet. Bring to a boil over high heat, and cook until the wine is reduced by half, about 3 minutes.

Add the fennel to the pan along with enough of the stock just to

the vegetable to permeate the dish absolutely. The braised fennel is then caramelized and the same vegetable is also used raw, as a garnish. Each of these variations demonstrates a different fennel preparation, all of which are useful in a variety of contexts, such as using it for a stand-alone side dish (braised) or in a salad (raw).

I haven't even mentioned the halibut, which provides a clean, sweet, and moist backdrop for this gathering of fennel.

cover the fennel. Bring to a boil, cover, and reduce the heat to low. Cook, turning the fennel halfway through the cooking time, until the fennel is barely tender when pierced with the tip of a knife, 10 to 12 minutes. Remove from the heat and let the fennel cool in its cooking liquid. Using a slotted spoon, transfer the fennel to a clean kitchen towel and pat the fennel dry. Strain the liquid into a bowl and reserve ⅔ cup for the vinaigrette.

In a 12-inch nonstick sauté pan, heat the remaining 2 tablespoons of oil over medium heat. Add the braised fennel and cook until tender and nicely caramelized on all sides, about 10 minutes. Set the fennel aside.

FENNEL CURLS

1 small (8-ounce) fennel bulb, feathery tops discarded

Using a mandoline, shave the fennel lengthwise into very thin slices, less than ⅛ inch thick. Place in a large bowl of iced water and refrigerate until crisp and curled, about 1 hour. (Do not prepare this more than 2 hours ahead of serving, or the fennel will absorb too much water and wilt.)

SWISS CHARD

2 cups water

3 tablespoons unsalted butter

1½ pounds Swiss chard, washed, stems removed

Coarse salt and freshly ground white pepper to taste

In a large saucepan, bring the water and 2 tablespoons of the butter to a boil over high heat. Add the Swiss chard, season with salt and pepper, and cover. Cook until the chard wilts, 3 to 4 minutes. Drain, cover, and keep warm.

HALIBUT AND ASSEMBLY

3 tablespoons extra-virgin olive oil

4 (6-ounce) halibut fillets, about 1¼ inches thick

Coarse salt and freshly ground white pepper to taste

Warm Coriander Seed Vinaigrette (recipe follows)

Whole green or purple basil leaves and flat-leaf parsley sprigs, with stems, for garnish

In a large sauté pan, heat 2 tablespoons of the oil over medium-high heat, until very hot but not smoking. Season the halibut on both sides with salt and pepper. Cook the halibut, until golden brown, about 4 minutes. Turn the fish and cook until it's barely opaque in the center, about 3 minutes.

While the fish is cooking, drain the fennel curls and spin them dry in a salad spinner. Transfer them to a large bowl, dress with the remaining tablespoon of oil, and salt and pepper. Reheat the Swiss chard if necessary.

On each of 4 warmed dinner plates, or on a large oval serving platter, make mounds of warm Swiss chard. Place a piece of roast fennel on each mound, fanning it out slightly, then a halibut fillet. Crown with handfuls of the dressed fennel curls, rolling up the largest slices into freestanding vertical shapes. Spoon the warm vinaigrette around and over each serving. (If serving on a platter, pour the extra vinaigrette into a sauceboat and pass it on the side.) Garnish with the basil and parsley inserted between the fennel curls.

Warm Coriander Seed Vinaigrette

MAKES ABOUT 1 CUP

²/₃ cup reserved cooking liquid from the pan-roasted fennel (see page 190)

¼ cup extra-virgin olive oil

2 tablespoons fresh lemon juice

1½ teaspoons coarsely crushed coriander seed

2 tablespoons finely minced shallot

1 small garlic clove, minced

Coarse salt and freshly ground white pepper to taste

2 tablespoons chopped fresh basil

1 tablespoon chopped fresh flat-leaf parsley

VINAIGRETTES CAN BE interesting, quickly made sauces for grilled fish—this one is also fine with grilled snapper, sea bass, or grouper.

In a medium saucepan, whisk all the ingredients except the basil and parsley over low heat until warm. The vinaigrette can be prepared up to 2 hours ahead and kept at room temperature. However, wait until just before serving to stir in the basil and parsley.

Variations: You may vary the herbs in the vinaigrette using only dill. Or you might substitute cilantro, the fresh herb from which coriander is derived, for the basil and the parsley. Also, you may enjoy adding a handful of freshly cut chives just prior to serving.

Substitute sea bass, red snapper, or grouper fillets for the halibut, reducing the cooking times slightly for the thinner fillets.

Grilled Spanish Mackerel with Chick-peas, Arugula, and a Lemon-Rosemary Vinaigrette

MAKES 4 SERVINGS

CHICK-PEAS, ONIONS, arugula, and lemon-rosemary vinaigrette would make for a delicious summer salad on their own. But each one offers a new complexity when served with grilled mackerel. The vinaigrette cuts the fattiness and richness of the mackerel, and will produce the same pleasing effect on virtually any grilled fish.

It's important to note that mackerel is highly perishable; within a day or so of purchase, it will develop a strong, unpleasant taste. Also be careful to adhere to the recommended amount of rosemary. It makes a great accompaniment to the other flavors here, but if presented out of proportion, it can be overwhelming.

Thinking Ahead: Marinate the mackerel up to 4 hours in advance, cover with plastic wrap, and refrigerate. The chick-pea salad *must be* made at least 1 hour in advance and kept covered at room temperature.

Special Equipment: perforated vegetable grilling rack, optional

MACKEREL AND MARINADE

4 (5-ounce) mackerel fillets

1/3 cup olive oil

1 small lemon, thinly sliced

1 medium shallot, thinly sliced

2 garlic cloves, thinly sliced

1 teaspoon coarsely ground white peppercorns

4 sprigs flat-leaf parsley, stems included, coarsely chopped

4 sprigs thyme, stems included, coarsely chopped

2 sprigs rosemary, stems included, coarsely chopped

Using a thin, sharp knife, make an incision at one end of the mackerel fillet. Locate the thin transparent skin that lays on top of the dark blue skin. Carefully pull off the transparent skin without removing the skin underneath.

In a shallow, nonreactive (glass or enameled) dish, combine the marinade ingredients. Add the mackerel fillets and cover tightly with plastic wrap. Refrigerate for at least 1 hour or for up to 4 hours.

VINAIGRETTES

1/3 cup plus 1 tablespoon champagne or white wine vinegar

1/4 cup fresh lemon juice

1 teaspoon Dijon mustard

1 cup extra-virgin olive oil

2 teaspoons finely chopped fresh rosemary

1 tablespoon minced shallot

1 clove garlic, peeled and mashed to paste with a pinch of salt

Coarse salt and freshly ground white pepper to taste

In a blender (or in a medium bowl using a handheld immersion blender), combine the vinegar, lemon juice, and mustard. With the machine running, gradually add the oil until it's emulsified. Transfer ²/₃ cup of the vinaigrette to a small bowl and stir in the rosemary, shallot, and garlic. (This is the lemon-rosemary vinaigrette.) Transfer the remaining vinaigrette to another small bowl. (This is the plain vinaigrette.) Season both vinaigrettes with salt and pepper.

CHICK-PEA SALAD

1 cup dried chick-peas, soaked in cold water to cover for at least 4 hours, or overnight, and drained

Coarse salt and freshly ground black pepper to taste

¹/₂ cup plain vinaigrette (see above)

> Whenever cooking dried beans in advance, refrigerate them in their cooking liquid, and they won't get hard.

Place the drained chick-peas in a medium saucepan and add enough cold water to cover them by 2 inches. Bring to a boil over high heat. Reduce the heat to low and simmer, uncovered, for 20 minutes. Add salt, and continue cooking until the chick-peas are tender, about 30 minutes more. You should have about 2¹/₂ cups. Drain well and transfer the hot chick-peas to a bowl.

Add the plain vinaigrette. Season with salt and pepper. Cover and let stand at room temperature for at least 1 hour or for up to 4 hours.

ASSEMBLY

3 tablespoons vegetable oil, for the grill grate

1 medium sweet Vidalia, Maui, or Bermuda onion, sliced crosswise into 8 thick rounds

1 tablespoon extra-virgin olive oil

Coarse salt and freshly ground pepper to taste

1 bunch arugula, stems removed, well washed

Build a charcoal fire in an outdoor grill and let the coals burn until covered with white ash. Lightly oil the grill grate. Brush the onion rounds with the olive oil and season with salt and pepper. Grill the onion rounds until tender, turning them halfway through cooking, about 8 minutes total. (An oiled, perforated vegetable-grilling rack is useful to keep the onions from slipping through the regular grill rack onto the coals.) Separate into rounds, and set the grilled onions aside.

Take the mackerel fillets from the marinade and gently scrape off the marinade ingredients with the back edge of a knife. Cut the fillets in half on a bias and season them on both sides with salt. Grill the fillets, skin side down, until nicely browned, about 3 minutes. Turn the fillets and grill until the fish is just opaque in the center, about 1 more minute.

Toss the arugula with the plain vinaigrette. Season with salt and pepper.

Everyday Presentation: Arrange the mackerel and onions on a large platter, and pass the chick-pea salad and vinaigrette on the side.

Gotham Presentation: On each of 4 dinner plates, stack 1 mackerel fillet, some grilled onions, and another mackerel fillet. Garnish with equal amounts of the arugula and chick-pea salads, then spoon the rosemary vinaigrette over the fish.

Flavor Building: I happen to love this combination of elements and wouldn't touch a thing, but if you'd like to experiment with some additional flavors, try substituting Potato-Shallot Salad (page 62), Ratatouille (page 172), or Caponata (page 221) for the chick-peas. Charred Tomatoes (page 238) also make a fine addition to the chick-peas.

If you live on the East Coast, fresh blue fish or sardines make great substitutions for the mackerel.

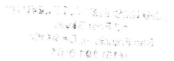

Monkfish with Savoy Cabbage, Smoked Bacon, and Fingerling Potatoes

MAKES 4 SERVINGS

Thinking Ahead: Prepare the stock and bacon up to 4 hours in advance. The cabbage and potato ragout may be prepared up to 2 hours in advance. Both may be kept covered, and refrigerated.

CHICKEN-BACON STOCK

1 tablespoon canola oil

2 ounces slab bacon, rind removed, cut into 4 pieces

1/3 cup chopped onion

3 garlic cloves, peeled and crushed

1 1/2 cups White Chicken Stock (page 33)

In a medium saucepan, heat the oil over medium-high heat. Add the bacon and cook until very lightly browned, about 5 minutes. Add the onion and garlic and reduce the heat to medium-low. Cook, covered, until the onion softens, about 7 minutes. Pour off any fat.

Add the stock and bring to a boil over high heat. Cook until reduced to 1 cup, about 10 minutes. Remove from the heat and let stand for 20 minutes. Strain the stock into a medium bowl. Dice and reserve the bacon.

SAVOY CABBAGE AND POTATO RAGOUT

4 fingerling or new potatoes, unpeeled

1 small carrot, cut into 1/4-inch dice

1 small (1-pound) head Savoy cabbage, outer leaves discarded, cut into 1/2-inch-wide shreds

Reserved stock

1/4 cup heavy cream

Reserved bacon

2 tablespoons unsalted butter

Coarse salt and freshly ground white pepper to taste

THE FOLLOWING uncommonly hearty fish dish combines the fortitude of monkfish with cabbage, smoked bacon, and red wine—elements one doesn't usually associate with fish. This combination is particularly suited to the cooler months, offering soothing comfort in the dead of winter.

I am particularly fond of this cabbage recipe because it breaks with the convention of overcooking the vegetable, which produces an unpleasantly strong flavor and odor. Here, it's cooked quickly in boiling water, then shocked in ice water to yield a bright green color and slightly crisp texture—a good technique to remember when you're looking for a simple accompaniment to chicken or duck.

This recipe also offers a rare opportunity to pair a red wine with fish—try it with a soft French Burgundy or an Oregon Pinot Noir.

In a pot of boiling salted water, cook the potatoes until tender when pierced with the tip of a knife, 10 to 15 minutes. When cooled, cut the potatoes in half lengthwise and set aside.

Cook the carrots in a pot of boiling salted water until barely tender, about 2 minutes. Drain and set aside.

Cook the cabbage in boiling salted water over high heat until barely tender, 3 to 4 minutes. Drain and shock in ice water. Using your hands, squeeze out all the excess moisture from the cabbage.

In a medium saucepan, bring the reserved chicken-bacon stock and the heavy cream to a boil over high heat. Add the potatoes, reserved diced bacon, carrots, and cabbage. Reduce the heat to low and simmer for 10 minutes. Gently stir in the butter and season with salt and pepper. Set aside.

ASSEMBLY

Spice Rub: $^1/_2$ teaspoon *each* ground star anise, ground coriander seed, and ground fennel; $^1/_4$ teaspoon ground cardamom

3 tablespoons canola oil

4 monkfish steaks (about 2 pounds total), backbones removed to yield 8 boneless fillets

Coarse salt and freshly ground white pepper to taste

2 tablespoons minced fresh chives, for garnish

In a 12-inch sauté pan, heat the oil over medium-high heat. Season the monkfish on both sides with the spice mixture, then season lightly with salt and pepper. Cook the monkfish until golden, about 3 minutes. Turn and cook until the other side is golden, about 3 minutes more. Reduce the heat to medium and cook until the monkfish is opaque in the center, about 2 minutes.

With a slotted spoon, transfer the vegetables to a warmed serving platter or individual plates. Arrange the monkfish fillets on top and spoon some of the extra sauce around the vegetables and fish. Garnish with the chives.

Variation: Use the cabbage and potato mixture as a side dish for sautéed duck breast, roast chicken, pork, or game.

Flavor Building: Stir any of the following into the cabbage and potato ragout: fresh, cooked fava, cranberry, or white beans; sautéed morel or chanterelle mushrooms; braised pearl onions; or sautéed chopped leeks.

Monkfish, Mussels, and Leeks in a Spiced Blue Crab Broth

MAKES 4 SERVINGS

Thinking Ahead: The spiced crab broth may be prepared up to 1 day in advance, covered, and refrigerated. The vegetables may be prepared 2 hours in advance, covered, and refrigerated.

USING BROTHS TO accompany fish can be very tricky; they often register with me as not integrated or assertive enough to "carry" the dish. This recipe uses a spicy seafood soup perfumed with white peppercorns, garlic, coriander, fennel seed, tarragon, parsley, and thyme. These flavors work extraordinarily well with the monkfish, also pointing out the crucial role that aroma can play in a taste experience. The delicately translucent leeks round out the dish.

SPICED CRAB BROTH

3 tablespoons vegetable oil

12 small blue crabs, cleaned (ask your fish market to do this)

1 medium onion, chopped

1 medium carrot, chopped

1 small celery rib, chopped

4 garlic cloves, sliced

1/4 cup Cognac or brandy

1 teaspoon white peppercorns

1/2 teaspoon coriander seed

1/2 teaspoon fennel seed

1 sprig tarragon

1 sprig flat-leaf parsley

1 sprig thyme

1 dried bay leaf

2 ripe plum tomatoes, seeded and chopped

3 tablespoons tomato paste

1/2 cup dry white wine

About 5 cups water

In a large stockpot, heat the oil over high heat. Add the crabs and cook, turning occasionally, until they take on a reddish color, about 10 minutes. Reduce the heat to medium-low and add the onion, carrot, celery, and garlic. Cook, stirring occasionally, until the vegetables soften, about 5 minutes. Turn up the heat to medium-high and add the brandy. Cook for 2 minutes to evaporate the alcohol and then add the peppercorns, coriander, fennel, tarragon, parsley, thyme, and bay leaf. Cook for 2 minutes to develop their flavor. Add the chopped tomatoes, tomato paste, and wine. Cook for 5 minutes to reduce slightly. Add enough water to cover the ingredients and bring to a boil. Reduce the heat to low, and simmer uncovered until well flavored, about 45 minutes. Remove from the heat and let stand for 10 minutes. Strain into a large bowl and press hard on the solids to extract as much flavor as possible; discard the solids. Skim off any fat from the surface of the stock. Return to the stockpot and boil over high heat until reduced to about 2 cups, 20 to 30 minutes. If not using immediately, cool to room temperature, cover, and refrigerate.

VEGETABLES

4 large fingerling or new potatoes, unpeeled

2 cups water

2 large leeks, white part only, cut into 1/4-inch-thick rounds, well washed

2 medium carrots, shaved into long ribbons with a vegetable peeler

Coarse salt

In a medium saucepan of lightly salted boiling water, cook the potatoes over high heat until tender when pierced with the tip of a knife, 10 to 15 minutes. Set the potatoes aside in their cooking liquid.

In a medium saucepan, bring the 2 cups water to a boil over high heat. Add the leeks and cook until they're tender, about 5 minutes. Using a slotted spoon, transfer the leeks to a bowl and set aside.

Add the carrots to the leek-cooking water and cook for 1 minute. Drain and transfer to the bowl with the leeks, and set aside at room temperature.

ASSEMBLY

3 tablespoons vegetable oil

8 boneless monkfish fillets (about 1 1/2 pounds total)

Coarse salt and freshly ground white pepper to taste

Crab broth

24 mussels, preferably cultivated, washed

Vegetables

4 tablespoons Herbed Garlic Butter (page 231)

Chervil and tarragon sprigs, for garnish

There's not a lot of meat on Eastern blue crabs, so it's not necessary to salvage them from the crab broth. However, cooks on the West Coast will have access to meaty Dungeness crabs. Substitute 3 Dungeness crabs, cut up into pieces and cracked, for the blue crabs. After sautéing the crabs until the shells turn red, pick out the crab meat. Reserve the crab meat, cool, and refrigerate. Return the shells to the stock. Continue making the stock as directed. Stir the crab meat into the broth with the vegetables to heat through.

In a 12-inch sauté pan, heat the oil over medium-high heat. Season the monkfish fillets with the salt and pepper. Place in the sauté pan and cook until golden, about 3 minutes. Turn and cook until the other side is golden, about 3 minutes more. Reduce the heat to medium and cook until the fish is opaque in the center when pierced with the tip of a knife, about 2 minutes.

Meanwhile, in a large saucepan, bring the crab broth to a boil over high heat. Add the mussels and cover. Cook until the mussels open, about 5 minutes. Discard any mussels that do not open. Transfer the mussels to a bowl. Add the vegetables to the broth and cook until they are heated through, about 1 minute. Using a slotted spoon, divide a quarter of the vegetables among 4 warmed deep soup bowls. Return the broth to a boil and whisk in the garlic butter, 1 tablespoon at a time.

Place 2 overlapping monkfish fillets in the center of each bowl. Ladle the enriched broth and remaining vegetables around the fish. Using tongs, arrange the mussels in the bowl. Garnish with the chervil and tarragon.

Salmon **with Artichokes** *à la Grecque*

MAKES 4 SERVINGS

THIS RECIPE WILL TEACH you how to create a thick, rich, creamy sauce without using any cream at all. It's based on some techniques I learned from Michel Guérard, one of the first chefs to explore spa cuisine *(cuisine minceur* in France) on a *haute* level. The sauce, an emulsion of stock, pureed artichokes, and extra-virgin olive oil, allows the flavor of the artichokes to really stand out.

This technique is a useful addition to one's repertoire, because, by varying the vegetable and herb garnishes, the possibilities are endless.

Thinking Ahead: The artichokes may be prepared as much as 8 hours in advance, covered, and refrigerated. The vinaigrette and Swiss chard may be prepared as much as 2 hours in advance, covered, and refrigerated.

ARTICHOKES *À LA GRECQUE*

3 cups water

2 tablespoons fresh lemon juice

5 medium artichokes

2 tablespoons extra-virgin olive oil

1 medium onion, sliced

1 head garlic, halved crosswise

$^1/_2$ cup dry white wine

1 sprig thyme

$^1/_2$ teaspoon coriander seed

$^1/_2$ teaspoon whole white peppercorns

$1^1/_2$ cups White Chicken Stock (page 33)

Coarse salt

In a medium bowl, combine the water and lemon juice.

Using a paring knife, pare away the thick green skin from the base of 1 artichoke. Trim away the dark green outer leaves to reveal the light green center cone.

Cut away the leaf tip to reveal the choke. Place the artichoke bottom in the lemon water. Repeat with the remaining artichokes.

In a medium saucepan, heat the oil

over medium-low heat. Add the onion and garlic and cover. Cook gently until the onion softens, about 6 minutes. Add the white wine, thyme, coriander seed, and peppercorns, and increase the heat to high. Cook until the wine is almost completely evaporated, about 3 minutes. Add the stock, the drained artichoke bottoms, and salt and bring to a simmer. Reduce the heat to medium and cover. Cook until the artichokes are tender, about 20 minutes. With a slotted spoon, transfer the artichokes to a plate and let stand until cool enough to handle. Using the tip of a dessert spoon, scoop out and discard the hairy chokes from the centers of the artichokes. If the artichokes are large, cut the bottoms in half vertically. Cover and set aside. Strain the cooking liquid into a medium bowl and set aside. Using the tip of a small knife, pick out 4 garlic clove halves from the solids and set aside.

ARTICHOKE SAUCE

   $^3/_4$ cup reserved cooking liquid (see above)

   4 reserved garlic halves

   2 reserved artichoke halves

   1 tablespoon fresh lemon juice, plus more as needed

   About $^1/_2$ cup extra-virgin olive oil

   Coarse salt and freshly ground white pepper to taste

In a blender, combine the reserved cooking liquid, garlic halves, artichoke halves, and the fresh lemon juice. With the machine running, gradually add enough of the oil to make a thick, pourable sauce. Taste, adding more lemon juice or olive oil as needed to balance the acidity, and season with salt and pepper.

SWISS CHARD

2 cups water

3 tablespoons unsalted butter

3 pounds Swiss chard, thick stems removed, well rinsed

Coarse salt and freshly ground white pepper

In a large saucepan, bring the water and 2 tablespoons of the butter to a boil over high heat. Add the Swiss chard, season with salt and pepper, and cover. Cook until the chard wilts, 3 to 4 minutes. Drain, then gently press out the excess moisture. Spread out the chard on a clean kitchen towel and cool. Just before serving, reheat the chard in a medium saucepan over low heat with the remaining tablespoon of butter. Reseason with salt and pepper, if necessary.

ASSEMBLY

3 tablespoons canola oil

4 (7-ounce) skinless salmon fillets

Coarse salt and freshly ground white pepper to taste

3 ripe plum tomatoes, peeled, seeded, and cut into ¼-inch dice

⅓ cup black Mediterranean olives, pitted and coarsely chopped

2 tablespoons chopped fresh flat-leaf parsley

In a medium saucepan, heat the remaining artichoke bottoms in the remaining cooking liquid over low heat until heated through, about 3 minutes. Keep warm.

In a 12-inch sauté pan, heat the oil over high heat until very hot but not smoking. Season the salmon with salt and pepper. Cook the salmon, skinned side up, until golden brown, about 3 minutes. Turn and cook until the other side is browned, about 2 minutes more.

While the salmon is cooking, add the tomatoes and olives to the artichoke sauce and warm over low heat, stirring constantly, about 1½ minutes. Remove from the heat and cover to keep warm.

In the center of 4 warmed dinner plates, place mounds of Swiss chard. Top each with 2 artichoke bottoms and a salmon fillet. Stir the parsley into the sauce, then spoon a few tablespoons onto each plate.

Seared Salmon, Potato Puree, Peas, and an Herbed Butter Sauce

MAKES 4 SERVINGS

THIS SIMPLE DISH features a light, herbaceous sauce—my favorite for salmon.

The presentation of this dish owes a nod to José Lampreia, who used to stack salmon atop a potato puree (made with extra-virgin olive oil, another Lampreia innovation) at his Maison Blanche restaurant in France. The Gotham Mashed Potatoes vary this dish drastically, providing the fish with an exceptionally rich foundation.

Thinking Ahead: The potatoes and sauce may be prepared as much as 2 hours in advance and kept warm.

GOTHAM MASHED POTATOES

5 large (2¼-pound) Idaho or russet baking potatoes, peeled and quartered

10 tablespoons unsalted butter, cut up

½ cup sour cream

Coarse salt and freshly ground white pepper to taste

In a pot of boiling salted water, cook the potatoes until tender, 15 to 20 minutes. Drain well.

Return the potatoes to the saucepan and cook over medium heat, stirring often, until the excess moisture evaporates and they begin to stick slightly to the bottom of the pan, about 3 minutes. Pass through a potato ricer into a large bowl or, using a potato masher, mash the potatoes with the butter and sour cream. Season with the salt and pepper. If necessary, keep warm in the top of a double boiler set over simmering water.

ASSEMBLY

1 cup fresh peas (from 1 pound peas in the pod)

¼ cup vegetable oil

4 (7-ounce) skinless salmon fillets

Coarse salt and freshly ground white pepper to taste

1½ tablespoons extra-virgin olive oil

2 teaspoons fresh lemon juice

Herbed Butter Sauce (recipe follows)

In a large saucepan of boiling salted water, cook the peas over high heat until just tender, 2 to 3 minutes. Drain in a strainer and transfer the peas to a bowl of iced water to cool completely. Drain again and set aside.

In a 12-inch sauté pan, heat the oil over medium-high heat. Season the salmon fillets on both sides with salt and pepper. Cook, skinned side up, until nicely browned, about 3 minutes. Turn and cook until the other side is browned and the fillets are barely opaque in the center, 2 to 3 minutes.

Just before serving, dress the peas with the olive oil and lemon juice, and season with salt and pepper.

Spoon a portion of the potato puree in the center of 4 warmed dinner plates. Top each with a salmon fillet. Spoon the butter sauce around and over the fish. Garnish with the peas.

Herbed Butter Sauce

MAKES ABOUT 1 CUP

1 tablespoon olive oil

2 tablespoons minced shallot

3 garlic cloves, minced

4 sprigs flat-leaf parsley

2 sprigs tarragon, plus 1 teaspoon finely chopped fresh tarragon leaves

1 large ripe tomato, peeled, seeded, and chopped

$^3/_4$ cup White Chicken Stock (page 33)

$^1/_4$ cup heavy cream

12 tablespoons (1$^1/_2$ sticks) unsalted butter, cut into 12 pieces

2 tablespoons dry white wine

1 teaspoon chopped fresh thyme leaves

Coarse salt and freshly ground white pepper to taste

2 tablespoons minced fresh chives

4 large basil leaves, cut into chiffonade (page 44)

4 sprigs chervil

> **Variations:** I find this sauce works well with other white fish such as halibut or grouper—either steamed or sautéed. You might also vary the herbs, or alter the amounts, to suit your own taste preferences.

In a small saucepan, heat the oil over low heat. Add the shallot and half the garlic. Cook, covered, until the shallot is soft, about 7 minutes. Tie the parsley and tarragon sprigs with kitchen string and add to the saucepan along with the chopped tomatoes. Cook until the tomatoes are heated through, about 2 minutes. Add the chicken stock and bring to a boil over high heat. Remove from the heat and let stand for 10 minutes. Strain the stock into a medium bowl. Discard the herb bundle, but save the shallot and tomato mixture.

Return the stock to the cleaned saucepan and add the cream. Bring to a boil and cook over medium-high heat, whisking constantly, until slightly reduced, about 3 minutes. Remove the saucepan from the heat. One piece at a time, whisk in the butter. Whisk in the reserved shallot mixture, the remaining garlic, the wine, and the thyme. Season with salt and pepper. Keep the sauce warm. Just before serving, stir in the chives, chopped tarragon, basil, and chervil.

Whole Roast Red Snapper with Tomatoes, Lemon, and Thyme

MAKES 4 TO 6 SERVINGS

1 (6-pound) whole red snapper, cleaned and scaled

Coarse salt and freshly ground white pepper

$^3/_4$ cup thinly sliced shallots

6 garlic cloves, thinly sliced

1 cup peeled, seeded, and chopped ripe tomatoes (or use canned tomatoes if ripe are not available)

1 small lemon, thinly sliced, seeds removed

1 tablespoon coarsely cracked coriander seeds

4 sprigs thyme

4 sprigs flat-leaf parsley; plus 2 tablespoons chopped, for garnish

$^1/_2$ cup extra-virgin olive oil

Preheat the oven to 400° F. Lightly oil the bottom of a roasting pan large enough to hold the whole fish. (If necessary, trim the fins with scissors to get a better fit.) Rinse the red snapper inside and out with cold running water and pat it dry with paper towels. Slash 4 X's about $^1/_4$ inch deep into the thickest parts on both sides of the fish to ensure even cooking. Season well with salt and pepper. Place the fish in the roasting pan, and scatter a few of the shallots and garlic in the cavity.

Strew the tomatoes, lemon, the remaining shallots and garlic, the coriander seeds, thyme and parsley sprigs over the fish, and drizzle with olive oil. Cover with aluminum foil.

Roast until the fish is cooked, 35 to 40 minutes. To test the fish for done-

THIS FISH DISH—QUICK, delicious, and presented whole—makes an impact. It requires just 15 minutes of preparation and 30 minutes of cooking time. The ingredients are simple. Just prep the fish, place it in the oven, and—presto!—it actually makes its own colorful sauce, replete with Provençal flavors.

I learned this recipe on my first day working in Michel Guérard's three-star restaurant in France. Toward the end of the morning's preparation, the chef stunned me when he handed me a whole snapper and casually told me to prepare lunch for him and the entire staff. Lunch for the whole staff . . . at Guérard's restaurant? I was, to say the least, terrified. When I was on the verge of a nervous breakdown, a young French chef showed me the simple preparation for this dish, as well as his method for boning cooked fish. I've made my own adjustments over the years, but this still remains very much as he taught me. The recipe was tested with a 6-pound snapper, but you may also make it with a group of smaller fish, cooking them in the same pan.

ness, make a small incision near the head. It should be just opaque near the bone. Using 2 large metal spatulas, transfer the fish to a warmed serving platter. Spoon the vegetable garnish over the fish, sprinkle with the chopped parsley, and present the whole fish at the table.

To serve, use a long, thin-bladed knife to cut vertically through the top fillet to the backbone. Make an incision down the backbone, and remove the back and dorsal fins. Use a large fork to lift off the 2 portions of the top fillet and place on warmed dinner plates. Lift off the bone structure and head and discard. Cut the bottom fillet in half horizontally. Transfer to dinner plates. Serve with the vegetables.

Variations: Substitute a whole wild striped bass for the red snapper. Or use smaller, farm-raised striped bass (about 2 pounds each), cooking the smaller fish for 20 to 30 minutes.

Flavor Building: Niçoise or green olives enhance this dish very well; use approximately 1 cup pitted olives. Sage, rosemary, and/or thyme may also be added to taste.

Red Snapper with Baby Clams, Merguez Sausage, and Romesco

MAKES 4 SERVINGS

Thinking Ahead: The romesco may be prepared up to 4 hours in advance and kept covered at room temperature. The Swiss chard may be prepared up to 2 hours in advance, covered, and refrigerated.

ROMESCO

2 tablespoons olive oil

1 large onion, halved and thinly sliced

1 large red bell pepper, seeded and thinly sliced

8 large garlic cloves, thinly sliced

$1^1/_2$ tablespoons sweet Hungarian paprika

$^1/_2$ teaspoon cayenne

Coarse salt

In a medium saucepan, heat the oil and gently cook the onion, covered, until soft, about 10 minutes. Add the pepper, cover, and cook until it softens, about 5 minutes. Add the garlic, cover, and cook for 5 minutes. Stir in the paprika, cayenne, and salt. Uncover and cook everything together for 5 more minutes, allowing the spices to permeate the vegetables and release their flavor. Transfer to a bowl and set aside.

SWISS CHARD

$1^1/_4$ pounds Swiss chard, thick stems discarded, well rinsed

2 tablespoons unsalted butter

Coarse salt and freshly ground white pepper

In a large pot of boiling water, cook the Swiss chard flavored with the butter, salt, and pepper, until the chard wilts, about 2 minutes. Drain well, pressing on the chard to remove the excess moisture. Set aside.

THIS IS A HIGHLY fragrant and spicy dish that combines richly spiced sausage with seafood, a time-honored combination that works brilliantly. This romesco sauce is based on a Catalan classic made with pulverized almonds, sweet peppers, onions, and garlic. (The actual birthplace of romesco is the ancient city of Tarragona.) When the romesco sauce hits the clams, their juice turns a brilliant, bright red, providing a stunning backdrop for the other ingredients. In fact, the effect is so exceptional that I'll often just steam open clams and serve them in a big bowl of romesco. The primary colors and bold flavors need very little augmentation, though the introduction of spicy sausage and red snapper into this context is absolutely delicious.

SNAPPER

4 (6-ounce) red snapper fillets, skin removed

Coarse salt and freshly ground white pepper

3 tablespoons olive oil

8 ounces merguez (spicy lamb sausage), cut into 4-inch lengths

Season the fillets on both sides with salt and pepper. In a 12-inch nonstick sauté pan, heat the oil over medium-high heat. Add the snapper and sausage and cook until the fish is golden brown, about 3 minutes. Turn the fish and sausage and cook until the other side of the fish is browned, another 4 minutes.

ASSEMBLY

16 small Manila or 12 littleneck clams

2–3 cups Clam Broth (page 40)

8 pieces Confit Tomatoes (page 46)

Chopped fresh flat-leaf parsley and cilantro, for garnish

Merguez, a spicy, fresh lamb sausage of North African heritage, can be found at specialty butchers. If necessary, substitute hot Italian sausage, preferably long, thin sausages about $3/4$ inch in diameter. To use larger sausages, cook them first until firm enough to slice, then cut into 2-inch lengths.

While the red snapper and sausage are cooking, place the clams and stock in a large saucepan, cover, and cook over high heat until the clams open, about 4 minutes. Add the romesco and stir until heated through, about 1 minute.

Mound the warm chard, a few clams, and tomato confit in 4 warmed, deep soup bowls. Place a red snapper fillet on each mound and spoon the romesco, remaining clams, and sausages around the chard. Add a ladle of the clam broth to each bowl and garnish with the parsley and cilantro.

Variation: Substitute monkfish fillets for the snapper.

Red Snapper Braised with Rosemary, New Potatoes, and Garlic Confit

MAKES 4 SERVINGS

ONE REASON MANY HOME cooks are hesitant to prepare fish is that they are afraid they might overcook it. If this applies to you, here is a very forgiving recipe. Even if you accidentally exceed the ideal cooking time by several minutes, you won't dry out the fish. It's also fun, perfumed with rosemary and adorned with whole cloves of garlic that allow the diner essentially to "play" with his food, mixing and matching the flavors that comprise each bite. Be sure to use a high-quality, extra-virgin olive oil; it makes a difference here.

I developed this recipe to satisfy my longing for an entrée that would evoke the pleasures of Provence, where I've spent a lot of time over the years. My most spectacular memories of the region are of summertime, when just about everything in the region—the food, the wine, and the weather—comes together almost poetically. When I presented this dish to the service staff at the Gotham, they were all skeptical—the simple, rustic presentation at first seemed out of character for the restaurant, but that was the point; it's a richly flavored, relaxed entrée you can feel very confident about making.

Thinking Ahead: The potatoes, garlic, and onions may all be prepared 8 hours in advance, covered, and refrigerated.

Special Equipment: mandoline-type slicer

NEW POTATOES

$1/4$ cup extra-virgin olive oil

1 pound small new potatoes, preferably ruby crescents, Yukon gold, or yellow Finn, washed and cut into $1/8$-inch-thick rounds (a mandoline-type slicer does the best job)

2 medium onions, quartered lengthwise, then cut into $1/4$-inch-thick slices

1 tablespoon chopped fresh rosemary

1 tablespoon chopped fresh thyme

Coarse salt and freshly ground white pepper

In a 12-inch nonstick sauté pan, heat the oil over medium-low heat. Add the potatoes and cook without coloring, stirring often to separate any slices that cling together, until the potatoes begin to soften, about 10 minutes. Add the onions, rosemary, and thyme, and season with salt and pepper. Cook, covered, until the onions soften, about 5 minutes. Transfer to a bowl and set aside.

RED SNAPPER

$1/2$ cup extra-virgin olive oil, or more if needed

20 cloves Roasted Garlic (page 47)

1 sprig rosemary

1 sprig thyme

4 (7-ounce) red snapper fillets, skin on

Coarse salt and freshly ground white pepper

$^3/_4$ cup dry white wine

2 cups Clam Broth (page 40), or more if needed

2 ripe medium tomatoes, peeled, seeded, and cut into $^1/_4$-inch dice

16 black Mediterranean olives, such as niçoise or kalamata, pitted and coarsely chopped (about $^1/_3$ cup)

2 tablespoons roughly chopped fresh flat-leaf parsley

Preheat the oven to 400° F. Add the oil to an ovenproof 12-inch nonstick sauté pan. Arrange the potatoes and onion in 4 thick mounds in the sauté pan, and scatter around the garlic, rosemary, and thyme. Season the snapper with salt and pepper. Place 1 fillet on top of each mound. Heat the skillet over medium heat until the oil begins to give off crackling sounds. Add the wine, bring to a boil, and cook until the wine is reduced by half, about 2 minutes.

Pour in the clam broth. Bring to a boil, cover, and place in the oven. Braise until the fish is barely opaque in the center, 7 to 8 minutes.

Using a slotted spatula, transfer the potato mounds with the fish fillets to the center of 4 warmed dinner plates or a large platter. Return the pan to the stove. Bring the cooking liquid to a boil over high heat. Cook the sauce until slightly thickened, 1 to 2 minutes. (This reboiling distributes the potato starch, a natural thickener, through the sauce, giving it body.) Add the tomatoes, olives, and parsley and cook for 15 seconds. Taste for balance, adding some olive oil or more clam broth if needed, and season if necessary with salt and pepper. Spoon half the sauce over the fish fillets and pour the rest into a warmed sauceboat. Serve immediately, with the sauce passed on the side.

Variation: Substitute sea bass or another firm, white-fleshed fish for the red snapper fillets.

Seared Tuna with Caponata, Pappardelle, and Red Wine Sauce

MAKES 4 SERVINGS

Thinking Ahead: The caponata may be prepared as much as 3 days in advance, covered, and refrigerated.

HERB SAUCE

¹/₄ cup heavy cream

8 tablespoons (1 stick) unsalted butter, cut into 8 pieces

1 teaspoon finely chopped fresh rosemary

Coarse salt and freshly ground white pepper to taste

Red Wine Sauce

2 cups dry red wine

¹/₄ cup red wine vinegar

1 tablespoon finely chopped shallot

1 garlic clove, peeled and crushed

1 stick (8 tablespoons) unsalted butter, cut into 8 pieces

Coarse salt and freshly ground white pepper to taste

In a medium saucepan, bring the wine, vinegar, shallot, and garlic to a boil over high heat. Cook, uncovered, until reduced to about ¹/₄ cup, 15 to 20 minutes. Remove from the heat. One piece at a time, whisk in the butter. Season with salt and pepper and strain. Keep the sauce warm.

In a medium saucepan, cook the cream over high heat until the cream is reduced to 2 tablespoons, about 5 minutes. Remove from the heat. One piece at a time, whisk in the butter. Whisk in the rosemary. Season with salt and pepper. Keep the sauce warm by placing the saucepan in a skillet of hot water over very low heat.

THERE ARE 2 COMPONENTS of this dish that are very versatile. The seared tuna is actually a tuna *au poivre* in which whole peppercorns are cracked and pressed into the fish before cooking. The combination is ideal: The pepper flavor fuses well with that of the tuna, adding a spicy undercurrent to the meaty texture of the fish.

The other versatile element here is the caponata, a mixture of eggplant, bell pepper, onion, plum tomatoes, olives, and capers, cooked together. A Mediterranean standard, caponata may be served on its own, tossed with pasta, or used to add a rich counterpoint or complement to many meats, fish, or poultry.

This dish was the result of a happy accident. One summer a few years back, my wife and I threw a Saturday night party at our home in East Hampton. Among the dishes we served were seared tuna, caponata, and pasta. On Sunday morning, we headed off to the beach, armed with a picnic basket full of

(continued)

TUNA AND ASSEMBLY

1 (1½-pound) loin of tuna, all skin and dark areas removed

2 tablespoons extra-virgin olive oil

½ teaspoon coarsely cracked white pepper

Coarse salt to taste

8 ounces fresh or dried pappardelle or fettuccine

1 tablespoon fresh lemon juice

1 tablespoon finely chopped fresh flat-leaf parsley

1 teaspoon finely chopped fresh chives

1¼ cup caponata (recipe follows)

Red Wine Sauce (page 217)

Rosemary, thyme, and chervil sprigs, for garnish

leftovers. I loaded my plastic plate with these items and was instantly struck by how well they complemented each other. As soon as we got back to the city, I began tweaking the recipe that led to this dish. At the Gotham, I began twirling the pappardelle up into the air in a sort of graduated cylinder—which became a stylistic signature.

Bring a large pot of salted water to a boil over high heat. Keep the water boiling for cooking the pasta.

Prepare the tuna by cutting it in half lengthwise and then down the middle to make 4 equal-size blocks. Brush the fish all over with the oil and rub it with the cracked pepper. Season with salt.

Heat a 12-inch, preferably cast-iron, skillet or a nonstick sauté pan over high heat. When the pan is very hot, add the tuna and cook, turning as each side is seared, 1 to 1½ minutes per side. Remove the fish from the pan and cover loosely with foil to keep warm.

Meanwhile, cook the pasta in the boiling water until just tender, 2 to 3 minutes for fresh, 8 to 10 minutes for dried. Drain well. In a bowl, coat the pasta with the herb sauce and add the lemon juice, parsley, and chives. Mix well.

Use a slicing knife to cut each piece of tuna crosswise (see photo) into ½-inch-thick slices. Slip a knife under one portion of sliced tuna, and transfer it to the bottom half of a warmed dinner plate. Overlap the slices into a fan.

Twirl a quarter of the pappardelle onto a carving fork with straight long tines, and place it in the center of the plate. Spoon about ¹/₂ cup of the caponata in an arch behind the pasta. Spoon a few tablespoons of the red wine sauce in front of the tuna. Garnish with the rosemary, thyme, and chervil. Repeat with the remaining plates.

Variations: You may leave the pappardelle out of this dish, substituting mixed greens and warm vinaigrette to create a tuna salad. Or, if you'd like to create a somewhat lighter version, leave the butter and cream out of the pasta sauce and toss the pasta with herbs and extra-virgin olive oil. (You may also leave out the red wine sauce if you elect to prepare the dish in this fashion.)

Caponata

MAKES ABOUT 2½ CUPS

1 small (12-ounce) eggplant, cut into ¼-inch cubes

1 teaspoon coarse salt, plus extra to taste

3 small celery ribs, cut into ¼-inch dice

⅓ cup olive oil, plus more if needed

Freshly ground white pepper to taste

1 small onion, chopped

¼ cup red wine vinegar

1½ tablespoons sugar

1 cup peeled, seeded, and chopped ripe plum tomatoes (or use canned if fresh are not ripe)

1 small red bell pepper, roasted (page 48), seeded, and cut into ¼-inch dice

¼ cup chopped pitted black Mediterranean olives

1½ tablespoons small capers, rinsed and coarsely chopped

2 salt-packed anchovies, soaked, bones discarded, and fillets finely chopped (see Sidebar, page 64)

MY RECIPE FOR caponata ensures that each vegetable retains its shape, color, and texture. For one of my favorite quick pasta dishes, perfect for summer picnics, toss room-temperature caponata with penne, lots of freshly grated Parmigiano-Reggiano cheese, chopped parsley, and a little extra-virgin olive oil to moisten it all.

In a large colander, toss the eggplant with the teaspoon salt. Let stand at room temperature for 1 hour to release some of the eggplant's bitter juices.

Meanwhile, in a medium saucepan of boiling salted water, cook the celery over high heat for 3 minutes. Drain, then rinse under cold running water. Set aside.

Rinse the eggplant quickly under cold running water to remove all the salt, and then gently squeeze handfuls of the eggplant to remove any excess liquid. In a 12-inch nonstick sauté pan, heat ¼ cup of the oil over medium-high heat. In batches, if necessary, sauté the eggplant, seasoned with salt to taste, until nicely browned, about 8 minutes. Using a slotted spoon, transfer the eggplant to a bowl.

In the same pan, heat the remaining oil over medium heat. Add the onion and cook, stirring often, until softened, about 5 minutes. Add the vinegar and sugar and cook until the vinegar is reduced to a glaze, about 7 minutes. Add the tomatoes and cook until thickened, about 10 minutes.

Add the tomatoes to the bowl with the eggplant, and fold in, along with the celery, the roasted pepper, olives, capers, and anchovies. Season with salt and pepper to taste. Cool to room temperature.

Gotham Shellfish Bouillabaisse

MAKES 8 SERVINGS

I SUPPOSE EVERY YOUNG chef has one dish that eludes or intimidates him or her. For me, whatever the reason, this world-renowned seafood soup was it. I spent a lot of time thinking about how to tackle this dish, but the catalyst came when I bought a set of rare cookbooks at auction in Paris. One of them featured an antique Provençale recipe that oddly included butter.

In time, I devised my own special butter, which I've nicknamed "bouilli butter," that is loaded with saffron, garlic, dried orange peel, star anise, and fennel seed. It finishes the bouillabaise (and other dishes) with a last-minute flavor boost.

Before I started tampering with this time-honored recipe, I made a trip to the South of France. I sampled the best bouillabaisse in the world, spoke with the chefs who cooked them every day, and began thinking about how to make the Gotham's both true to tradition yet somehow unique. The classic recipe uses only fish, so I based my recipe more on the Bouillabaisse Royale, which

(continued)

Thinking Ahead: The bouilli butter and aioli may be prepared as much as 2 days in advance and kept refrigerated, or frozen for up to 1 month. The lobsters may be prepared as much as 8 hours in advance, covered, and refrigerated. The vegetables for the bouillabaisse may be prepared up to 2 hours in advance and stored covered at room temperature.

LOBSTER

$1/4$ cup distilled white vinegar

4 ($1^1/4$-pound) live lobsters

Bring a large stockpot of salty water (at least 10 quarts) and the vinegar to a boil over high heat. In batches if necessary, place the lobsters in the pot and cover. Cook for about 4 minutes (this kills the lobsters and sets the meat).

Using tongs, transfer the lobsters to a work surface. Protecting your hands with a towel, twist off the claws and return them to the water to cook for an additional 4 minutes.

Meanwhile, working over a bowl to catch the juices, separate the heads from the tails.

Cut the tails in half lengthwise. Place the tails in a bowl. When the claws have finished cooking, add to the tails, cover, and refrigerate.

Using a heavy knife, roughly chop the lobster heads for the stock.

BOUILLABAISSE STOCK

$1/2$ cup olive oil

Reserved lobster heads (see above)

2 pounds fish bones and heads, from white-fleshed fish such as bass, snapper, flounder, cod, or halibut

1 medium onion, chopped

$1/2$ cup chopped fennel

uses langoustines or lobsters. Then I expanded on this, adding a range of other shellfish—shrimp, clams, mussels, and calamari. I hope you like it.

$^1/_2$ cup chopped leeks, white part only

1 head garlic, cut in half horizontally

3 (3-inch) strips orange zest, removed with a vegetable peeler

2 teaspoons ground fennel seed

2 teaspoons freshly ground white pepper

10 sprigs thyme

2 sprigs tarragon

1 star anise, broken into points

$^1/_2$ teaspoon saffron threads

$^3/_4$ teaspoon sweet Hungarian paprika

$^1/_8$ teaspoon cayenne

$^1/_2$ dried bay leaf

4 tablespoons tomato paste

1 cup chopped ripe tomatoes, including juices (use canned tomatoes if ripe are not available)

1 cup dry white wine

1 quart White Chicken Stock (page 33)

Coarse salt to taste

In a large stockpot, heat the oil over medium-high heat. Add the chopped lobster heads and cook, stirring occasionally, until the shells are bright red, about 10 minutes. Add the fish bones, onion, fennel, leeks, and garlic. Reduce the heat to low and cover. Cook the vegetables without coloring until they soften, about 5 minutes.

Add the aromatics and seasonings: the orange zest, fennel seed, white pepper, thyme, tarragon, star anise, saffron, paprika, cayenne, and bay leaf. Cook for 5 minutes to release their perfume. Add the tomato paste, chopped tomatoes, and wine. Raise the heat to high and cook until the wine reduces by half, about 3 minutes.

Add the stock, and, if needed, enough water to cover the ingredients. Season with salt. Bring to a boil over high heat, skimming as needed. Reduce the heat to low and simmer uncovered for 45 minutes. Remove from the heat and let stand for 20 minutes. Strain through a colander set over a large container. Press hard on the solids to extract as much flavor as possible, then discard the solids. If not using immediately, cool to room temperature, cover, and refrigerate.

ASSEMBLY

Bouillabaisse stock

8 medium fingerling or new potatoes, unpeeled

$^1/_4$ cup olive oil

1 large onion, thinly sliced

1 (10-ounce) fennel bulb, thinly sliced

1 medium red bell pepper, seeded and thinly sliced

1 medium yellow bell pepper, seeded and thinly sliced

$1/8$ teaspoon saffron threads

24 large shrimp, preferably with heads attached, unpeeled

24 Manila or 12 littleneck clams, well scrubbed

40 mussels, preferably cultivated, well scrubbed

8 ounces squid, cleaned, cut crosswise into $1/4$-inch-thick rings, tentacles reserved

2 tablespoons Pernod, or to taste

4 tablespoons Bouilli Butter (recipe follows)

Coarse salt and freshly ground white pepper to taste

Aioli (recipe follows)

In a pot of boiling salted water, cook the potatoes until they're tender when pierced with the tip of a knife, 10 to 15 minutes. Set the potatoes aside in their cooking liquid.

In a large stockpot, heat the oil over low heat. Add the onion and fennel and cook gently without coloring for 5 minutes. Add the red and yellow peppers and the saffron. Continue cooking gently until the vegetables soften, about 15 minutes. The vegetable mixture can be prepared up to 2 hours ahead and kept at room temperature.

Add the strained bouillabaisse stock and bring to a boil over high heat. Drain the potatoes and add to the stock along with the shrimp, clams, and mussels. Cover and cook for 3 minutes. Add the cooked lobster with its juices and the squid, and cook until all the shellfish open, about 3 more minutes.

Strain through a large colander set over a large bowl. Transfer the shellfish and vegetables to a large soup tureen. Pour the liquid back into the stockpot and bring to a boil over high heat. Add the Pernod and whisk in the bouilli butter. Taste and season with salt and pepper, if necessary. Pour about half the soup into the tureen and keep the rest warm on the stove.

Serve in large deep soup bowls, passing the aioli on the side.

Bouilli Butter

MAKES ABOUT ¾ CUP

3 (3-inch-long) strips orange zest, removed with a vegetable peeler

8 tablespoons (1 stick) unsalted butter, softened

1 large garlic clove, mashed to a paste with a sprinkle of coarse salt

½ teaspoon chopped fresh tarragon

Coarse salt to taste

½ teaspoon sweet Hungarian paprika

¼ teaspoon ground star anise

¼ teaspoon ground fennel seed

¼ teaspoon saffron threads

¼ teaspoon cayenne

¼ teaspoon freshly ground white pepper

EXTRA BOUILLI BUTTER can be used to dress grilled fish or vegetables

In a small saucepan, blanch the zest in boiling water over high heat for 1 minute. Drain and rinse under cold water. Finely mince the zest and place it in a small bowl with the butter, garlic, tarragon, and salt to taste.

In a small dry sauté pan over low heat, stir the paprika, star anise, fennel, saffron, and cayenne and white pepper, until fragrant, about 1 minute. Turn out onto a plate and cool. Add to the butter and combine well. Scrape out onto a piece of plastic wrap, form into a thick log, and wrap tightly. Refrigerate until firm, at least 1 hour.

Aioli

MAKES ABOUT 1½ CUPS

2 large egg yolks at room temperature

2 large garlic cloves, mashed to a paste with a sprinkle of coarse salt

1 teaspoon fresh lemon juice, or more as needed

¼ teaspoon Dijon mustard

¼ teaspoon cayenne

1 cup canola oil

½ cup olive oil

6 tablespoons heavy cream

Coarse salt to taste

AIOLI, THE FAMOUS Provençale garlic mayonnaise, is traditionally made with olive oil, but a bit of heavy cream gives it a smoother finish. I use it as a sandwich spread, or as a dip for steamed vegetables.

Place the egg yolks in a medium bowl.

Drape a kitchen towel in a medium saucepan and place the bowl in the saucepan to steady it. Whisk in the garlic, lemon juice, mustard, and cayenne. Combine the canola and olive oils in a glass measuring cup. Drop by drop, very slowly whisk in the oil. This will take at least a couple of minutes. If the aioli gets too thick to whisk, you can add a little of the cream to thin it slightly. When all the oil is incorporated, whisk in the cream. Season with salt, and balance the acidity with more lemon juice, if needed. Cover and refrigerate. Let stand at room temperature for 30 minutes before serving.

Soft-Shell Crabs with New Potatoes, Broccoli Rabe, and Brown Butter Sauce

MAKES 4 SERVINGS

Thinking Ahead: The vegetables and sauce may be prepared as much as 2 hours in advance and stored at room temperature.

VEGETABLES

4 medium creamer or new potatoes, unpeeled

1 cup fava beans

1 pound broccoli rabe, tough stems discarded

In a pot of boiling salted water, cook the potatoes over high heat until tender, about 15 minutes. Remove from the heat and let stand in their liquid.

Cook the fava beans in a pot of boiling salted water until tender, 2 to 3 minutes. Remove with a slotted spoon and transfer to a bowl of iced water to cool. Drain again, and peel off the tough skins from the beans.

Cook the broccoli rabe in the same pot of boiling salted water until barely tender, about 2 minutes. Drain, and keep warm.

SOFT-SHELL CRABS AND ASSEMBLY

12 medium soft-shell crabs, cleaned

Coarse salt and freshly ground white pepper to taste

6 tablespoons canola oil

2 tablespoons unsalted butter

Brown Butter Sauce (recipe follows)

2 tablespoons finely minced fresh chives

12 large salt-packed caper berries (see Sidebar, page 230) well rinsed; or 1 tablespoon regular capers

Preheat the oven to 450° F. Season the crabs with salt and pepper. Divide the oil between two ovenproof 12-inch sauté pans and set over

BROWN BUTTER SAUCE IS usually nothing more than butter cooked in a sauté pan until the milk solids are browned, which gives the resulting sauce a toasted, nutty quality. It's a fine, quick way to dress a piece of sautéed fish, but I wanted something more to offset the bitterness of the broccoli rabe in this dish—really a sauce, not just melted butter. The result is a fascinating example of the saucier's art. Butter and cream are boiled until the milk solids separate from the liquid fat, cooked until the fat solids brown, then carefully blended with lemon juice to emulsify the sauce. It's an advanced method, but such an unusual, delicious sauce that I'm confident passionate cooks will want it in their repertoire.

high heat until very hot but not smoking. Add the crabs, shell side down, and cook until crisp, about 4 minutes. Turn the crabs and place the sauté pans in the oven. Roast until the crabs are golden brown and cooked through, about 5 minutes.

Meanwhile, slice the reserved potatoes into ¼-inch-thick rounds and return them to the saucepan with 1 cup of their cooking liquid. Add the reserved fava beans and the butter and bring to a simmer over medium heat. Simmer to heat the vegetables through, about 1 minute. If necessary, reheat the broccoli rabe in a small sauté pan in the oven.

In the center of 4 warmed dinner plates, use a slotted spoon to place equal amounts of the potatoes and fava beans. Place the broccoli rabe on top, and then 3 crabs. Spoon the brown butter sauce over the crabs and vegetables. Scatter with the chives and caper berries.

Large caper berries, about the size of blueberries and packed in vinegar, are available at specialty and gourmet food shops. They should be well rinsed under cold running water to remove the excess vinegar.

Brown Butter Sauce

MAKES ABOUT 1 CUP

½ cup heavy cream

8 tablespoons (1 stick) unsalted butter

3 tablespoons fresh lemon juice, plus more as needed

Coarse salt and freshly ground white pepper to taste

In a medium saucepan, bring the cream and butter to a boil over high heat. Do not let it boil over. Stirring constantly, reduce until the mixture breaks and the milk solids brown and separate from the clear butter fat, 10 to 12 minutes.

Remove from the heat and let stand for 10 minutes, allowing the toasted milk solids to settle and the sauce to cool slightly before proceeding.

Pour off the layer of butter fat and set aside. Place the solids in a blender and, with the machine running, pour in the butter fat, creating a smooth, creamy emulsion. Add the lemon juice, and season with salt and pepper. Taste to check for acidity, and add more lemon juice if necessary. Keep the sauce warm, but not hot (see Sidebar, page 234).

Roast Lobster with Beet Couscous and Baby Bok Choy

MAKES 4 SERVINGS

Thinking Ahead: The couscous may be prepared up to 4 hours in advance and kept at room temperature. The sauce may be made up to 1 hour in advance and kept warm (see Sidebar, page 234). The lobster meat may be prepared for cooking as much as 2 hours in advance and stored in the refrigerator. The vegetables may be prepared up to 6 hours in advance, covered, and refrigerated.

HERBED GARLIC BUTTER

8 tablespoons (1 stick) unsalted butter, at room temperature

2 large garlic cloves, mashed to a paste with a sprinkle of coarse salt

1 teaspoon fresh lemon juice

$^{1}/_{2}$ teaspoon chopped fresh thyme

$^{1}/_{2}$ teaspoon freshly ground black pepper

Coarse salt to taste

In a small bowl, combine all of the ingredients, mashing them to-gether with a rubber spatula. If making ahead, transfer to a piece of plastic wrap and form into a cylinder. Wrap tightly and refrigerate. Otherwise, cover and store at room temperature. (The garlic butter must be softened for spreading onto the lobster tails.)

BEET COUSCOUS

$1^{1}/_{2}$ cups White Chicken Stock (page 33) or water

1 small (6-ounce) beet, peeled and sliced into thin rounds

2 teaspoons unsalted butter

$1^{1}/_{3}$ cups quick-cooking couscous

2 to 3 tablespoons fresh lemon juice

1 tablespoon extra-virgin olive oil

Coarse salt and freshly ground white pepper to taste

Season stock with salt and pepper. In a medium saucepan, bring the

VISUALLY, THIS DISH IS as lush and colorful as a tropical underwater scene, and the recipe will teach you how to organize your time properly to cook lobster for a party of 4 to 6 people by doing most of the work ahead of time.

The port and ginger sauce I created for this dish is a tantalizing combination of flavors concealed within an innocent-looking white sauce. It can be used to dress any number of other shellfish, too.

The other invention here is the beet couscous, a unique variation on the traditional version. The couscous is cooked in stock with pureed beets stirred into the mix. The result is a deep, rich, and unexpected combination of texture, flavor, and color.

The delicate green bok choy and red lobster, set off by the brilliant burgundy-colored couscous and white sauce render this an absolute stunner, even when the individual elements are presented separately.

beet and stock to a boil over high heat. Reduce the heat to low and cook until the beet is tender, about 15 minutes. Measure out $^3/_4$ cup cooking liquid and set aside. Transfer the beet and the remaining cooking liquid to a blender and puree.

In a saucepan, bring the reserved $^3/_4$ cup cooking liquid and the butter to a boil over high heat. Place the couscous in a medium bowl and pour in the boiling beet liquid. Mix, cover tightly with plastic wrap, and let stand until the couscous is tender, about 7 minutes. Uncover and let cool.

Fold in the beet puree. Dress with the lemon juice and oil, and if necessary, season with salt and pepper. Cover and let stand at room temperature until ready to serve.

VEGETABLE GARNISH

4 baby bok choy, bottoms trimmed so they will stand

2 bunches (1$^1/_2$ pounds) watercress, thick stems discarded

Bring a large pot of lightly salted water to a boil over high heat. Add the baby bok choy and cook until the thickest part is tender when pierced with the tip of a knife, about 4 minutes. Using a slotted spoon, transfer the bok choy to a large bowl of iced water and cool. Remove the bok choy from the water, squeeze gently to remove excess moisture, and set aside.

Add the watercress to the boiling water and cook until tender, about 1 minute. Drain well. Squeeze any excess water from the watercress. Set aside.

ASSEMBLY

$^1/_4$ cup distilled white vinegar

6 (1$^1/_4$-pound) live lobsters

2 tablespoons canola oil

Coarse salt and freshly ground white pepper

White Port and Ginger Sauce (recipe follows)

3 scallions, thinly sliced on an extreme bias, for garnish

Cilantro sprigs, for garnish

Bring a large stockpot of salty water (at least 10 quarts) and the vinegar to a boil over high heat. Place the lobsters in the pot and cover. Cook until the lobsters stop moving, 3 to 4 minutes. (This kills the lobsters and sets the meat.) Transfer the lobsters to a work surface.

With a heavy knife, cut off the tails and claws. Crack the claws and cut the tails in half lengthwise. Put the lobster claws and tails on a plate, cover, and set aside. This step can be done 4 hours in advance.

Position 2 oven racks in the center and top third of the oven and preheat the oven to 450° F. In a 12-inch ovenproof sauté pan, heat the oil over high heat until very hot but not smoking. Place the lobster claws in the sauté pan, season with salt and pepper, and cook until the claws deepen in color, about 1 minute. Transfer to the top rack of the oven and roast until the claws turn red, 4 to 5 minutes. Transfer to a plate and set aside to cool slightly.

Arrange the lobster tails, cut sides up, in a large shallow roasting pan. Season with salt and pepper. Spread the garlic butter over the tails. Roast on the top rack of the oven until the lobster meat is cooked through, about 7 minutes. While the lobster tails are roasting, remove the meat from the claws, and set aside.

Place the bok choy and watercress in a shallow baking dish and cover loosely with foil. Bake on the center rack of the oven until heated through, about 5 minutes.

In the center of each of 4 warmed dinner places, stand up a baby bok choy. Place a spoonful of the couscous above the bok choy to the right, and mound a quarter of the watercress next to the couscous. Stand 2 half lobster tails up on the couscous, leaning them against the bok choy, and add 2 lobster claws. Spoon a few tablespoons of the sauce around each plate. Garnish with the scallions and cilantro sprigs.

Variations: To create a potent herb sauce, leave out the ginger, substituting 2 teaspoons of chopped fresh tarragon or chervil into the finished sauce in its place.

If the beets have fresh, young, tender greens, you should *absolutely* substitute them for the watercress.

If baby bok choy are unavailable, substitute 1 medium head of bok choy, cut into 1-inch-wide pieces.

White Port and Ginger Sauce

MAKES ABOUT ¾ CUP

¼ cup plus 2 tablespoons imported white port

¼ cup fresh lemon juice

THE SWEETNESS OF THE port is set off by fresh ginger, which gives an Asian spin to this sauce.

2 tablespoons chopped shallot

1 tablespoon grated fresh ginger

1 large garlic clove, minced

2 tablespoons heavy cream

1 stick (8 tablespoons) unsalted butter, cut into 8 pieces

Coarse salt and freshly ground white pepper to taste

In a medium saucepan, bring the port wine, lemon juice, shallot, ginger, and garlic to a boil over high heat. Cook until reduced to a thick syrup (about 2 tablespoons), about 8 to 10 minutes. Add the cream and bring to a boil. Remove from the heat. One piece at a time, whisk in the butter. Season with salt and pepper. Strain through a fine wire sieve into a small bowl. Keep warm (see Sidebar).

To keep butter-based sauces warm for up to 2 hours, transfer the sauce to the top of a double boiler set over hot, not simmering, water. Or, keep the sauce in its saucepan in a warm spot on the stove. Another method is to store the sauce in a wide-mouthed vacuum bottle, if you have one.

Grilled Marinated Octopus with Chick-peas and Charred Tomatoes

MAKES 4 SERVINGS

Thinking Ahead: The octopus must be braised and marinated at least 1 day prior to serving. The vinaigrette and chick-peas may be prepared as much as 1 day in advance. The fennel curls should not be made more than 2 hours before serving. All should be stored covered and refrigerated.

BRAISED OCTOPUS

4 pounds (2 medium) octopus

6 cups water

3 cups dry red wine

1 cup chopped fennel with feathery tops, if still attached

1 medium onion, chopped

1 medium carrot, chopped

1 head garlic, halved horizontally

1 tablespoon coarse salt

6 sprigs flat-leaf parsley

1 sprig thyme

1 dried bay leaf

1 teaspoon whole black peppercorns

Coarse salt to taste

THIS RECIPE EMPLOYS a 3-step process (braising, marinating, and grilling) that tenderizes and brings out the full spectrum of flavors in the octopus. While this may seem to be a lot of trouble for one dish, the rewards are substantial.

The sweet, smoky charred tomatoes deepen the flavor of this dish. Their soft texture offers a foil for the octopus, which is extremely toothsome. The braising liquid, made with red wine, is transformed into the vinaigrette for the dish with the addition of extra virgin olive oil and a dash of aged red wine vinegar.

Using a large knife, cut off the octopus heads and discard them. Locate the beak in the center of each octopus; cut it out and discard it.

In a large pot, combine all the remaining ingredients, seasoning carefully with coarse salt to give the liquid a briny edge. Add the octopus and cover with a heatproof plate that fits into the pot to keep the octopus submerged. Bring to a boil over high heat. Reduce the heat to low and simmer, uncovered, until tender, 2 to 2½ hours (the tentacles will begin to pull away from the body, but cut off a small piece to taste for tenderness). Remove from the heat and cool in the liquid.

Remove the octopus, reserve ⅓ cup of the braising liquid for the vinaigrette, and discard the rest. Using a clean kitchen towel, rub off the skin and remove the suction cups from the octopus. Set the cleaned octopus aside.

MARINADE

½ cup olive oil

½ cup sliced shallots

⅓ cup reserved braising liquid

2 garlic cloves, sliced

¼ teaspoon dried oregano, preferably Greek

½ teaspoon coarsely crushed black peppercorns

In a shallow glass or enamel container, whisk all the marinade ingredients until combined. Add the braised octopus and cover. Refrigerate, turning the octopus occasionally in the marinade, at least overnight and for up to 3 days.

OCTOPUS VINAIGRETTE

⅓ cup remaining reserved braising liquid

⅓ cup extra-virgin olive oil

¼ cup red wine vinegar

1 teaspoon minced shallot

¼ teaspoon minced garlic

⅛ teaspoon chopped fresh thyme leaves

⅛ teaspoon dried oregano, preferably Greek

Coarse salt and freshly ground black pepper to taste

Dash of cayenne

In a medium bowl, mix together all the ingredients. The vinaigrette should not be emulsified, but should leave pools of red wine and vinegar scattered throughout the plate. Cover and refrigerate for at least 1 hour before serving. Mix well before serving.

CHICK-PEA SALAD

½ cup dried chick-peas, rinsed and soaked in cold water to cover for at least 4 hours or overnight

Coarse salt and freshly ground white pepper to taste

2 teaspoons red wine vinegar

4 teaspoons fresh lemon juice

2 tablespoons finely chopped fresh flat-leaf parsley

2 teaspoons finely chopped shallot

1 small garlic clove, mashed to a paste with a sprinkle of salt

¼ cup extra-virgin olive oil

Place the soaked and drained chick-peas in a medium saucepan and add enough cold water to cover by 2 inches. Bring to a boil over high heat. Reduce the heat to low. Simmer, uncovered, for 20 minutes. Add salt and continue cooking until tender, about 20 minutes more. Drain well. Immediately transfer the hot chick-peas to a medium bowl.

In a small bowl, whisk the vinegar, lemon juice, parsley, shallot, and garlic. Gradually whisk in the oil. Season with salt and pepper. Pour over the warm chick-peas and mix well. Cover and let stand for at least 2 hours at room temperature. Reseason before serving, if necessary.

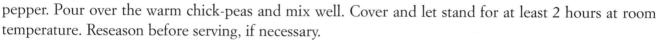

CHARRED TOMATOES AND ASSEMBLY

4 ripe plum tomatoes, halved lengthwise

2 tablespoons olive oil

Coarse salt and freshly ground white pepper to taste

1 medium red onion, quartered and thinly sliced

Flat-leafed parsley sprigs, for garnish

Build a hot charcoal fire in an outdoor grill and let the coals burn until covered with white ash. Brush the tomatoes with the oil and season with the salt and pepper. Cook, turning once, until charred, 4 to 5 minutes altogether. Transfer to a plate and cover with foil to keep warm.

Remove the octopus from the marinade. Lightly oil the grill. Grill the octopus, turning once, until lightly browned and heated through, about 6 minutes. Transfer to a plate, season with salt and pepper, and cover with foil to keep warm.

Arrange the chick-peas in the center of a large serving platter, and top with the octopus. Surround with spoonfuls of vinaigrette and the charred tomatoes. Scatter with the onion slices and parsley.

Variations: The fennel adds even more interest to this dish, but can be omitted from the braising liquid without sacrificing any great depth of flavor. The chick-peas may be replaced with boiled new potatoes dressed in the broken vinaigrette. The charred tomatoes provide crucial relief to the octopus, but if you like, you may go the more traditional route with a salad of tomato, red onion, and flat-leaf parsley.

Grilled Prawns with Lime, Cilantro, and Chiles

MAKES 4 SERVINGS

Thinking Ahead: The prawns must be marinated 3 hours in advance, covered, and refrigerated.

MARINADE

$1/2$ cup vegetable oil

Grated zest of 2 limes

Grated zest of 1 orange

$1/3$ cup fresh lime juice

$1/3$ cup fresh orange juice

3 tablespoons finely chopped fresh ginger

4 scallions, finely sliced

8 garlic cloves, sliced

1 or 2 fresh hot chile peppers, such as jalapeño, seeded and finely chopped

1 tablespoon sweet Hungarian paprika

5 cilantro sprigs

8 sprigs flat-leaf parsley

1 teaspoon coriander seed, crushed

$1/2$ teaspoon cayenne

2 dried hot red chile peppers, or $1/4$ teaspoon crushed hot red pepper flakes

$1/4$ teaspoon freshly ground white pepper

In a large bowl, combine all the marinade ingredients. Transfer half (including the solids) to a smaller bowl and set aside.

PRAWNS AND ASSEMBLY

2 pounds (10 to 15 per pound) large prawns, preferably head on, unpeeled

Coarse salt

2 tablespoons chopped fresh cilantro leaves

2 tablespoons chopped fresh flat-leaf parsley

I MAKE THIS SPICY DISH all summer long, serving a steaming, aromatic platter of prawns as a small meal to be enjoyed casually. It's also an easy recipe to multiply for a crowd. Serve it on a sweltering afternoon with ice cold beer or margaritas, and watch everyone forget about the heat.

The Asian-accented marinade is so rich and spicy that I use it again as a dressing after the prawns have been grilled. Head on, unpeeled prawns (the largest size marine shrimp, 10 to 15 pieces per pound) are dramatic on the grill and the shells keep the juices trapped inside.

Add the prawns to the large bowl of marinade and toss well. Cover and refrigerate both bowls, turning the prawns occasionally in the marinade. After 3 hours, remove the prawns from their marinade and season with coarse salt. Let stand at room temperature for 40 minutes before grilling.

Meanwhile, build a hot charcoal fire in an outdoor grill and let it burn until the coals are covered with white ash. Lightly oil the grill grate. Grill the prawns, turning once, until they turn pink and firm, 3 to 5 minutes.

Strain the reserved small bowl of marinade through a wire strainer into a medium bowl, pressing hard on the solids. Check for seasoning and spoon over the prawns. Garnish with the chopped cilantro and parsley.

Variation: While I prefer the large, head-on prawns, medium-size shrimp (under 20 pieces per pound, with or without heads), can be substituted. Some people find their shells tender enough to eat along with the shrimp.

Scallops with Potatoes, Leeks, Sea Urchin, and Sevruga Caviar

MAKES 4 SERVINGS

YEARS AGO I MADE A tour of seafood purveyors in New England with a friend of mine who was starting up a specialty company (with the irresistible name Wild Edibles) in New York City. At a weigh station, we casually seared a few freshly shucked scallops and spread sea urchin on them for an impromptu snack. The combination of simple seafood flavors and textures was incredible—smooth, sweet, salty sea urchin and voluptuous scallops. Back at the Gotham, I rounded out the combination with potatoes, leeks, and caviar, making it even more complex and luxurious.

If you're using diver-harvested sea scallops (which I recommend you do), remove the small flap of muscle for use in the scallop butter. Otherwise, purchase an extra ounce of scallops and chop coarsely as a substitute.

Thinking Ahead: The potatoes may be cooked up to 2 hours in advance and kept covered at room temperature. The scallop butter sauce may be prepared as much as 1 hour in advance and kept warm (see Sidebar, page 234).

POTATO AND LEEK RAGOUT

6 small fingerling or new potatoes, unpeeled

3 medium leeks, white parts only, cut on a bias into $1/4$-inch-thick slices, well rinsed to remove all grit

1 cup water

2 tablespoons unsalted butter

Coarse salt and freshly ground white pepper to taste

$1/4$ cup heavy cream

In a pot of lightly salted boiling water, cook the potatoes over high heat until tender, 15 to 20 minutes. Drain, cut into $1/3$-inch-thick rounds, and place in a bowl. Cover and keep warm.

Meanwhile, in a medium saucepan, combine the leeks, the cup of water, and the butter. Season with salt and pepper. Bring to a simmer over medium heat and cook until the leeks are tender, about 5 minutes. Add the sliced potatoes to the leeks and then add the cream. Season with salt and pepper and keep warm.

ASSEMBLY

2 tablespoons vegetable oil

12 large sea scallops, preferably diver-harvested (about 1 pound), small muscle flaps removed and reserved (see Sidebar)

Coarse salt and freshly ground white pepper

Scallop Butter Sauce (recipe follows)

1 medium tomato, peeled, seeded, and cut into $1/4$-inch dice

2 tablespoons chopped chives

Meat from 4 sea urchins

2 ounces fresh caviar, either sevruga or ossetra

In a 12-inch nonstick sauté pan, heat the oil over high heat until very hot but not smoking. Season the scallops with salt and pepper. Cook the scallops until golden brown, about 3 minutes. Using kitchen tongs, turn the scallops and reduce the heat to medium. Cook until the other side is browned and the scallops are on the rare side, about 2 minutes.

Using a slotted spoon, place equal amounts of the potato and leek ragout in the centers of 4 warmed dinner plates. Arrange 3 scallops on top, then more of the ragout. Spoon scallop butter sauce around the plates. Scatter with the chopped tomatoes and chives. Garnish each with equal amounts of sea urchin and caviar.

Variation: You may omit the sea urchin to simplify the dish or to accommodate your own personal taste.

Scallop Butter Sauce

MAKES ABOUT ½ CUP

Scraps from 12 diver-harvested sea scallops, or 1 large sea scallop, coarsely chopped

¼ cup water

¼ cup dry white wine

½ cup heavy cream

8 tablespoons (1 stick) unsalted butter

Coarse salt and freshly ground white pepper to taste

Preparing Sea Urchin: While there are many species of sea urchin, the green sea urchin found on the Pacific and Atlantic coasts is most commonly used in the United States. Sea urchins are approximately 4 inches in diameter and look like pin cushions. If you are using fresh urchins, cut around the bottom half of the shell with scissors. Inside you will find five orange-to-yellow-colored ovaries, also known as *corals* (often mistakenly referred to as "roe"). There is no need to cook or adorn them, except perhaps with a drop of lemon juice. Sea urchin may also be purchased in Japanese fish markets already cleaned and presented on small wooden trays. The Japanese name is *uni*.

In a small nonreactive saucepan, bring the scallop scraps, water, and wine to a boil over medium-high heat. Cook until the liquid is reduced by half, about 7 minutes. Add the cream and boil until reduced by half, about 10 minutes. Remove from the heat and whisk in the butter. Season with salt and pepper. Keep the sauce warm until ready to serve (see Sidebar, page 234).

8 Poultry, Game Birds, and Rabbit

Chicken Curry with Broccoli, Sticky Rice, and Pineapple Chutney

Grilled Asian Chicken, Grilled Asparagus, and Ginger Aioli

Chicken Breasts with Roasted Shiitake Mushrooms and Braised Endive

Grilled Breast of Chicken with Portobello Mushrooms and Green Herb Pesto

Duck Breast with Chinese Five-Spice Powder and Asian Vegetables

Duck Breast, Caramelized Endive, Sweet Potatoes, and Green Peppercorn Sauce

Duck Breast with Turnips and Medjool Dates

Pheasant Choucroute with Pureed Potatoes and Lady Apples

Squab with Polenta, Peas, and Pearl Onions

Roast Turkey Stuffed with Mashed Potatoes, Sausage, and Chanterelles

Braised Rabbit with Green Olives, Whole Roasted Shallots, and White Bean Puree

I must confess an affinity for chicken. And, while there's nothing better than a simple whole roasted chicken, I have included a few spicy recipes that boast more complex flavors.

Among the Far Eastern influences I've drawn upon in this chapter are: Chicken Curry with Broccoli, Sticky Rice, and Pineapple Chutney (page 250); Grilled Asian Chicken, Grilled Asparagus, and Ginger Aioli (page 254); and Chicken Breasts with Roasted Shiitake Mushrooms and Braised Endive (page 256). All these recipes are relatively simple and ideal for summer entertaining.

Even with all of these Asian-influenced dishes, I couldn't resist making just a bit more room for Duck Breast with Chinese Five-Spice Powder and Asian Vegetables (page 260), which grew out of my love for Peking duck, which I used to eat with alarming frequency on my nights off.

In this chapter, as much as anywhere else in the book, I've also presented some of the classic recipes I first learned in culinary school and while working in France. This is especially true of duck, which I grew to appreciate during the six months I spent seemingly surrounded by them in the south of France.

The Duck Breast, Caramelized Endive, Sweet Potatoes, and Green Peppercorn Sauce (page 264) is a deeply satisfying fall dish, rooted in tradition. The same may be said of the Braised Rabbit with Green Olives, Whole Roasted Shallots, and White Bean Puree (page 280), a cooking school staple that I simply love to make.

The duck breast recipe also demonstrates the technique of pan-roasting, which is used often for lean poultry and meats. This technique sears the meat over high heat, and continues the cooking slowly—sometimes on top of the stove and sometimes in the oven. If you have a twelve-inch sauté pan with a metal handle, it can go directly into the oven.

A few notes on the poultry, game birds, and rabbit used in this chapter:

Chicken

Even while growing up, I was never fond of supermarket-quality chicken. Today, however, with the availability of free-range and organic chicken, it is possible to secure a quality bird more easily. Marinating a chicken will help to coax out as much of its subtle flavor as possible. For this same reason, many of the recipes in this book recommend cutting up the chicken, both to allow it more intimate contact with the marinade and to allow greater control over doneness while cooking.

At the Gotham, we have direct contact with farmers who raise superb poultry and rabbits for us and other restaurants, and many of them supply the mail order companies that are recommended on page 375. Similarly, you should buy your poultry from a high-quality source who will guarantee that it has never been frozen.

If you can't get free-range or organic chicken, a kosher chicken would be the next best thing.

Duck

Most home cooks are familiar with Pekin or Long Island ducks, which are found in every supermarket. Unfortunately, these birds are quite fatty and don't have much meat on them. (A Pekin, for instance, weighs about five pounds, and most of that is fat and bone.) I prefer the relatively lean, larger, more flavorful Muscovy or Moulard ducks.

Muscovy ducks are meaty, have a good, developed game flavor, and are what I use most often.

Moulard ducks, a cross between Muscovy and Pekin, are primarily used to produce foie gras, but their abundant breast meat—*magret* in French—is delicious grilled or sautéed. If, for example, you are making a boneless duck recipe, you may prefer to buy *magrets,* but keep in mind that they will not leave you with bones to use in a sauce. (You would have to use the Brown Chicken Stock on page 34.)

Mallard ducks, which I do not use in this book, are wild, with a pronounced gamey taste. They can also be a little tough and are often braised.

I encourage you to buy whole ducks that you can cut up to suit your needs, since they yield bones, trimmings, wing tips, necks, and giblets to turn into a duck stock, and ultimately, a sauce. It is recommended to cook the breasts, which are best done medium-rare, separately from the legs, which should be cooked medium-well. If you cook a whole duck, you are likely to get a dry, gray, overcooked breast meat.

Pheasant

Farm-raised pheasant has a much less assertive flavor than the wild pheasant you may have had from a hunter's prize, so don't be concerned that the domesticated bird will be too gamey. Pheasant is very lean, and care should be taken not to overcook it—the flesh should be tinged pink and juicy.

Rabbit

Pan-roasting and grilling are common cooking methods for rabbit, but I like the extra moisture provided by braising, as in the recipe for Braised Rabbit with Green Olives, Whole Roasted Shallots, and White Bean Puree (page 280). This method helps ensure that the rabbit—especially farm-raised rabbit—will not turn tough and dry.

Rabbit plays a very large role in the cuisine of France and Italy, but has never been very popular in the United States. Braised rabbit is a classic, important recipe that every culinary student must master, so I've been eating this particular dish for a long time. I also enjoy a pasta sauce with braised rabbit for which I have provided recipe notes on page 282.

Squab

My favorite game bird might be squab. Very often people confuse squab with pigeon because of its French name, but it's not pigeon. Despite the fact that its not very popular in the United States, squab *is* very popular at the Gotham. If you can get a squab whole, including feet and head, that would be ideal because it signals freshness. You can buy these at many ethnic markets. I recommend buying squabs at eighteen to twenty ounces in weight.

Squab is best when served medium-rare. At the Gotham, we cook squab several ways, but here I offer a relatively simple alternative to the classic method of roasting a whole bird, with a recipe that allows the breast and wings to sauté in just eight to twelve minutes. The dish itself, Squab with Polenta, Peas, and Pearl Onions (page 273), is a perfect springtime meal.

Turkey

As with chicken, you should always buy an organic or free-range turkey, and buy it fresh. Under no circumstances should you purchase a "self-basting" turkey, which is loaded with chemicals.

Domesticated wild turkeys are excellent as well, but rarely grow over twelve pounds, so if you are thinking of trying one, you should know that they don't serve a crowd.

Chicken Curry **with Broccoli, Sticky Rice, and Pineapple Chutney**

MAKES 6 SERVINGS

THIS DISH IS ACTUALLY A "fusion" of Thai, Indian, and Japanese cuisines. It offers many elements for you to add to your personal repertoire—an exotic marinade, a great curry sauce, and a pineapple and red pepper chutney. Even served family-style, these components are extremely vivid and complementary.

Making your own curry can be a lot of fun. For me it brought back memories of when I was a child and got my first chemistry set. I experimented with about 20 versions of this recipe, visited a few restaurants, and—after reading a small stack of books on curry—hit on the following "formula."

The marinated chicken is delicious simply roasted or grilled without a sauce, but I wanted to share this favorite recipe, which gives the dish a significant boost of flavor.

Thinking Ahead: Marinate the chicken for at least 8 hours. The sauce may be prepared as much as 1 day in advance, covered, and refrigerated. The chutney may be prepared as much as 3 weeks in advance and stored, covered, in the refrigerator.

MARINATED CHICKEN

$2^1/_2$ teaspoons coriander seed

5 green cardamom pods

$^1/_2$ teaspoon whole cloves

3 ounces fresh ginger, chopped (about $^2/_3$ cup)

1 head garlic, peeled, halved, and crushed

$^1/_4$ cup chopped shallots

1 stalk lemongrass, tender bottom part only, finely chopped (about 3 tablespoons); or the grated zest and juice of 1 small lemon

2 teaspoons Madras-style curry powder

1 cup vegetable oil

2 ($3^1/_2$-pound) chickens, quartered

In a dry sauté pan over medium heat, separately cook the coriander seed, cardamom pods, and cloves until lightly toasted, and very fragrant, 1 to 2 minutes each. Remove the cardamom seed from the pods and discard the pods. In an electric coffee grinder or spice mill, grind the spices together. Reserve $^1/_2$ teaspoon of the ground spices and transfer the rest to a large bowl.

Add the remaining marinade ingredients to the bowl and stir well. Add the chicken and toss to coat with the marinade. Cover tightly and refrigerate, turning the chicken occasionally, for at least 8 hours or overnight.

THAI CURRY SAUCE

1 tablespoon vegetable oil

2 stalks lemongrass, tender bottom part only, chopped (about $^1/_2$ cup); or grated zest of 1 medium lemon

3 tablespoons finely chopped shallots

1 teaspoon finely chopped fresh ginger

2 garlic cloves, sliced

1 small dried hot red chile pepper

1 small banana, peeled and sliced

$^1/_2$ teaspoon reserved marinade spice mixture

$^1/_2$ teaspoon Madras-style curry powder

$^1/_4$ teaspoon ground turmeric

$^1/_8$ teaspoon ground mace

2 cups White Chicken Stock (page 33)

Coarse salt and freshly ground black pepper to taste

In a medium saucepan, heat the oil over medium heat. Add the lemongrass, shallots, ginger, garlic, and chile pepper. Cover and cook slowly until the ingredients soften, 2 to 3 minutes. Add the banana and cook uncovered for 2 minutes. Stir in the reserved spice mixture, the curry powder, turmeric, and mace and stir until fragrant, about 1 minute Add the chicken stock and bring to a boil over medium-high heat. Cook until reduced to about 1 cup, about 20 minutes.

Pour the sauce into a blender (or use an immersion hand blender) and puree. Pass the sauce through a fine mesh strainer, discarding the solids. Season with salt and pepper. Return to the saucepan and keep warm.

ASSEMBLY

Coarse salt and freshly ground black pepper

2 tablespoons canola oil

2 cups Japanese-style medium-grain rice

2 cups broccoli florets

$^1/_3$ cup Pineapple and Red Pepper Chutney (recipe follows)

12 sprigs cilantro, for garnish

2 scallions, thinly sliced, for garnish

Preheat the oven to 400° F. Remove the chicken from the marinade, wiping off the vegetables and spice. Season the chicken with salt and pepper.

In a 12-inch ovenproof sauté pan, heat the oil over medium-high heat. In batches, add the chicken, skin side down, and cook until browned, then turn and brown the other side, about 8 minutes total. As the chicken is browned, transfer it to a shallow roasting pan. Roast chicken in the oven until it shows no sign of pink when pierced near a bone and the juices run clear, 15 to 20 minutes.

Wash the rice under cold running water, then place it in a medium saucepan with enough cold water to cover by $3/4$ inch. Soak for 15 minutes. Add $1/2$ teaspoon of coarse salt and bring slowly to a boil. Reduce the heat to low, cover, and simmer until the rice is tender and the water is absorbed, 20 to 30 minutes. Turn off the heat and let the rice rest until ready to serve. (The rice will stay warm, covered, for up to 20 minutes.)

Bring a medium saucepan of lightly salted water to a boil over high heat. Add the broccoli florets and cook until just tender, about 3 minutes. Drain, and keep warm.

In the centers of 6 warmed dinner plates, place spoonfuls of the rice and the broccoli. Overlap a chicken breast and a leg at the bottom half of each plate, and spoon the sauce around the chicken. Garnish with a spoonful of chutney, and the cilantro and scallions.

Pineapple and Red Pepper Chutney

MAKES ABOUT 2 ¼ CUPS

2 tablespoons vegetable oil

1 small red onion, finely chopped

1 small red bell pepper, seeded and cut into $1/4$-inch dice

2 tablespoons grated fresh ginger

2 large garlic cloves, minced

2 cups chopped ($1/2$-inch dice) fresh pineapple

$3/4$ cup distilled white vinegar

$1/2$ cup orange juice

$1/2$ cup sugar

2 tablespoons dried currants

2 small dried hot red peppers, soaked in water for 10 minutes, drained, seeded, and finely chopped

$1/2$ teaspoon coarse salt

In a medium-size heavy-bottomed saucepan, heat the oil over medium heat. Add the onion and red bell pepper and cook without browning until the onion is soft, about 4 minutes. Add the ginger and garlic. Stir until fragrant, about 2 minutes. Add the remaining ingredients and bring to a boil, stirring, over high heat. Reduce the heat to very low. Simmer, uncovered, stirring occasionally, until the chutney thickens, about 35 minutes. Cool completely.

Grilled Asian Chicken, Grilled Asparagus, and Ginger Aioli

MAKES 6 SERVINGS

THE MARINADE RECIPE used here features bold flavors—ginger, lemongrass, garlic, and chile pepper—to create a spicy grilled chicken. The chicken and asparagus can be cooked in advance and eaten cold, making them ideal for, say, a picnic, or to take to someone's house for a "pot luck" dinner. The ginger aioli unites the ingredients on the plate.

One trick to remember here, or any time you grill chicken, is to let the chicken come to room temperature before grilling it, and to season it with coarse salt 20 minutes in advance of cooking. This technique will produce a pronounced flavor.

When cooking asparagus on the grill, be sure to cook it slowly over indirect heat, and don't allow it to brown too much.

Thinking Ahead: The aioli may be made as much as 6 hours in advance. The chicken must be marinated at least 8 hours in advance. Both should be refrigerated until ready to use.

MARINATED ASIAN CHICKEN

4 stalks lemongrass, tender bottom parts only, finely chopped (about 1 cup); or grated zest of 2 medium lemons

$^1/_3$ cup soy sauce

2 tablespoons canola oil

2 tablespoons chopped fresh ginger

2 scallions, finely sliced

1 small dried hot red chile pepper, chopped

$1^1/_4$ teaspoons Madras-style curry powder

12 sprigs cilantro, including stems, coarsely chopped

2 (3-pound) free-range chickens, quartered

Combine all of the marinade ingredients in a large bowl, add the chicken, and turn to coat it on all sides. Cover tightly with plastic wrap and refrigerate for at least 8 hours or overnight, turning occasionally.

GRILLED ASPARAGUS

$1^1/_2$ pounds large asparagus, ends trimmed, spears peeled with a vegetable peeler

2 tablespoons extra-virgin olive oil

Coarse salt and freshly ground pepper to taste

In a shallow dish, toss the asparagus with the oil, salt, and pepper. Let stand for at least 30 minutes or for up to $1^1/_2$ hours.

ASSEMBLY

Coarse salt and freshly ground white pepper

2 cups Ginger Aioli (page 140)

Build a charcoal fire in a grill and let the coals burn until covered with white ash. Lightly oil the grill.

Remove the chicken from the marinade, wiping off as much of the marinade as possible. Season the chicken with salt and pepper and grill it first skin side down, turning once, until nicely browned, about 8 minutes total. Arrange the chicken around the perimeter of the grill away from direct heat. Cover the grill and cook the chicken until it shows no sign of pink when pierced in the thickest part, about 25 minutes. During the last 5 minutes of grilling the chicken, place the asparagus in the center of the grill, arranging them perpendicular to the grid. Cover and grill until lightly browned, about 2½ minutes. Using a large spatula, roll the asparagus over to grill the other side, about 2½ minutes.

Arrange the chicken and asparagus on platters. Serve with individual bowls of the ginger aioli for dipping.

Variations: Sticky Rice (page 253), Apricot-Cherry Chutney (page 74), Grilled Potato and Onions (page 290), Grilled Vegetables (page 303), and Grilled Mangoes (page 81) all make suitable substitutes or additions to the asparagus.

Chicken Breasts with Roasted Shiitake Mushrooms and Braised Endive

MAKES 4 SERVINGS

THE COOKING METHOD described in this recipe is identical to the one we use at the Gotham, a pan-roasting technique that produces a crisp golden skin.

I've written of my fondness for Belgian endive elsewhere in the book; this is another way to serve it, using its beautiful pale color and sophisticated bitter flavor as a vegetable rather than a salad.

Cooking shiitake mushrooms in the oven produces a one-of-a-kind aroma, but more importantly, it preserves more of their flavor than sautéing them. (Because they are so absorbent, they soak up too much butter in a pan.) Here, just a splash of olive oil produces the desired effect.

Thinking Ahead: The endive may be braised as much as 8 hours in advance, kept refrigerated in their cooking liquid, and reheated.

4 Belgian endive

$1/4$ cup extra-virgin olive oil

$1/4$ cup fresh lemon juice

Coarse salt and freshly ground white pepper to taste

1 quart water

$1/4$ cup canola oil

4 half free-range chicken breasts, wing tips removed

4 tablespoons unsalted butter

16 shiitake mushrooms, stems discarded

1 tablespoon chopped shallot

$1/2$ cup dry white wine

2 tablespoons minced fresh chives

About 1 hour before serving, place the endive in a medium nonreactive saucepan. Sprinkle with 2 tablespoons of the olive oil and the lemon juice, and season with salt and pepper. Pour in the water. Place an ovenproof weight of some kind (a plate, or a smaller saucepan lid) on top of the endive to submerge them completely. Bring to a boil over high heat. Reduce the heat to low and simmer about six minutes until almost tender when pierced with the tip of a sharp knife. Remove from the heat and let cool in the liquid.

Position 2 racks in the center and upper third of the oven and preheat to 400° F. In a 12-inch ovenproof sauté pan, heat the canola oil over high heat. Season the chicken with salt and pepper. Cook the chicken, skin side down, until nicely browned, about 5 minutes. Turn and add 1 tablespoon of the butter to the sauté pan. Cook until the butter is foamy, about 1 minute. Transfer the chicken to the center rack of the oven and roast for 5 minutes.

Meanwhile, toss the mushrooms with the remaining 2 tablespoons of olive oil and season with salt and pepper. After the chicken has roasted for 5 minutes, place the mushrooms in a shallow roasting pan on the top rack of the oven.

Roast the chicken and mushrooms, basting often, until the chicken shows no sign of pink when pierced near the bone and the juices run clear, about 20 minutes total roasting time.

Turn off the oven and leave the door ajar, keeping the mushrooms in the oven. Transfer the chicken to a platter and tent it loosely with foil to keep warm.

Pour off all but 1 tablespoon of the fat from the sauté pan. Place the pan on top of the stove over medium heat. Add the shallot and cook, stirring often, until softened, about 2 minutes. Add the wine and bring to a boil, scraping up the browned bits with a wooden spoon. Cook until the wine is reduced to about $1/4$ cup, 5 to 7 minutes.

Meanwhile, remove and discard the chicken breastbones. (They are easy to pull off in one piece, but use a small knife to help, if you wish.) Pour any of the collected juices from the platter into the sauté pan and bring to a boil. Off the heat, stir in the remaining 3 tablespoons of butter, 1 tablespoon at a time. Add the chives and season with salt and pepper.

If necessary, reheat the endive in their cooking liquid until hot. Remove and cut each endive in half lengthwise. On each warmed dinner plate, cross 2 endive halves in the center. Place a chicken breast against the endive and garnish with 4 mushrooms. Spoon the pan sauce over all.

Grilled Breast of Chicken
with Portobello Mushrooms and Green Herb Pesto

MAKES 4 SERVINGS

WE HAVE PLENTY OF HOT summer days in New York where simple outdoor cooking is the preferred way to make a meal. Portobello mushroom caps are spread with a bright green herb pesto after cooking, and are simply delicious when eaten with the chicken. Potato salad is a classic accompaniment to grilled chicken, so why buck tradition when it tastes this good—serve the dish with a double batch of creamy Potato Salad (page 91).

Thinking Ahead: The chicken can be marinated up to 8 hours in advance. The pesto can be prepared up to 1 hour in advance and kept at room temperature.

MARINATED CHICKEN

$1/4$ cup fresh lemon juice

$1/4$ cup extra-virgin olive oil

2 sprigs rosemary, coarsely chopped

2 sprigs thyme, coarsely chopped

6 garlic cloves, thinly sliced

$1/4$ teaspoon crushed hot red pepper flakes

4 free-range chicken breasts, wing tips removed

In a nonreactive shallow dish (glass is best), whisk together all the marinade ingredients and add the chicken breasts. Cover tightly with plastic wrap and refrigerate, turning occasionally, for at least 4 hours and up to 8 hours.

GREEN HERB PESTO

$1/4$ cup extra-virgin olive oil

2 tablespoons finely chopped fresh flat-leaf parsley

2 tablespoons minced fresh chives

1 teaspoon finely chopped fresh tarragon

1 garlic clove, mashed to a paste with a sprinkle of coarse salt

$1/2$ teaspoon coarse salt

$1/2$ teaspoon coarsely cracked black peppercorns

In a small bowl, combine all the ingredients. Cover tightly and let stand at room temperature for up to 1 hour.

ASSEMBLY

Coarse salt and freshly ground white pepper

4 large Portobello mushrooms, stems removed and reserved

2 tablespoons extra-virgin olive oil

Build a charcoal fire in a grill and let the coals burn until covered with white ash. Lightly oil the grill.

Remove the chicken from the marinade and wipe off as much of the marinade as possible. Season the chicken with salt and pepper and grill it, skin side down, until nicely browned, about 5 minutes. Turn and arrange the breasts around the perimeter of the grill, away from the direct heat. Cover the grill and cook the chicken until it shows no sign of pink when pierced at the bone near the wing joint, about 15 minutes.

During the last 10 minutes, brush the mushroom caps and stems with the oil, and season with salt and pepper. Grill directly over the coals, cap side facing down, until they're browned, 3 to 5 minutes. Turn and brush with some of the pesto. Cook until tender, about 4 minutes. Transfer the chicken and mushrooms to a large platter, and finish with more of the herb pesto.

Duck Breast with Chinese Five-Spice Powder and Asian Vegetables

MAKES 4 SERVINGS

ROASTING A WHOLE DUCK at home is a formidable prospect that requires a lot of effort—roasting it over high heat, managing the huge amount of fat that cooks off. It's a real project. This dish, which evolved out of my love for Peking duck, offers the less labor-intensive alternative of boning and sautéing the duck breast. By starting the duck in a cool pan and gradually increasing the temperature, the fat melts evenly, leaving a crispy skin. Seasoning the duck breasts with Chinese five-spice powder gives the duck a distinctive Asian kick.

This dish makes unique use of Chinese or Napa cabbage, cooking wedges of it in a sauté pan rather than simply shredding it as most recipes do. The pleasing, crisp flavor of the vegetable develops during the cooking process, transforming into a very enjoyable complement to the duck. The snow-pea pods, baby bok choy, and shiitake mushrooms provide visual interest as well as a myriad of vegetable textures and flavors.

Thinking Ahead: The sauce may be prepared as much as 1 day in advance. The Asian vegetables may be prepared 2 hours in advance. Both should be covered and stored in the refrigerator.

DUCK SAUCE

2 tablespoons canola oil

1 scallion, chopped

2 large garlic cloves, peeled and crushed

1 tablespoon chopped fresh ginger

1 cup Brown Chicken or Duck Stock (pages 34 and 38)

$1/2$ cup water

1 dried Chinese black (shiitake) mushroom

1 tablespoon mushroom soy or regular soy sauce

$1^1/2$ teaspoons hoisin sauce

$1/2$ teaspoon Chinese chile paste with garlic

Pinch of Chinese five-spice powder (see Sidebar, page 263)

Coarse salt, if needed

In a medium saucepan, heat the oil over medium heat. Add the scallion, garlic, and ginger and cook, stirring often, until softened and fragrant, about 3 minutes. Add the remaining ingredients except salt and bring to a boil over high heat. Reduce the heat to low and simmer until well flavored and reduced to 1 cup, about 30 minutes. Taste carefully and add salt if needed. Strain the sauce into a small bowl.

ASIAN VEGETABLES

4 baby bok choy (1 pound total), bottoms trimmed so the bok choy will stand

16 snow peas, trimmed

2 tablespoons vegetable oil

12 medium shiitake mushrooms, stems discarded

Coarse salt and freshly ground white pepper

1/2 small head Napa cabbage

Bring a large pot of lightly salted water to a boil over high heat. Have a large bowl of iced water nearby. Add the bok choy to the boiling water and cook until they're barely tender, 4 to 5 minutes. Using a skimmer or a slotted spoon, transfer the bok choy to the iced water.

Add the snow peas to the boiling water and cook until just bright green, about 1 minute. Using the skimmer, transfer the snow peas to the iced water. When the vegetables have cooled, drain and set aside.

In a large nonstick sauté pan, heat 1 tablespoon of the oil over medium heat. Add the mushroom caps and cook, turning once, until tender, about 5 minutes. Season with salt and pepper. Transfer to a plate and set aside.

Cut the cabbage into quarters without removing the core, leaving the leaves attached at the root end. In the sauté pan, heat the remaining oil over high heat until very hot but not smoking. Add the cabbage, cut side down, quarters and cook until golden brown, about 3 minutes. Turn and cook until the other side is browned, about 3 minutes more. Season with salt and pepper and set aside.

DUCK BREAST

4 (10-ounce) Muscovy duck breasts

2 teaspoons Chinese five-spice powder

Coarse salt and freshly ground black pepper

Trim away any excess skin and fat from the duck. Using a sharp knife, score the skin lightly in a cross-hatch pattern, but do not cut into the flesh. Season the duck breasts on both sides with the five-spice powder, salt, and pepper. Place in a cold, large nonstick sauté pan and set over medium heat. Cook until the skin is beautifully browned and crisp, about 10 minutes. Turn the breasts and cook until medium-rare, about 3 minutes. Transfer to a plate and lightly tent with foil to keep warm. Let stand for 5 minutes before slicing.

ASSEMBLY

2 scallions, thinly sliced on an extreme bias

8 sprigs cilantro

Bring a large pot of salted water to a boil over high heat. Add the bok choy and snow peas and cook until heated through, about 1 minute. Drain. If necessary, reheat the mushrooms, cabbage, and duck sauce. Keep warm.

> The sauce recipe yields a complex interplay of duck stock, black mushrooms, scallions, ginger, and hoisin sauce—thick enough to stand up to the duck, and just sweet enough to balance the fattiness of its meat.
>
> The Chinese ingredients are all available at Asian grocers as well as most supermarkets.

Chinese five-spice powder is a blend usually including equal parts ground Chinese cinnamon (cassia), aniseed, star anise, Sichuan peppercorns, and cloves. Like all spice mixtures, homemade versions are the best, since they are fresher. You can grind all of the ingredients in a spice mill or coffee grinder, and store it in a covered glass jar. Many supermarkets carry it in their spice displays.

Mushroom soy sauce is flavored with dried black mushrooms, but regular soy sauce is an acceptable substitute.

Hoisin sauce is a sweet bean paste.

Gotham Presentation: Slice the duck breasts into ¼-inch-thick slices. Slip the blade under a sliced breast and transfer it to the bottom half of a warmed dinner plate, fanning out the slices. Arrange the bok choy and cabbage together in the center. Pull back a few of the bok choy layers to create a petal effect, and garnish with the snow peas and mushroom caps. Finish with the scallions and cilantro.

Everyday Presentation: Place the snow peas, mushrooms, bok choy, and cabbage in the center of a large warmed platter. Arrange the sliced duck breasts around the edges. Serve with the sauce passed on the side.

Variations: This dish mixes well with Sticky Rice (page 253). Squab and lamb also make suitable substitutes for the duck (follow the general instructions for pan-roasting squab on page 274).

Duck Breast, Caramelized Endive, Sweet Potatoes, and Green Peppercorn Sauce

MAKES 4 SERVINGS

DUCK WITH GREEN peppercorn sauce was an old idea, even 20 years ago when I started cooking, but it is a sauce I still use from time to time with excellent results. The flavors and colors of this dish—rare duck breast, caramelized endive, and orange sweet potatoes (flavored with maple syrup), are an ideal autumn combination. While most Americans don't think of endive when trying to settle on a vegetable, it's remarkably easy to prepare and is the perfect accompaniment in dishes like this one, where the slightly bitter flavor contrasts the other components.

Thinking Ahead: The sweet potato puree may be made up to 1 hour in advance and kept warm. The green peppercorn sauce may also be prepared up to 1 day in advance, covered, and refrigerated.

SWEET POTATO PUREE

4 large sweet potatoes (2 pounds total), pierced with a fork

4 tablespoons unsalted butter

1 tablespoon Grade B maple syrup (if Grade B is unavailable, use Grade A)

Coarse salt and freshly ground white pepper to taste

Preheat the oven to 400° F. Bake the sweet potatoes until tender, about 1 hour. When cool enough to handle, peel and place the flesh in a medium saucepan. Add the butter and maple syrup. Mash the potatoes over very low heat until they are smooth and the butter is incorporated, about 1 minute. Season with salt and pepper. Keep warm by placing the saucepan in a skillet of simmering water over low heat.

DUCK

4 (10-ounce) Muscovy duck breasts, wing tips removed

Coarse salt and freshly ground white pepper

Trim away any excess skin and fat from the duck. Using a sharp knife, score the skin lightly in a crosshatch pattern, but do not cut into the flesh. Season the duck breasts with salt and pepper. Place in a large cold nonstick sauté pan and set over medium-high heat. Cook until the skin is beautifully browned and crisp, about 10 minutes. Turn and cook until medium-rare, about 3 minutes. Transfer the duck to a plate and cover loosely with aluminum foil to keep warm. Let rest for 5 minutes before slicing.

ASSEMBLY

4 Belgian endives

1 tablespoon olive oil

Green Peppercorn Sauce (recipe follows)

Heat a tablespoon of olive oil in a sauté pan. Sauté endives cut side down until nicely caramelized. Turn endives and keep warm over low heat. Cut each duck breast into $1/4$-inch slices. Slip the knife blade under a sliced breast, and transfer it to the bottom half of a warmed dinner plate, fanning out the slices. At the "ten o'clock" position, place a spoonful of warmed sweet potato puree. Fold back a few of the outside leaves, and place the endive in the "two o'clock" position. Spoon the sauce around the edge of the plate and serve.

Variations: In seasons other than fall, substitute Gotham Mashed Potatoes (page 206) or Creamy Polenta (page 276) for the sweet potato puree.

Green Peppercorn Sauce

MAKES ABOUT 1 CUP

1 tablespoon canola oil

1 tablespoon finely chopped shallot

1 garlic clove, finely chopped

$1^{1}/_{2}$ teaspoons brine-packed green peppercorns, drained and rinsed

1 cup dry red wine, preferably Cabernet Sauvignon

1 cup Brown Chicken Stock (page 34)

$1/2$ cup water

2 tablespoons unsalted butter

Coarse salt and freshly ground white pepper to taste

TRY THIS SAUCE WITH grilled steak. Be sure to use the green peppercorns packed in brine, not dried green peppercorns, which are better used for grinding.

In a medium saucepan, heat the oil over medium heat. Add the shallot and cook, stirring often, until it's lightly browned, about 2 minutes. Add the garlic and half the green peppercorns and cook until the garlic is fragrant, about 1 minute. Pour in the wine and bring to a boil over high heat. Cook until the wine is reduced to a syrup, about 10 minutes.

Add the stock and water and cook until well flavored and reduced to 1 cup, about 10 minutes. Strain the sauce into a small saucepan. Whisk in the butter, 1 tablespoon at a time. Stir in the remaining green peppercorns and season with salt and pepper.

Duck Breast with Turnips and Medjool Dates

MAKES 4 SERVINGS

Thinking Ahead: The turnips and dates may be prepared as much as 2 hours in advance and kept at room temperature.

Special Equipment: mandoline

TURNIPS AND DATES

2 tablespoons unsalted butter

3 large turnips, peeled and very thinly sliced into rounds with a mandoline-type slicer

4 Medjool dates, pitted and thinly sliced lengthwise (see Sidebar)

Coarse salt and freshly ground white pepper to taste

In a large sauté pan, heat the butter over medium heat. Cook the turnips until soft and lightly browned around the edges, 3 to 4 minutes. During the last minute of cooking, add the dates. Season with salt and pepper and cover to keep warm.

DUCK

4 (10-ounce) boneless Muscovy duck breasts

Coarse salt and freshly ground white pepper

1 cup Duck Stock (page 38)

4 tablespoons unsalted butter

Trim away any excess skin and fat from the duck. Using a sharp knife, score the skin lightly in a crosshatch pattern, but do not cut into the flesh. Season the duck breasts with salt and pepper. Place in a cold 12-inch nonstick sauté pan and set over medium-high heat. Cook until the skin is beautifully browned and crisp, about 10 minutes. Turn and cook until medium-rare, about 3 minutes. Transfer the duck to a plate and cover loosely with aluminum foil to keep warm. Let rest for 5 minutes before slicing.

I'VE ALWAYS APPRECIATED the pairing of duck with the natural sweetness of fruit, and this dish was developed when I began experimenting to find a new pleasure in this vein. The honeyed quality of the Medjool dates complements the duck in a profoundly classic way.

This recipe features an unusual method for cooking turnips, slicing them thin, and sautéing them slowly in a bit of butter. They cook quickly, browning a little around the edges, and take on a wonderfully buttery, caramelized, sweet flavor that rounds out the other flavors in the dish.

Meanwhile, in a small saucepan, bring the brown duck sauce to a boil over medium heat. Reduce heat and whisk in the butter 1 tablespoon at a time. Season with salt and pepper and keep warm.

Medjool dates are especially large, plump, and sweet. They can be found at Mideastern grocers and many specialty food stores.

Gotham Presentation: Using a sharp knife, cut each duck breast crosswise into $1/4$-inch slices. Slip the blade under each breast and transfer the slices to the bottom half of 4 warmed dinner plates, fanning out the slices. Gather together some date slivers and wrap them with a few turnip slices. Set this bouquet in the center of each plate along with some more turnip slices gently folded and positioned to help support the bundle. Garnish with a few extra date slivers. Spoon the sauce around the duck and turnips.

Everyday Presentation: Mound the turnips and dates in the center of a platter and arrange the sliced duck breasts around the outside of the garnish. Spoon a little of the sauce around the edge of the platter and pass the rest in a sauceboat.

Variations: Try substituting other dried fruits, such as apricots or figs, for the dates. Of course, fresh figs, peaches, or pears are great, too.

Pheasant Choucroute **with Pureed Potatoes and Lady Apples**

MAKES 6 SERVINGS

Thinking Ahead: The choucroute may be prepared as much as 3 days in advance, covered, and refrigerated.

POACHED LADY APPLES

12 lady apples

2 tablespoons fresh lemon juice

6 cups water

1 cup sugar

1 vanilla bean, split lengthwise

Using the tip of a sharp paring knife, dig out the tough core from the bottom of each apple, reaching about halfway into the middle. Toss the apples with the lemon juice.

In a medium saucepan, bring the water, sugar, and vanilla to a boil over high heat. Add the apples and return to the boil. Remove from the heat and cover. Or, if not using them right away, cool, cover, and refrigerate.

APPLE CIDER SAUCE

2 tablespoons canola oil

1 small onion, chopped

2 garlic cloves, sliced

1 sprig thyme

$1/2$ teaspoon whole black peppercorns

$3/4$ cup dry white wine

$1/2$ cup apple cider

2 cups Brown Chicken Stock (page 34)

Coarse salt and freshly ground white pepper to taste

2 tablespoons unsalted butter

1 to 2 tablespoons Calvados or applejack (optional)

I CREATED THIS DISH one winter when I found myself faced with the task of preparing a Christmas dinner in Florida. For a native of Buffalo, the Southeast felt like a strange place to spend Christmas, and the 80° weather made it difficult to get into the right state of mind. To get over this obstacle, I began thinking about Alsace and the hearty, restorative foods for which it is known—braised sauerkraut, bacon, smoked sausages, apples, and juniper berries. All of these foods put me in mind of snow-covered landscapes and the sanctuary of a warm fireplace. After a while, I was inspired. It's not a traditional choucroute, because the sauerkraut is served with pheasant, which seemed a more appropriate choice for the holiday than the usual sausages. Lady apples, which are available in the autumn and winter, provide a tart counterpoint.

This dish is topped with an apple cider sauce composed of a reduction of fresh apple cider and Calvados, concentrating the fruit and

(continued)

In a medium saucepan, heat the oil over medium heat. Add the onion and cook, stirring often, until lightly browned, about 5 minutes. Add the garlic, thyme, and peppercorns and stir until fragrant, about 1 minute. Add the wine and cider, bring to a boil over high heat, and cook until thick and reduced to about $\frac{1}{3}$ cup, 10 to 15 minutes.

Add the chicken stock and bring back to a boil. Lower the heat to medium and cook until slightly reduced and well flavored, about 10 minutes. Strain into another saucepan and season with salt and pepper. Off the heat, whisk in the butter, 1 tablespoon at a time. If desired, add the Calvados. Keep the sauce warm by placing the saucepan in a skillet of hot water over very low heat.

PHEASANT

3 (3-pound) pheasants, cut into quarters

Coarse salt and freshly ground white pepper

4 tablespoons canola oil

4 tablespoons unsalted butter

providing notes of both sweetness and acidity. It is combined with rich brown chicken stock and mixed with a touch of butter to soften its flavor. Rounding out this Alsatian theme are creamy mashed potatoes with lots of sour cream and chives.

Pheasant has a tendency to dry out because the anatomy of its breast is unusual—fat at one end, long and tapered at the other—making it very difficult to cook it evenly. You might want to cook this a little pink at the bone as a safeguard, or accept the fact that it's going to be somewhat dry.

Preheat the oven to 400° F. Season the pheasant pieces with salt and pepper. Divide the oil equally between two 12-inch sauté pans, and heat over medium-high heat. Add the pheasant, skin side down, and cook until the skin is browned, about 6 minutes. Turn the pheasant quarters and cook for another 4 to 5 minutes. Add 2 tablespoons butter to each pan. Place the sauté pans in the oven and roast, basting occasionally, until the breasts feel springy to the touch, about 5 minutes. Remove the breast quarters to a plate and cover loosely with foil to keep warm. Continue cooking the legs until they show just a little pink at the bone, 3 to 4 more minutes.

ASSEMBLY:

1 recipe Gotham Mashed Potatoes (page 206)

1 recipe Choucroute (recipe follows)

In the center of 6 warmed dinner plates, place mounds of mashed potatoes. Arrange a breast and leg next to the potatoes. Add equal portions of choucroute, and garnish with the drained apples. Spoon the sauce over and around the pheasant.

Choucroute

MAKES 6 SERVINGS

1 pound fresh sauerkraut

2 ounces smoked bacon, cut into ¼-inch dice

2 ounces smoked kielbasa sausage, cut into ¼-inch dice

1 small onion, finely chopped

1 tart cooking apple, such as Granny Smith, peeled, cored, and coarsely grated

½ teaspoon ground juniper berries (grind in a spice or coffee grinder)

¼ teaspoon ground caraway seed

¾ cup apple cider

¾ cup champagne vinegar or white wine vinegar

THIS VARIATION ON THE classic choucroute has a sweet freshness provided by the apple that plays off the smoked meats beautifully.

Place the sauerkraut in a large bowl and add cold water to cover. Let stand for 10 minutes to remove some of the brine. Repeat once, then drain and gently squeeze out the excess moisture.

Meanwhile, in a medium saucepan, cook the bacon and sausage over medium heat until the bacon is lightly browned, about 5 minutes. Add the onion, apple, ground juniper berries, and ground caraway. Reduce the heat to medium-low and cover. Cook until the onion softens, 5 to 7 minutes. Add the cider and vinegar, increase the heat to high, and cook uncovered until the liquids are reduced to about ½ cup, 15 to 20 minutes. Add the sauerkraut, reduce the heat to medium, and cook until the liquids have reduced entirely, about 10 minutes. Cover and keep warm.

Squab with Polenta, Peas, and Pearl Onions

MAKES 4 SERVINGS

Thinking Ahead: The vegetables can be prepared up to 4 hours ahead, covered, and refrigerated. The sauce can be prepared up to 2 hours ahead and kept warm.

PEARL ONIONS AND PEAS

1 cup fresh peas (from 1 pound peas in the pod)

2 tablespoons butter

4 ounces pearl onions (about 20), peeled (see Sidebar, page 274)

Coarse salt and freshly ground white pepper to taste

Bring a medium saucepan of salted water to a boil over high heat. Add the peas and cook until just tender, 2 to 3 minutes. Use a slotted spoon to transfer the peas to a bowl of iced water to cool completely. Drain again and set aside.

Pour out all but 1 cup of the water. Add the butter and bring to a boil over high heat. Add the onions, reduce the heat to low, and simmer until the onions are almost tender, about 10 minutes. Stir in salt and pepper to taste. Remove from the heat, keeping the onions in their liquid.

SQUAB PAN SAUCE

2 (18-ounce) squabs

2 tablespoons canola oil

Coarse salt and freshly ground white pepper to taste

1 tablespoon unsalted butter

2 shallots, finely minced

$^1/_2$ cup dry red wine

$^3/_4$ cup Brown Chicken Stock (page 34)

Using a sharp knife, cut the wing tips off the squabs. Cut down each side of the backbones and remove. Place the squabs, breast side up,

THIS RECIPE OFFERS THE model for a squab dish that may be adapted year-round (see Variations). Here, squab and polenta are paired with springtime peas and pearl onions. As stunning as this dish is, it's not that difficult to produce. The polenta can be made ahead and kept warm; the peas and onions can be cooked early and reheated; and the squab sautés in 10 minutes. While the squab is resting, you make a pan sauce, so the entire dish can be produced with less than 1 hour's preparation!

The polenta recipe here calls for milk and cream instead of water, and this liquid is first infused with fresh thyme and crushed garlic cloves, making it a rich, creamy foil for the squab. At the Gotham, I serve this with Grilled Foie Gras (page 81) in addition to the squab.

To sauté squab, keep the breastbones in and baste frequently to ensure that it cooks evenly. While it requires attention and effort, it's a viable method for use in a home setting.

on the work surface. Press down on the breast with the heel of your hand to crack the breast keel bone. Turn the squabs over and pull out the keel bone. Cut each squab in half. Coarsely chop the wing tips, backs, and neck bones, and the gizzards and hearts, and set aside.

In a 12-inch sauté pan, heat the oil over medium-high heat. Season the squab halves with salt and pepper. Place in the sauté pan, skin side down, and add the butter. Cook, basting occasionally, until the squabs are browned, about 8 minutes. Turn and continue cooking, basting occasionally, until the other side is browned and the breasts are medium-rare, about 4 minutes. Remove to a plate, pull out the remaining rib bones, and add them to the reserved rough-chopped bones. Cover loosely with foil to keep warm.

> To peel pearl onions, cook them in boiling water for 1 minute to loosen the skins. Drain and rinse under cold water. Peel with a sharp knife, trimming off the tops and bottoms.

To make the pan sauce, pour off all but 1 tablespoon of fat from the sauté pan. Add the reserved bones and cook over medium-high heat, stirring occasionally, until browned, about 10 minutes. Add the shallots and stir until they soften, about 1 minute. Add the wine and bring to a boil, scraping up the browned bits on the bottom of the sauté pan with a wooden spoon. Cook until the wine is reduced to ¼ cup, about 5 minutes. Add the stock and collected juices from the plate with the squab and bring to a simmer. Reduce the heat to low, and simmer to concentrate the flavors, about 3 minutes. Strain the sauce through a fine wire strainer, pressing hard on the solids. Taste and season with salt and pepper.

ASSEMBLY

1 recipe Creamy Polenta (recipe follows)

Bring the onions back to a simmer over medium heat. Add the peas and cook just until heated through, about 1 minute.

Using a large serving spoon, set a portion of the polenta just off the center of 4 warmed dinner plates. (If desired, large polenta quenelles can be made by using 2 serving spoons; one to scoop and the other to shape.) Place a squab half next to the polenta and spoon the pearl onions and peas next to both. Spoon the sauce around the plate.

Variations: Fava beans and (in the summertime) fresh corn mingle well with these ingredients, or may be used as substitutes for the peas and onions.

Creamy Polenta

MAKES 4 SERVINGS

1 cup milk

1 cup heavy cream

1 garlic clove, peeled and crushed with a knife

1 sprig thyme

$\frac{1}{2}$ cup quick-cooking polenta

Coarse salt and freshly ground white pepper to taste

THIS IS A DELICIOUSLY rich recipe for polenta. By substituting White Chicken Stock (page 33) for some or all of the cream, you can lighten it to suit your own taste.

In a medium saucepan, bring the milk, cream, garlic, and thyme to a simmer over medium heat. Be careful that it does not boil over. Remove from the heat and let stand for 10 minutes. Pick out the garlic and thyme. Whisk in the polenta, bring back to a gentle boil, and cook over low heat, whisking constantly, until thick, about 5 minutes. Season with salt and pepper. Keep warm, covered, on the side of the stove. It will stay warm for 10 to 15 minutes.

Roast Turkey **Stuffed with Mashed Potatoes, Sausage, and Chanterelles**

MAKES 12 TO 16 SERVINGS

Thinking Ahead: The turkey giblet stock can be prepared as much as 1 day in advance, covered, and refrigerated.

TURKEY STOCK

Turkey neck and giblets (no liver)

10 cups Double Turkey Stock or White Chicken Stock (pages 37 or 33)

Chop the turkey neck into large pieces. In a large saucepan, combine the turkey neck, giblets, and stock. Slowly bring to a boil over medium-high heat, skimming off any foam that rises to the surface. Reduce the heat to very low and simmer for 3 to 4 hours. Strain the stock into a large bowl. You should have 2 quarts of turkey stock; add more stock if necessary. Finely chop the turkey neck meat and the giblets, discarding the bones. Cool the stock and chopped turkey meat to room temperature. Cover separately and refrigerate.

TURKEY

1 (16- to 18-pound) whole fresh turkey, rinsed with cold water and patted dry

1 recipe Mashed Potato, Sausage, and Chanterelle Stuffing (recipe follows)

2 tablespoons vegetable oil

1 teaspoon ground juniper berries (grind in a spice or coffee grinder)

Coarse salt and freshly ground white pepper

Preheat the oven to 325° F.

Loosely stuff the turkey body and neck cavities with the stuffing. Transfer the remaining stuffing to a shallow baking dish, cover with aluminum foil, and refrigerate (see Sidebar). Rub the turkey all over with the oil, the ground juniper berries, salt, and pepper.

Place on a rack set in a large, shallow roasting pan. Pour 2 cups of

FOR THANKSGIVING, MY father-in-law, an inspired cook, makes a remarkable and unconventional stuffing of mashed potatoes and chanterelles, which are at the height of their season in November. In sharp contrast, my mother has always served a traditional sausage and bread stuffing. When I became the designated cook *for both families* every November, I devised this recipe to honor both traditions without betraying either one. It features the mashed potatoes and chanterelles of my wife's family's stuffing, but also incorporates elements of my mother's recipe. A rich give-and-take occurs when this stuffing cooks, absorbing the bird's juices as the turkey literally swells with flavor.

A few notes on the turkey itself: It's absolutely essential that you use a *fresh* free-range, organic, or kosher turkey from the best local source. The flavor is incomparable. You should never defrost a frozen turkey, or use one that has been artificially preserved, or is declared "self-basting."

Turkey Tips: A few useful observations I've picked up over the years:

✳ Figure 1 pound of meat per person for birds up to 12 pounds, and ¾ pound per person for birds over 12 pounds. This will leave you with ample leftovers.

✳ Use ¾ cup stuffing for each pound of turkey.

✳ Hens tend to be more tender than toms, though more expensive. Hens usually weigh between 12 and 18 pounds. Save the wishbone!

To reheat the extra stuffing: After the turkey has been roasted, increase the oven temperature to 400° F. and bake for about 30 minutes while the turkey is resting. Baste stuffing with some stock to keep moist and flavorful.

the turkey stock into the pan. Roast, allowing about 20 minutes per pound, until a meat thermometer inserted in the thickest part of the thigh reads 175° F., 5½ to 6 hours. About every 20 minutes, baste the turkey with the stock. If the stock evaporates, add more to the pan. You want nice, dark, reduced drippings: Do not let them burn. Toward the end of the roasting, tent the turkey with foil if necessary to protect the skin from becoming too dark. Transfer the turkey to a large serving platter. Let rest for 20 to 30 minutes, tented with foil, while you prepare the sauce.

TURKEY SAUCE

4 teaspoons cornstarch dissolved in 2 tablespoons water

⅛ teaspoon ground juniper berries (grind in a spice or coffee grinder)

½ teaspoon chopped fresh rosemary

4 tablespoons unsalted butter, cut into pieces

Coarse salt and freshly ground white pepper to taste

Pour the turkey drippings into a glass bowl. Skim off and discard the yellow fat that rises to the surface. Set the drippings aside.

Place the roasting pan over 2 burners on top of the stove and turn the heat to high. Pour 2 cups of the turkey stock into the roasting pan and bring to a boil, scraping up the browned bits on the bottom of the pan with a wooden spoon.

Pour the stock into a large saucepan and add the remaining stock and reserved drippings. Bring to a boil over high heat and cook until richly flavored and reduced to about 4 cups, 15 to 20 minutes. Stir in the chopped giblets and turkey meat. Whisk in the cornstarch mixture, ground juniper berries, and rosemary. Cook until the sauce is lightly thickened, about 1 minute. Remove from the heat and whisk in the butter, a piece at a time. Season with the salt and pepper. Pour into a warmed sauceboat.

Present the turkey with the stuffing and sauce.

Mashed Potato, Sausage, and Chanterelle Stuffing

MAKES 12 TO 16 SERVINGS

3 pounds Idaho or russet baking potatoes, peeled and cut into 2-inch chunks

1 cup sour cream

12 tablespoons (1½ sticks) unsalted butter

1¼ cups thinly sliced shallots (6 large shallots)

4 garlic cloves, minced

2 pounds fresh mushrooms, preferably chanterelles, thinly sliced

2 tablespoons vegetable oil

2 pounds sweet Italian sausage, casings removed

1 cup chopped fresh flat-leaf parsley

½ cup chopped fresh chives

2 teaspoons chopped fresh thyme

1½ teaspoons chopped fresh rosemary

1¼ teaspoons ground juniper berries (grind in a spice or coffee grinder)

Coarse salt and freshly ground white pepper to taste

IF YOU WISH, SUBSTITUTE the lamb sausage mixture (see Sidebar, page 213) for the Italian sausage.

Bring a large pot of lightly salted water to a boil over high heat. Add the potatoes and cook until tender, 20 to 25 minutes. Drain well and return to the empty pot. Stir the potatoes over medium heat until the excess moisture is evaporated and they seem somewhat drier, about 3 minutes. Pass through a potato ricer into a large bowl, or mash with a potato masher. Mix in the sour cream and 8 tablespoons of the butter.

In a large sauté pan, heat 2 tablespoons of the remaining butter over medium-low heat. Add the shallots and garlic and cook, stirring often, until they're softened, about 3 minutes. Add to the potatoes.

Heat the remaining 2 tablespoons of butter in the sauté pan over medium-high heat. Add the mushrooms and cook, stirring occasionally, until the mushrooms have given off their liquid, it evaporates, and they are beginning to brown, 10 to 15 minutes. Add to the potatoes.

Heat the oil in the sauté pan over medium-high heat. Add the sausage and cook, breaking it up with a spoon, until lightly browned, about 10 minutes. Add the sausage to the potatoes. Add the parsley, chives, thyme, rosemary, and juniper berries, then season with salt and pepper to taste. The stuffing is best freshly prepared. Do not stuff the turkey until ready to roast.

Braised Rabbit with Green Olives, Whole Roasted Shallots, and White Bean Puree

MAKES 4 SERVINGS

RABBIT BRAISED WITH olives is something all culinary students are taught to prepare, and I have developed a special fondness for this particular dish. New ideas about how to augment it came to me often enough that I have changed the recipe over the years. This current version uses a combination of fennel seed and wine vinegar that contribute a rich undercurrent of spice flavor and a soft acidity that is particularly well suited to rabbit. The white bean puree, almost as thick as mashed potatoes, makes the perfect foil because of its uncommonly lush texture, while the slow-roasted cippolini onions—sweet and golden—round out the dish and add interest to the plate. Olives contrast the other flavors here; be sure to add them at the end to keep their potentially strong flavor from overwhelming the dish.

BRAISED RABBIT

2 (2^1/$_2$-pound) rabbits

Coarse salt and freshly ground white pepper to taste

^{1}/$_4$ cup olive oil

1 medium onion, chopped

1 small carrot, chopped

1 celery rib, chopped

6 garlic cloves, unpeeled, crushed

2 cups dry white wine

^{1}/$_4$ cup red wine vinegar

2 teaspoons fennel seed, toasted until fragrant in a dry sauté pan

^{1}/$_2$ teaspoon whole black peppercorns

4 cups White Chicken Stock (page 33)

1 cup pitted green Mediterranean olives, such as picholine or Sicilian

Using a heavy knife or cleaver, cut up each rabbit into 7 pieces:
Remove and reserve the front and hind legs.

Remove the bony lower 2 to 3 inches of the rib section, chop coarsely, and reserve.

Separate the saddle from the loin and cut the saddle into 2 pieces.

You now have 2 saddle sections, the loin, 2 front legs, and 2 hind legs. Season all the rabbit pieces with salt and pepper.

In a large ovenproof casserole or sauté pan, heat the oil over medium-high heat. In batches, brown the rabbit on all sides, turning occasionally, about 8 minutes total. Transfer to a plate and set aside.

Add the reserved rabbit bones to the casserole and brown, about 8 minutes. Lower the heat and add the onion, carrot, celery, and garlic. Cook, stirring often, until lightly browned, about 5 minutes. Add the wine, vinegar, fennel seed, and peppercorns. Bring to a boil over high heat and cook until reduced by half, about 10 minutes. Add the stock and bring back to a boil.

Return the browned rabbit to the casserole. Reduce the heat to low and cover tightly. Braise the rabbit, removing the individual pieces as they cook through, placing them on a platter, and covering with foil to keep them from drying out. The loin will take about 15 minutes; the saddle, 25 minutes; the front legs, 45 minutes; and the back legs, 1 hour and 20 minutes. Strain the sauce through a wire sieve into a medium bowl. Skim off the fat from the surface.

Return the strained sauce to the cleaned casserole and cook until the sauce is richly flavored and reduced to about 2 cups, 20 to 30 minutes. Add the rabbit and olives and heat through, about 5 minutes. Season with salt and pepper.

WHOLE ROASTED SHALLOTS

12 whole unpeeled shallots

2 tablespoons water

1 tablespoon extra-virgin olive oil

Coarse salt and freshly ground white pepper to taste

Preheat the oven to 400° F. Place the shallots in a small baking dish that holds them snugly in a single layer. Drizzle them with the water, oil, salt, and pepper and toss to coat. Cover tightly with aluminum foil and bake until tender, 40 to 50 minutes.

WHITE BEAN PUREE

1$\frac{1}{2}$ cups (12 ounces) dried cannellini (white kidney) beans, soaked overnight in cold water, drained

2 cups White Chicken Stock (page 33)

2 cups water

1 small onion, halved

2 garlic cloves, peeled and crushed

1 sprig thyme

Coarse salt and freshly ground white pepper to taste

6 tablespoons extra-virgin olive oil

In a medium saucepan, bring the soaked beans, the stock, water, onion, garlic, and thyme to a boil over high heat. Reduce the heat to low and simmer for 20 minutes. Add the salt and continue cooking until the beans are tender, 20 to 30 minutes. Drain through a colander set over a bowl, reserving the garlic and cooking liquid. Discard the onion and thyme.

In a food processor fitted with the metal blade, pulse the beans and reserved garlic. With the machine running, gradually add the oil. If necessary, add enough of the reserved bean cooking liquid to make a smooth puree. Season with salt and pepper.

To assemble, place a mound of white bean puree in the center of each warmed dinner plate. Place a few pieces of rabbit around the puree. Spoon some sauce onto the plate, and garnish with the roasted shallots.

Variations: If you love black truffles, substitute 2 to 3 ounces of them, thinly sliced, for the olives to finish this dish. Also, you may remove the rabbit meat from the bones, return it to the sauce, and toss with pappardelle or fettuccine for a classic pasta sauce. Chicken braised with olives is another classic dish that you can make by substituting chicken for the rabbit and adjusting the cooking time to allow for the larger chicken pieces (approximately 25 minutes for the breasts and approximately 45 minutes for the legs and thighs).

9 Meats and Game

Every year, when my family asks me what I want for my Fourth of July birthday dinner, I always say the same thing, "grilled lamb." Its full flavor needs very little coaxing. Not coincidentally, the Rack of Lamb with Herbed Crust, Garlic Flan, Flageolets, and a Merlot Sauce (page 294) has been the centerpiece of my New Year's Eve celebration for many years, as well.

Lamb, like many meats, is the food of celebration and ritual—from steak dinners enjoyed to commemorate business triumphs, to Independence Day cookouts where friends and family enjoy barbecued ribs. The substantial, primal rewards of meat appeal to a timeless craving . . . even the most civilized of our species remains carnivorous by nature.

Some of the dishes in this chapter are, appropriately enough, among the most hearty and substantial in the book. Simply put, it takes a certain amount of weight to accompany steak, lamb, or venison, so side dishes must be suitable matches. The one steak dish in the book, for example, is accompanied by a rich potato and bacon "cake" (page 292).

With some meats, I've demonstrated braising techniques designed to amplify the flavor through slow-cooking with simple aromatics. Short ribs of beef, for example, demonstrate an inexpensive way to elevate a humble cut of meat with rich mashed potatoes and a colorful and tasty root vegetable garnish. And the pork roast (page 309) owes its flavor both to the braising process and to the mustard spaetzle and poached lady apples that accompany it.

In strong contrast, venison has a one-of-a-kind natural flavor, best suited to fall and winter. American diners today can avail themselves of farm-raised venison, which is far less gamey than wild venison. I've offered venison here grilled (page 321), which is a great alternative to the same old steaks on the grill, and in an autumn dazzler, Loin of Venison with Rosemary Poached Pears, Root Vegetables, and Pumpkin Puree (page 317).

Many of these dishes, like Lamb Shanks with Creamy White Beans and Yellow Turnip Puree, and Braised Short Ribs with Baby Root Vegetables and Mashed Potatoes (pages 305 and 288), are perfect for casual entertaining and family meals. (They are so appealing, in fact, that we often offer them on Gotham's menu, though not family-style.) Long-simmered, with the tender meat practically falling off the bone, these are extremely satisfying dishes. They take little last-minute attention and can be made well ahead of time.

In this country, mass production has affected the flavor of meat, so you have to know your butcher and his or her commitment to quality. Luckily, there are small farmers and ranchers who are producing excellent meat from animals that have been fed on natural diets. Some mail order sources for such meats are listed on page 375, though you can often find high-quality meat at your local supermarket.

Pan-roasting

Quick cooking with little fat in a shallow pan over a high flame, this method develops a flavorful brown crust that holds in the juices. It is important to sauté in a pan large enough to hold the meat without crowding, or the steam created will not be able to escape the pan, and the excess moisture will hinder the browning process. I tested these recipes in a 12-inch heavy-gauge, stainless steel pan, which is easy to find at well-stocked kitchenware stores. It is a very versatile utensil, and I encourage you to purchase one if you don't own one already. This pan will usually cook all of a recipe's serving portion at once. (If it won't, I'll suggest that you brown the meat in batches). Otherwise you will have to use 2 smaller sauté pans.

Be sure your pan is hot enough before adding the meat. The cooking oil should be shimmering, but not smoking. Once the meat is in the pan, don't move it around, and let it cook long enough for it to brown nicely. Restaurant stove burners are much hotter than home stoves (although many home cooks own professional stoves), and restaurant dishes are cooked over a more intense flame. All the recipes in this book were tested on a home stove, so the estimated timings will work in your kitchen. However, it is better to judge by the way the food looks and smells than to set a stopwatch, so be somewhat flexible. If you have a restaurant stove with high B.T.U.s (Bunsen Thermal Units), the timings for your stovetop-cooked foods will naturally be shorter.

Braising

Gentle, slow cooking in liquid that tenderizes tough cuts of meat and keeps them moist is called "braising." While you can braise over low heat on top of the stove, I prefer to braise in the oven at approximately 300° F, as the heat is more even and there is less chance of burning the bottom of the pan. The braising liquid must be kept at a simmer, not a boil. Check occasionally to be sure, and if it is boiling, reduce the oven temperature by 25° or so.

Beef

As a nod to American culinary tradition, we always have a well-aged steak on the menu at the Gotham Bar and Grill. You should purchase prime or choice grade—the better the meat is marbled with fat, the higher the grade and the more tender the steak will be when cooked. While we are all at the mercy of what our butcher carries, you can special-order prime meat. Dry-aged steaks are especially worth seeking out, or mail-ordering. To achieve this effect, whole sirloin cuts are stored under special conditions for about three weeks to develop their flavor and tenderize the meat, which is then well trimmed and cut into steaks. The amount of shrinkage caused by the aging and the trimming contributes to the high cost of these steaks, but also fully justifies it.

Veal

When purchasing veal, look for pale pink flesh with snow-white fat (unless you're buying organic veal, which will be red). Some of the best veal in America can be mail-ordered. (See source on page 375.)

Lamb

The best-flavored lamb should have deep red flesh and white fat. At home, I like to cook leg of lamb. While you may ask the butcher to do the boning for you, I prefer to cut the boned lamb into 2 or 3 smaller "roasts," following the natural seams of the meat. It is much easier to control the cooking of these smaller roasts than of a butterflied leg, which is thick in some parts and thin in others. (See recipe for Grilled Leg of Lamb with Moroccan Spices, page 302.) If you do have the butcher bone your lamb, be sure to ask him to give you the bones, sawed into 2-inch pieces, to use in a lamb stock.

Pork

It is harder and harder to get moist, good-tasting pork these days. To be sure of juicy results, I like braised pork shoulder. If you can get farm-raised pork, you will appreciate the difference.

Venison

For those diners who remember hunted, aged venison as an unpleasantly gamey taste experience, the gentle, slightly beefy flavor of farm-raised venison will be a revelation. Venison is now farm-raised in many states, primarily from axis deer, which are native to India. In these recipes, I call for the cuts most easily ordered: boneless loin roasts (that can be cut into steaks) and a bone-in rack of venison.

Braised Short Ribs with Baby Root Vegetables and Mashed Potatoes

MAKES 6 SERVINGS

THIS IS A GREAT WINTER dish that offers the sturdy, hearty combination of short ribs, root vegetables, and mashed potatoes—foods that promise real sustenance.

Short ribs have an exceptionally deep, developed flavor that is coaxed out by searing, then slowly braising them, rendering much of their fat but none of their flavor. When braising, keep the bubble as slow and imperceptible as possible and check often to make sure the ribs don't dry out.

Sweet and tender turnips and carrots help moderate the richness of the short ribs. However, the mashed potatoes put this dish over the top—a fact respected by the suggested portion sizes.

Served with a simple salad, like the Endive, Parsley, and Shallot Salad (page 93), this would make for a very satisfying meal.

Thinking Ahead: The beef ribs and sauce, without the butter, may be braised as much as 2 days in advance. The baby root vegetables may be prepared as much as 8 hours in advance. Both should be stored, covered, in the refrigerator.

SHORT RIBS

2 tablespoons vegetable oil

6 large, meaty short ribs (about 6 pounds total)

Coarse salt and freshly ground white pepper to taste

1 medium onion, coarsely chopped

1 medium carrot, coarsely chopped

1 medium celery rib, chopped

3 large garlic cloves, minced

1 tablespoon tomato paste

1 (750 ml) bottle dry red wine, such as Zinfandel

4 cups White Chicken Stock (page 33)

1 teaspoon whole white or black peppercorns

2 sprigs thyme

2 sprigs rosemary

1 dried bay leaf

5 tablespoons unsalted butter

Preheat the oven to 300° F. In a large, heavy-bottomed, ovenproof casserole or sauté pan with a lid, heat the oil over medium-high heat. Season the short ribs with the salt and pepper. Cook in batches without crowding until nicely browned on all sides, about 8 minutes. Transfer to a plate.

Pour off all but 3 tablespoons of the fat. Return the casserole to medium-high heat and add the onion, carrot, and celery. Cook, stirring often, until the vegetables are nicely browned, 8 to 10 minutes.

Add the garlic and the tomato paste and cook for 1 minute. Add the red wine and cook until reduced by half, about 10 minutes. Add the stock, peppercorns, thyme, rosemary, and bay leaf and bring to a boil. Return the short ribs to the casserole and cover tightly.

Braise until the short ribs are tender, about 2 hours. About 15 minutes into the cooking time, check to be sure the liquid is barely simmering, and reduce the oven temperature, if necessary. When tender, transfer the ribs to a platter. Cover with foil to keep warm.

Let the braising liquid stand off the heat for 3 minutes. Skim off any fat that rises to the surface. Return the casserole to the stove and bring to a boil over high heat. Cook until the sauce is richly flavored and reduced to about 1½ cups, 10 to 15 minutes. Off the heat, whisk in the butter, 1 tablespoon at a time. Season with salt and pepper.

BABY ROOT VEGETABLES

12 ounces baby turnips, peeled

12 ounces baby carrots, peeled

Coarse salt and freshly ground white pepper to taste

Bring a large pot of salted water to a boil over high heat. Add the turnips and cook until tender, about 10 minutes. Using a slotted spoon, transfer the turnips to a bowl. Cover to keep warm.

Add the carrots to the boiling water and cook until tender, about 6 minutes. Drain and keep warm with the turnips. (If cooking ahead, plunge the vegetables into iced water to stop the cooking, drain, and set aside. When ready to serve, reheat briefly in boiling salted water.) Season with salt and pepper.

ASSEMBLY

1 recipe Gotham Mashed Potatoes (page 206)

Place a mound of mashed potatoes in the center of each warmed dinner plate. Lean a short rib up against the potatoes. Spoon the sauce around the potatoes, and garnish with the turnips and carrots.

Variation: Serve this dish cold, dicing the meat and combining it with diced red onion, celery, and green olives. Dress with olive oil and red wine vinegar to create a great salad.

Flavor Building: Horseradish Sauce (see Sidebar, page 325) makes a potent complement to the short ribs.

Charcoal-Roasted Prime Rib with Caribbean Spices

MAKES 6 TO 8 SERVINGS

COOKING PRIME RIB ON a barbecue is fun, exciting, and delicious! (A friend of mine used to do this on his rooftop in Brooklyn Heights, and the meal was always unforgettable.) If you really love roast beef, you simply have to try cooking it on a grill.

The grilling, coupled with Caribbean seasoning, gives prime rib a unique flavor, but you could alternate this seasoning with a more traditional herb rub (see Sidebar), which really enhances the natural flavor of the meat. (For the former, Dark and Stormies, or some other evocative tropical drink. For the latter, serve a red wine.)

Thinking Ahead: Let the meat sit with the spice rub for at least 4 hours.

SPICE RUB

$^{1}/_{2}$ cup chopped onion

8 garlic cloves, thinly sliced

3 tablespoons olive oil

2 tablespoons light brown sugar

2 tablespoons sweet Hungarian paprika

2 tablespoons freshly ground black pepper

1 tablespoon chopped fresh thyme leaves

1 tablespoon ground Jamaican allspice

1 teaspoon dried ginger

1 teaspoon cayenne

4 habañero chiles (optional), halved, seeded, and finely chopped

In a food processor fitted with the metal blade, process the onion, garlic, and oil until pureed. Transfer to a bowl, add the remaining ingredients, and stir to form a thick paste.

ASSEMBLY

1 (10-pound) prime rib of beef

Coarse salt and freshly ground white pepper

1 cup oak or other hardwood chips, soaked in water to cover for 30 minutes, drained, divided into thirds, wrapped separately in foil, the foil pierced in several places

10 medium (5-ounce) red onions

3 pounds small, whole fingerling potatoes, unpeeled, or use small new potatoes, cut in half

$^{1}/_{3}$ cup olive oil

Trim the top layer of fat on the roast to $1/4$-inch thickness. Using a sharp knife, slash the top of the roast to create a crosshatch marking about $1/4$ inch deep. Massage the roast all over—top, bottom, and sides—with $1/4$ cup of coarse salt, then with about half the spice paste. Spread the remaining paste over the top of the roast. Cover the roast and refrigerate it for 4 to 6 hours. Then let it stand at room temperature for 1 hour before cooking.

Build a good-size charcoal fire banked on one side of an outdoor grill. Place a disposable aluminum pan on the other side of the grill and add enough water to come $1/2$ inch up the sides of the pan. Let the coals burn just until they are covered with white ash and you can hardly hold your hand over them for 1 or 2 seconds. (The coals should be very hot.) Place one of the wood chip packets on the coals and let them begin to smolder. Lightly oil the grill grate.

Place the roast on the grill over the pan. Cover the grill and partially close all the vents to keep the fire from burning too quickly. Cook, adding a handful of charcoal (and another wood chip packet) to the fire every 40 minutes or so to keep the grill temperature at about 325° F., until a meat thermometer inserted in the thickest part of the meat reads 130° F., about $2 1/2$ hours. Be flexible with your estimated cooking time, as grilling is an inexact science. Let the meat stand for 20 minutes before carving.

To cook the vegetables with the meat, toss the onions and potatoes in a large bowl with the oil. Season with salt and pepper. About 1 hour before the end of the roast cooking time, place the onions around the meat over the foil pan. About 20 minutes before the end of the cooking time, add the potatoes to the grill, directly over the coals. Cook, turning occasionally, until all the vegetables are tender.

Instead of the Caribbean Spice Rub, try just to highlight the natural flavor of the meat with an herb rub. In a food processor, combine $1/2$ cup chopped onion, 8 garlic cloves, and 3 tablespoons olive oil. Liquefy. Add 2 tablespoons *each* chopped fresh rosemary and thyme, 1 tablespoon dried sage, and 3 tablespoons freshly ground black pepper. Massage the roast all over with coarse salt, and then with this herb rub.

Variations: The roast may also be cooked in an oven. Preheat the oven to 450° F. Place the roast in a large roasting pan, fat side up. Roast for 20 minutes. Lower the oven temperature to 325°, and continue roasting until a meat thermometer inserted in the thickest part of the roast reads 130°, about $2 1/4$ hours.

Sirloin Steak with Potato and Bacon "Cake" and Red Wine Butter

MAKES 4 SERVINGS

THIS MAIN-COURSE combination of steak and potatoes offers one of the more obvious, primal indulgences in the book, but it is elevated by 2 uniquely delicious components.

The centerpiece here is not the steak, but the potato-bacon cake, made with diced potatoes, chives, and smoked bacon, and designed to be served from the center of the table. The presentation converts these commonplace ingredients into something special. It's a stunning, hearty side dish—especially appropriate to accompany a meat entrée. The recipe for this "cake" was inspired by a similar version I once enjoyed at the restaurant Les Amis Louis in Paris.

The other component here is a flavored, or compound, butter—in this case a red wine butter—that melts over the steak. It is very simple to make: Red wine, shallots, and garlic are heated until the liquid is nearly evaporated, then the mixture is cooled and mashed together with butter and a small handful of herbs. The

Thinking Ahead: The red wine butter may be prepared as much as 1 week in advance and stored, tightly wrapped, in the refrigerator. The cake should be made just before serving, but may be kept warm for up to an hour in a 180° F. oven.

RED WINE BUTTER

1 cup dry red wine

2 tablespoons finely chopped shallot

1 small garlic clove, finely minced

8 tablespoons (1 stick) unsalted butter, softened

1 tablespoon finely chopped fresh flat-leaf parsley

Coarse salt and freshly ground white pepper to taste

In a small saucepan, bring the red wine, shallots, and garlic to a boil over high heat. Cook until the wine is almost completely reduced, about 15 minutes. Cool completely.

In a small bowl, use a rubber spatula to mash the cooled shallot mixture with the butter and parsley until well combined. Season with the salt and pepper. Transfer to plastic wrap and roll the butter into a cylinder about 4 inches long and 1 inch in diameter. Wrap tightly and refrigerate until firm, about 4 hours. Slice the chilled butter into 8 rounds.

POTATO AND BACON "CAKE"

5 large (2¼-pound) baking potatoes, such as russets, peeled and cut into 1-inch dice

1 tablespoon vegetable oil

3 ounces smoked slab bacon, cut into ¼-inch dice

8 tablespoons (1 stick) unsalted butter

¼ cup finely chopped shallots

2 tablespoons minced fresh chives

1 teaspoon minced garlic

Coarse salt and freshly ground white pepper to taste

Preheat the oven to 450° F. Bring a large pot of lightly salted water to a boil over high heat. Add the potatoes and cook halfway, about 10 minutes. Drain and transfer to a large bowl.

Meanwhile, add the oil to an ovenproof 8-inch nonstick sauté pan. Cook the bacon over medium heat until lightly browned, about 5 minutes. Transfer the bacon to paper towels to drain. Discard the fat. Combine the potatoes, bacon, 4 tablespoons of the butter, the shallots, chives, and the garlic. Season carefully with salt and pepper.

Transfer the potato mixture to the sauté pan and spread it evenly, pressing down on the potatoes to compress the cake. Dot the remaining 4 tablespoons of butter around the outside perimeter of the cake so the butter will melt down the sides as it heats. Cook over medium heat until sizzling around the edges, about 10 minutes. Transfer to the oven and bake until golden brown, about 40 minutes. Hold a serving platter over the skillet, and invert them together to unmold the potatoes onto the platter.

> "new" butter is then refrigerated until firm. This is just one of countless compound butters with which you might experiment. They are a great way to elevate a simple meat or fish course, and also work well with cooked vegetables.

> Many cookbooks will suggest that you keep a supply of compound butters in your freezer, but I find that it is more practical to prepare them on an as-needed basis, storing the leftover butter for some impromptu use. When holding steaks for a few minutes while finishing side dishes, place them on a wire cake rack. The juices will stay in the meat, rather than run out, as they would on a plate.

ASSEMBLY

4 (14-ounce) dry-aged sirloin steaks

Coarse salt

2 tablespoons coarsely cracked white peppercorns

1 recipe Swiss Chard (page 192), or any other cooked greens

Build a charcoal fire in a grill, and let the coals burn until covered with white ash (or preheat the broiler). Season the steak with the salt, then press the peppercorns into the steaks. Grill the steaks, turning once, until medium rare, about 8 minutes total.

Garnish each steak with red wine butter, and serve with the potato and bacon cake and Swiss chard (or other cooked greens).

Variations: The potato-bacon "cake" works well as a side dish with a great many meats and poultry. My favorite pairings are roast chicken, rack of lamb, and veal chops.

The red wine butter works very well with fish, especially grilled salmon, swordfish, or tuna. The butter provides a rich counterpoint to the fish itself.

Rack of Lamb with Herbed Crust, Garlic Flan, Flageolets, and a Merlot Sauce

MAKES 4 SERVINGS

DON'T BE AFRAID, IT'S just a rack of lamb. **That's what I feel like saying to home cooks who find preparing a rack of lamb intimidating. It's actually not that difficult. The method I recommend involves 3 basic steps: first, seasoning the racks with salt and pepper and browning them in a skillet to isolate their natural juices; second, roasting them in an oven; and, finally, coating them with mustard and a bread crumb and herb mixture and broiling them until the crust is browned. This relatively simple process yields a perfectly cooked and richly seasoned rack.**

The sauce technique used for this dish—a reduction of Merlot, lamb stock, and other supporting ingredients—can be used to underscore lamb in many other contexts. Good lamb sauces are difficult to come by, so don't be reluctant to rely on this one over and over.

The herbed crust recipe used here is actually more intense and flavorful than the classic mixture of bread crumbs, chopped parsley,

Thinking Ahead: The sauce may be prepared as much as a day in advance; the garlic flans and flageolets may be prepared up to 6 hours in advance. All should be stored covered, and refrigerated.

Special Equipment: four 6-ounce ceramic ramekins

LAMB

2 (4-pound) racks of lamb, 7 to 8 ribs per rack

Ask the butcher to saw off the chine bone and french the rib bones, reserving all the meat and bone trimmings from preparing the racks to use for the wine sauce. Have the chine bone sawed into 2-inch pieces. At home, trim away and discard all of the extraneous fat from the meat trimmings.

HERBED CRUST

$^1/_2$ cup fresh bread crumbs, made from firm white bread, crusts removed (see Sidebar, page 296)

$^1/_4$ cup chopped fresh flat-leaf parsley

$1^1/_2$ teaspoons chopped fresh mint

$1^1/_2$ teaspoons chopped fresh tarragon

1 garlic clove, minced

1 tablespoon extra-virgin olive oil

Coarse salt and freshly ground black pepper to taste

In a medium bowl, combine the bread crumbs, parsley, mint, tarragon, and garlic. Drizzle with the oil and toss to moisten the crumbs. Season with salt and pepper.

FLAGEOLETS

1 cup dried flageolets, soaked overnight in cold water to cover, drained

1½ cups White Chicken Stock (page 33)

1½ cups water

1 small onion, halved

2 garlic cloves, peeled and crushed

1 sprig thyme

Coarse salt and freshly ground pepper to taste

In a medium saucepan, bring the drained flageolets, stock, water, onion, garlic, and thyme to a boil over high heat. Reduce the heat to low and simmer for 20 minutes. Add the salt and pepper and continue cooking until the flageolets are tender, another 20 to 30 minutes. Off the heat, allow the flageolets to cool in their cooking liquid. Refrigerate and reheat the flageolets in the cooking liquid, if necessary.

and garlic. This one calls for mint and tarragon to highlight further the lamb's flavor.

The garlic custard is a useful component to add to your repertoire. It provides garlic flavor without the irrepressibly strong impact of whole cloves. The silken texture of the flan makes it an important presence on the plate; it both contrasts the texture of the lamb and melds supremely well with the Merlot sauce.

GARLIC FLAN

Unsalted butter, for the ramekins

1¼ cups heavy cream

3 large eggs

⅓ cup Roasted Garlic Puree (see Sidebar, page 47)

Coarse salt and freshly ground white pepper to taste

Position a rack in the center of the oven and preheat to 300° F. Lightly butter the ramekins.

Whisk all of the ingredients until smooth, by hand or using a blender. Place the ramekins in a larger baking dish. Pour the garlic cream into the ramekins. Place the baking dish in the oven. Pour enough hot water into the dish to come about ½ inch up the sides of the ramekins. Cover the pan with aluminum foil.

Bake until the custards are set, about 1 hour. (The centers will still seem a little loose.) If not serving immediately, cool completely, cover with plastic wrap, and refrigerate until ready to reheat. To reheat the flans, place the unwrapped ramekins in a large sautée pan and add enough water to come ½ inch up the sides. Bring to a simmer over low heat. Cook until the garlic flans are heated through, about 30 minutes. The flans will keep warm in the turned-off sauté pan for up to 30 minutes. Before unmolding, remove them from the water bath and set for a moment on a kitchen towel to dry.

ASSEMBLY

Coarse salt and freshly ground black pepper to taste

2 tablespoons canola oil

2 tablespoons Dijon mustard

Merlot Sauce (recipe follows)

To make fresh bread crumbs, trim the crusts and cut the bread into cubes. Process in a food processor fitted with the metal blade until fine. Rub the crumbs through a wire strainer.

Position a rack in the center of the oven and preheat to 400° F. Season the racks of lamb with salt and pepper.

In a 12-inch ovenproof sauté pan, heat the oil over high heat until very hot but not smoking. Add the lamb, meaty side down, and sear until nicely browned, 3 to 4 minutes.

Transfer the skillet to the oven and roast for 7 minutes. Turn the lamb and continue cooking for another 8 minutes, until a meat thermometer inserted in the center reads 120° to 125° F. (About 15 minutes total roasting time.) Remove the lamb from the oven and let it rest for 10 minutes. (The lamb will continue to cook by 5° to 10° as it stands. This timing will give you rare meat. If you like medium-rare meat, add about 3 minutes to the total cooking time; add about 8 minutes for medium meat.)

Position a broiler rack about 6 inches from the source of heat and preheat. Spread the mustard on the top of the racks. Cover with the herbed bread crumbs, pressing to make sure they adhere. Broil until the crust is golden brown, 2 to 3 minutes.

Gotham Presentation: Cut into double rib chops. In the center of 4 warmed dinner plates, cross pairs of chops, interlocking the bones. Run a knife around the inside of each ramekin, and unmold a flan onto each plate. Use a slotted spoon to add some flageolets. Spoon the sauce onto the plates.

Everyday Presentation: Serve the lamb and beans on a platter, the sauce in a sauceboat, and serve the garlic flans in their ramekins, instructing your guests to eat them with a spoon.

Variations: This dish can be simplified by leaving out the lamb sauce and garlic flans. It's also acceptable to use just about any bean with this dish, especially white beans or fava beans.

Merlot Sauce

MAKES ABOUT 1 ½ CUPS SAUCE

Reserved meat and bone trimmings from 2 racks of lamb

1 tablespoon vegetable oil, plus more as needed

2 medium shallots, sliced

4 garlic cloves, peeled and crushed

¾ cup Merlot wine

1 teaspoon coarsely crushed whole black peppercorns

1 sprig rosemary

1 sprig thyme

1½ quarts White Chicken Stock (page 33)

LONG SIMMERED, WITH hints of rosemary and garlic, this is the perfect sauce for lamb.

In a large saucepan, heat the oil over medium-high heat. In batches, if necessary, brown the lamb meat and bone trimmings for about 10 minutes. Transfer to a bowl and set aside.

Pour off all but 1 tablespoon of the fat from the saucepan. Reduce the heat to medium. Add the shallots and cook, stirring often, until browned, 3 to 5 minutes. Add the garlic and stir until fragrant, about 1 minute. Return the browned trimmings and bones to the pan. Add the red wine, peppercorns, rosemary, and thyme. Bring to a boil over high heat and cook until the wine is reduced to ¼ cup, 10 to 15 minutes. Add the chicken stock and bring to a boil. Reduce the heat to low and simmer very slowly until the stock is reduced to about 1 quart, about 3 hours.

Strain through a fine sieve into a large bowl. Let stand for 5 minutes, then skim off the fat that rises to the surface. Return the stock to the cleaned saucepan and bring to a boil over high heat. Cook until richly flavored and reduced to about 1½ cups, 15 to 20 minutes.

Grilled Leg of Lamb with Roasted Garlic, Braised Escarole, and Chick-pea Puree

MAKES 6 TO 8 SERVINGS

Thinking Ahead: The escarole may be prepared as much as 2 hours before serving, covered, and refrigerated.

LEG OF LAMB

4 tablespoons Roasted Garlic Puree (see Sidebar, page 47)

3 tablespoons coarsely chopped fresh flat-leaf parsley

2 tablespoons chopped fresh mint

1 tablespoon finely chopped fresh thyme

1½ teaspoons finely chopped fresh rosemary

Coarse salt and freshly ground white pepper to taste

1 (5½-pound) boneless leg of lamb, shank end, well trimmed

2 tablespoons olive oil

Preheat the oven to 350° F. In a small bowl, combine the garlic puree, parsley, mint, thyme, rosemary, 1 teaspoon of pepper, and salt.

Place the boned lamb, cut side up, on the work surface. Butterfly the meat by cutting into, but not through, the thickest parts of the muscle.

Open up the meat and spread with the garlic mixture, leaving a 1-inch border all around the edge.

Reshape the lamb and fold over the top, and then the bottom, to enclose the filling.

Use kitchen string to tie up the

THIS IS AN ORIGINAL way to cook leg of lamb: Spread a rich, aromatic puree of garlic and herbs inside the boned leg, then roll it up and grill it, letting the flavors seep into the meat. The roast garlic "stuffing" is a vast improvement over the more traditional method of inserting slivers of garlic into the meat. Not only does my technique distribute the flavor more evenly, but it eliminates the possibility of a diner biting into a piece of raw garlic.

The method for the chick-pea puree is useful—pureeing the peas in a Cuisinart with extra-virgin olive oil to create a delicious, creamy accompaniment to the leg of lamb.

Braised escarole is a rarity in most home kitchens in the United States, but well worth trying. Finally, if there's a mint jelly aficionado at your table, the mint in the "stuffing" will subtly satisfy their expectation.

 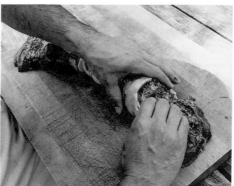 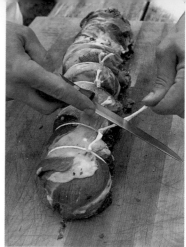

roast crosswise. Cut the lamb in half. Rub the lamb with oil and season it generously with salt and pepper.

Build a charcoal fire in an outdoor grill. Let the coals burn until covered with white ash. Grill the lamb, turning often, until a meat thermometer inserted in the center registers 130° F. for medium-rare lamb, 20 to 25 minutes. Or preheat the oven to 350° F. Heat the oil in a 12-inch skillet set over medium-high heat. Add the lamb and sear it turning often on all sides until nicely browned, aproximately 12 minutes. Transfer the meat to a roasting pan and roast in the preheated oven until a meat thermometer inserted in the center registers 130° F. for medium-rare, aproximately 20 to 25 minutes.

BRAISED ESCAROLE

1 tablespoon olive oil

1 medium onion, chopped

1 garlic clove, finely chopped

2 cups White Chicken Stock (page 33)

2 (1-pound) heads escarole, washed, and cut crosswise into 1-inch-wide pieces

Coarse salt and freshly ground white pepper to taste

In a large saucepan, heat the oil over medium heat. Add the onion and garlic and cook, stirring often, until the onion is soft, about 3 minutes. Add the stock and bring to a boil. In batches, add the escarole, letting the first batch wilt (this is a matter of seconds) before adding the next. Season with salt and pepper and cook just until the escarole is tender, about 5 minutes.

ASSEMBLY

Chick-pea Puree (see Sidebar)

Remove the strings from the roast. Using a sharp, thin-bladed carving knife, cut crosswise into ³/₄-inch-thick slices. On each warmed plate, arrange overlapping slices of the roast, and spoonfuls of the escarole and chick-pea puree.

Flavor Building: Whole Roasted Shallots (page 281) are a great side dish for the leg of lamb.

Chick-pea Puree: Make the White Bean Puree on page 281, substituting soaked, drained chick-peas for the white beans. The chick-peas could take up to 1 hour to cook until tender enough to puree.

Grilled Leg of Lamb **with Moroccan Spices, Grilled Vegetables, and Basmati Rice Salad**

MAKES 6 TO 8 SERVINGS

TOASTED CORIANDER, cumin, and cardamom combine to make an evocative marinade for the lamb in this Middle Eastern–inspired dish. The soft, slow-roasted vegetables offer an understated counterpoint to the meat, while a much more profound effect is provided by the basmati rice salad. Commonly used to accompany tandoori roasted poultry and beef, this salad is made with yogurt, which has a cooling effect on the palate that offers relief from the spiciness of the lamb.

Thinking Ahead: Marinate the lamb for at least 4 hours, covered and refrigerated, before grilling. The basmati rice salad may be prepared as much as 2 hours in advance and kept at room temperature.

MARINATED LEG OF LAMB

1 (5½-pound) boneless leg of lamb, either shank or butt end, well trimmed

2 teaspoons coriander seed

1 teaspoon cuminseed

6 teaspoons cardamom pods

1 small onion, coarsely chopped

¼ cup chopped fresh ginger

6 garlic cloves, peeled, crushed under a knife

2 tablespoons vegetable oil

1 teaspoon ground turmeric

1 teaspoon ground cinnamon

½ teaspoon coarse salt

4 small dried hot red chile peppers, crumbled; or ½ teaspoon crushed hot red pepper flakes

Using a sharp knife, "seam out" the lamb by cutting it into 2 or 3 smaller roasts, following the natural formation of the muscles. Set aside.

In a dry medium sauté pan over medium heat, cook the coriander, cumin, and cardamom, stirring often, until fragrant and lightly toasted, about 2 minutes. Cool on a plate, then grind in a spice mill or coffee grinder, and set aside.

In a food processor fitted with the metal blade, process the onion, ginger, garlic, and oil until finely chopped. Add the ground spices, including the turmeric and cinnamon, the salt, and the chile peppers. Pulse to mix, adding a few tablespoons of water if necessary, to make a smooth puree.

Place the lamb pieces in a large bowl and coat with the spice marinade. Cover and refrigerate for at least 4 or up to 6 hours.

GRILLED VEGETABLES

1 small (1-pound) eggplant, cut into 8 rounds

8 plum tomatoes, halved lengthwise

3 large red onions, cut into $1/4$-inch-thick rounds

3 tablespoons extra-virgin olive oil

Coarse salt and freshly ground white pepper to taste

Build a charcoal fire in a grill, and let the coals burn until covered with white ash. Lightly oil the grill grate. Brush the eggplant, tomatoes, and onion rings with the olive oil and season with salt and pepper. Grill, turning occasionally, and basting with more oil if needed, until the vegetables are tender, about 8 minutes for the eggplant and onions, and 5 minutes for the tomatoes. Transfer to a plate, season with salt and pepper, and set aside. Let cool to room temperature.

ASSEMBLY

Cilantro sprigs, for garnish

1 recipe Basmati Rice Salad (recipe follows)

Add more charcoal to the fire, bank the coals to one side of the grill, and let them burn until covered with white ash. Grill the lamb pieces directly over the coals, turning once to sear, about 5 minutes total. Move the lamb to the other side of the grill, away from the coals. Cover the grill and cook the lamb, turning halfway through cooking, until a meat thermometer inserted in the thickest part of the lamb reads 130° F. for medium-rare lamb, about 25 minutes total. Each piece of lamb will be a different size, with different cooking times. If you cook all of the lamb for about the same time, the smaller pieces will be more well done than the larger, thicker ones—which may be desirable if serving a group of people with varying tastes. If you want all the lamb medium-rare, start testing the smaller pieces for doneness after 20 minutes, and remove each piece from the grill as it reaches 130°. Place the lamb on a large platter and let it rest for 5 minutes before carving.

Using a sharp, thin-bladed carving knife, cut the lamb across the grain into $1/2$-inch-thick slices. Overlap the slices on a platter, and surround with the vegetables. Garnish the platter with the cilantro, and serve with the basmati rice on the side.

Variation: If you like, you can use the marinades and accompaniments to spice up lamb chops.

Flavor Building: Both the Thai Curry Sauce and Pineapple and Red Pepper Chutney (pages 252 and 253) work well with this dish.

Basmati Rice Salad

MAKES 6 TO 8 SERVINGS

1 cup basmati rice

1 tablespoon vegetable oil

1 teaspoon black mustard seed (or use yellow mustard seed)

1²/₃ cups plain yogurt

2 tablespoons minced fresh cilantro leaves

2 tablespoons seeded and minced jalapeño chile pepper

1 tablespoon peeled and minced fresh ginger

Coarse salt and freshly ground white pepper to taste

Bring a large pot of lightly salted water to a boil over high heat. Add the rice and cook until tender, about 15 minutes. Drain, rinse under cold water, and transfer to a medium bowl.

In a small sauté pan over medium heat, cook the mustard seed in the oil, stirring often, until the mustard seed start to pop, about 2 minutes. Scrape into the bowl of rice.

Add the yogurt, cilantro, jalapeño, and ginger and mix well. Season with salt and pepper. This can be made up to 2 hours ahead, but do not refrigerate it or the rice will get hard. Before serving, taste and re-season with salt and pepper, and add more yogurt if needed to return the salad to a creamy consistency.

Lamb Shanks with Creamy White Beans and Yellow Turnip Puree

MAKES 6 SERVINGS

Thinking Ahead: The beans must soak in water overnight. Everything but the puree may be prepared well in advance, or timed to be cooked while the shanks are braising, which takes several hours.

LAMB SHANKS

$^1/_4$ cup olive oil, or as needed

6 (1-pound) lamb shanks, trimmed

Coarse salt and freshly ground white pepper

1 medium onion, coarsely chopped

1 medium carrot, coarsely chopped

1 large head garlic, cloves separated, unpeeled

2 cups dry red wine

$1^1/_2$ cups Brown Chicken Stock (page 34)

$1^1/_2$ cups water

4 sprigs thyme

3 (4-inch-long) strips of lemon zest, removed from the lemon with a vegetable peeler

1 teaspoon whole black peppercorns

Preheat the oven to 300° F. In a large, flameproof casserole or roasting pan with a lid, heat the oil over medium-high heat. Season the lamb shanks with salt and pepper. In batches, without crowding, cook the lamb shanks, turning occasionally, until nicely browned on all sides, about 8 minutes. Transfer to a plate and set aside.

Pour off all but 2 tablespoons of the fat. Reduce the heat to medium and add the onion, carrot, and garlic. Cook, stirring often, until the vegetables brown deeply, about 10 minutes. Add the wine and bring to a boil. Cook until reduced to about $^1/_4$ cup, 10 to 15

BRAISING LAMB SHANKS properly makes the meat so tender that it comes off the bone with just the tug of a fork. It's impossible to overemphasize the importance of *slow*-cooking the shanks to achieve this effect, checking them every 15 to 20 minutes to be sure they are simmering ever so slightly. The slower, the better. If the heat is too high, the meat will contract and dry out.

You will find the recipe for creamy white beans to be a highly versatile addition to your repertoire. The beans are softened in their cream mixture, creating a combination of flavor and texture that complements a wide variety of dishes. They work just as well in this winter entrée as they do with, say, grilled shrimp in the summertime.

If you've ever wondered what to do with those big, wax-covered yellow turnips or rutabagas found in many markets, here is one answer.

minutes. Return the shanks to the casserole. Add the stock, water, thyme, lemon zest, and peppercorns and bring to a boil. Tightly cover the casserole.

Bake until the lamb shanks are very tender, about 1¾ hours. Turn the shanks occasionally and check that they are not cooking too fast—the braising liquid should be barely simmering. Lower the oven temperature, if necessary. Continue cooking for approximately 45 minutes longer until, when tested with a fork, the meat easily separates from the bone.

CREAMY WHITE BEANS

1 cup dried white beans (cannellini), soaked overnight in water to cover, drained

1 medium onion, halved

1 garlic clove, peeled and smashed

2 sprigs thyme

Coarse salt and freshly ground white pepper to taste

¼ cup heavy cream

2 tablespoons unsalted butter or Herbed Garlic Butter (page 231)

In a medium saucepan, combine the drained beans, onion, garlic, and thyme. Add enough cold water to cover by 2 inches. Bring to a boil over high heat. Reduce the heat to medium-low and simmer for 20 minutes. Season with the salt and continue cooking until the beans are just tender, about 15 minutes more, depending on the dryness of the beans. Drain the beans, reserving ½ cup of the cooking liquid.

Return the beans and the reserved liquid to the saucepan. Add the cream and bring to a simmer over medium heat. Cook until slightly thickened, about 5 minutes. Stir in the butter, and season with salt and pepper.

YELLOW TURNIP PUREE

3 medium yellow turnips (rutabagas), peeled, cut into 2-inch cubes

8 tablespoons (1 stick) unsalted butter

Coarse salt and freshly ground white pepper to taste

Bring a large saucepan of lightly salted water to a boil over high heat. Add the yellow turnips and return to the boil. Reduce the heat to medium and simmer until the turnips are tender when pierced with the tip of a sharp knife, about 30 minutes. Drain well. Return to the saucepan and place over medium heat. Cook, stirring constantly, until the excess moisture has evaporated and the turnips begin to stick to the bottom of the pan, about 3 minutes. Reduce the heat to low. Add the butter and mash the turnips with a potato masher. Season with salt and pepper. (If making ahead, leave the butter out; reheat the puree in a double boiler over boiling water, then stir in the butter, salt, and pepper just before serving.

Lighter White Beans: If creamy white beans are too rich for your taste, follow this method to create a lighter, no-less-satisfying alternative: Using a conventional blender or immersion hand blender, pour 1/2 cup of the cooking liquid from the pot in which the beans were cooked into the blender vessel. Blend, adding up to 2 tablespoons each of beans and extra-virgin olive oil, a little at a time, until the mixture reaches a creamy consistency. Use this mixture in place of the recipe above that features butter and cream.

ASSEMBLY

Coarse salt and freshly ground white pepper to taste

6 sprigs thyme, for garnish

Transfer the lamb shanks to a large platter and cover with aluminum foil to keep warm. Spoon off the fat on the surface of the braising liquid, and place the casserole over high heat. Bring the cooking liquid to a boil and cook until richly flavored and reduced to about 1 1/2 cups, about 10 minutes. Strain the sauce and season with salt and pepper.

Place a lamb shank in the center of each of 6 warmed dinner plates. Holding the meaty end with one hand, bring up the shank bone into a vertical position with the other hand, pressing down so the meat releases from the bone at the meaty end to form a base for the shank to stand in. Place a mound of turnips at the ten o'clock position, and a spoonful of beans at the two o'clock position. Spoon the sauce over and around the lamb shank and garnish with a sprig of thyme. Or, leave the lamb shanks on the platter and garnish with the thyme. Place the turnip puree and beans in individual serving bowls, and pour the sauce into a warmed sauceboat.

Variations: Creamy Polenta (page 276) may be substituted for the turnips to provide a very different counterpoint to the lamb and beans. Also, peas and pearl onions make an effective springtime alternative to the white beans.

Braised Pork Roast with
Mustard Spaetzle and Poached Lady Apples

Meats and Game 309

Thinking Ahead: The pork and apples may be prepared as much as 1 day in advance, covered, and refrigerated. The spaetzle themselves can be prepared up to 4 hours in advance, covered, and refrigerated, but warm them in the sauce immediately before serving.

Special Equipment: potato ricer (fitted with the large-holed disc) or a spaetzle press

BRAISED PORK AND SAUCE

2 tablespoons vegetable oil

1 (4^1/$_2$-pound) boneless pork shoulder, trimmed and tied (have your butcher do this)

Coarse salt and freshly ground white pepper to taste

1 medium onion, coarsely chopped

1 medium carrot, coarsely chopped

1 celery rib, coarsely chopped

6 medium garlic cloves, crushed with a knife

^{1}/$_3$ cup dry white wine

2 cups White Chicken Stock (page 33)

1 sprig marjoram

1 sprig thyme

1 sprig sage

1 teaspoon whole white peppercorns

2 tablespoons unsalted butter, softened

2 tablespoons all-purpose flour

Preheat the oven to 300° F. In a large flameproof casserole or roasting pan with a lid, heat the oil over medium-high heat. Season the pork with salt and pepper. Add the pork to the pan and cook, turning occasionally, until browned on all sides, about 10 minutes. Transfer the pork to a plate. Pour out all but 1 tablespoon of the fat.

THIS IS AN IDEAL FAMILY dinner for a snowy, winter day. Pork, spaetzle, and lady apples are traditional foods that offer invigorating relief from the chill of the season.

The braised pork featured here resulted from my effort to find an alternative to roast pork, which can often be dry and lack flavor. I devised a braising sauce of white wine, marjoram, garlic, and sage. After cooking for hours in this liquid, the pork becomes infused with these elements, and becomes so tender that you can cut it with a fork and it practically melts in the mouth.

Poached lady apples are both remarkably tart and sweet, complementing the pork in the same way that a good, homemade apple sauce would. The fresh spaetzle tossed in a creamy mustard sauce adds yet another counterpoint. Set against these backdrops, the flavor of the braised pork practically leaps from fork to mouth.

Add the onion, carrot, celery, and garlic to the pan. Cook, stirring often, until the vegetables are softened and browned, about 7 minutes. Add the wine and cook until almost completely evaporated, about 4 minutes. Add the stock, marjoram, thyme, sage, and peppercorns and bring to a boil. Return the pork to the pan and cover tightly. Place in oven.

Cook until the pork is fork-tender, 3 to 3½ hours. About 15 minutes into the cooking time, check to be sure the liquid is barely simmering, and reduce the oven temperature, if necessary. Remove the pork to a platter and cover loosely with foil to keep warm. Let the pan stand for 5 minutes. Skim the fat from the surface of the cooking liquid. Bring the cooking liquid to a boil over medium heat.

Meanwhile, in a small bowl, combine the butter and flour into a paste. Gradually whisk in about ½ cup of the cooking liquid to form a thin paste. Whisk the flour paste back into the pan juices. Reduce the heat and gently simmer, stirring occasionally, 10 to 15 minutes until the sauce thickens. Strain through a wire sieve. Season with salt and pepper. Keep warm.

MUSTARD SPAETZLE

⅔ cup milk

4 large eggs plus 2 large egg yolks

1¾ cups all-purpose flour

¼ teaspoon freshly grated nutmeg

½ teaspoon salt

¼ teaspoon freshly ground white pepper

2 teaspoons vegetable oil (optional)

½ cup heavy cream

½ cup water

4 tablespoons unsalted butter

3 tablespoons Dijon mustard

2 tablespoons finely minced fresh chives

In a medium bowl, whisk together the milk, whole eggs, and egg yolks. Add the flour, nutmeg, salt, and pepper and mix well.

Bring a large pot of lightly salted water to a boil over high heat. In batches, place the spaetzle batter in a potato ricer fitted with the large holes or in a spaetzle press. Press the batter into the boiling water; it will hold its shape when it hits the water. Return to the boil and cook for 1 minute, until the spaetzle are firm. Using a wire strainer, scoop the cooked spaetzle out of the water. (If making ahead, transfer to a bowl of iced water to cool completely, then drain well. Toss with the oil, cover, and refrigerate.)

In a large saucepan, bring the cream and water to a boil over high heat. Reduce the heat to medium-low and whisk in the butter and mustard. Add the spaetzle and chives and warm through, about 1 minute.

ASSEMBLY

1 recipe Poached Lady Apples (page 269)

1 recipe Baby Root Vegetables (page 289)

Slice the pork roast, and serve with the spaetzle, apples, baby vegetables, and sauce.

Variations: Gotham Mashed Potatoes (page 206) or fettuccine tossed with sweet butter make good substitutes for the spaetzle. Another idea would be to toss 1 pound of cooked, drained fettuccine in the mustard sauce until well coated and heated through.

Pan-Roasted Veal Chops with Baby Artichokes, Fava Beans, and Basil Butter

MAKES 4 SERVINGS

FOR ME, THERE'S something tremendously hopeful about spring. I'm always struck by the winter thaw, and how life almost seems to be starting over each March, when the sun's warmth can be felt for the first time, and new plants begin to poke up through the soil. This dish celebrates spring by including tender, braised baby artichokes, the season's first basil, and delicate fava beans. No sauce is used here. Instead, a fragrant basil butter—which derives its velvety texture from the inclusion of almond flour—finishes the dish with an aroma as fresh and enticing as the scent of a field after a good rain.

Thinking Ahead: The basil butter may be prepared as much as 3 days in advance and refrigerated. The artichokes and fava beans may be prepared separately as much as 4 hours in advance, refrigerated, and reheated immediately before serving.

BRAISED ARTICHOKES AND FAVA BEANS

2 tablespoons fresh lemon juice

4 medium artichokes

$1/2$ cup extra-virgin olive oil

$1/3$ cup thinly sliced shallots

$1/4$ cup thinly sliced garlic

1 teaspoon coriander seed

$1/2$ teaspoon fresh thyme leaves

$1/4$ cup dry white wine

$3/4$ cup White Chicken Stock (page 33)

$1^1/2$ pounds fresh fava beans

Add the lemon juice to a bowl of cold water. Working with 1 artichoke at a time, remove the tough, dark outer leaves to reveal the light green tender leaves. Using a small sharp knife, pare away the tough dark green skin from the base and stems. Cut off the top of the artichoke where the leaves indent at the base. Pull out the purple center leaves. Using the tip of a dessert spoon, dig out and discard the hairy choke. Cut lengthwise into $1/4$-inch-thick slices. As each artichoke is prepared, drop the slices into the bowl of lemon water to keep them from discoloring.

In a 10-inch nonreactive sauté pan, heat the oil over medium heat. Add the shallots, garlic, coriander seed, and thyme and cook until the shallots are soft, about 5 minutes. Reduce the heat to low and cover. Add the wine, increase the heat to high, and boil until almost completely evaporated, about 2 minutes.

Drain the artichokes and add them to the sauté pan. Cook for 1 minute, then add the stock. Bring to a boil, then reduce the heat to low. Cover and simmer until the artichokes are tender, 12 to 15 minutes. Set aside.

Meanwhile, bring a saucepan of salted water to a boil over high heat. Add the fava beans and cook for 1 minute. Drain and rinse under cold water. Remove the thick peel from each bean and set aside.

VEAL CHOPS

6 tablespoons canola oil

4 (14- to 16-ounce) loin veal chops, cut 1 inch thick

Coarse salt and freshly ground white pepper

Position the racks in the top third and center of the oven and preheat to 450° F. Heat two 12-inch oven-proof sauté pans over high heat until very hot. Add 3 tablespoons of oil to each sauté pan.

Season the veal chops with salt and pepper. Place 2 chops in each sauté pan. Cook until the chops are nicely browned on the bottom, about 4 minutes. Turn the chops and cook until the other side is seared, about 1 minute.

Transfer to the oven. Roast until the undersides of the chops are browned, about 5 minutes. Continue roasting until the veal feels somewhat resilient when pressed in the center, about 3 minutes more. This is for medium-rare veal. If you prefer it medium to medium-well, continue roasting for another 3 to 5 minutes.

ASSEMBLY:

2 tablespoons chiffonade of mint leaves (page 44)

Coarse salt and freshly ground white pepper to taste

1 recipe Basil Butter (recipe follows), cut into 8 rounds

Add the fava beans to the artichokes and cook over low heat until the beans are tender and heated through, about 2 minutes. Add the mint and season with the salt and pepper.

Using a slotted spoon, transfer equal portions of the vegetables to 4 warmed dinner plates. Add the veal chops, then garnish with rounds of basil butter.

Flavor Building: Vegetable custards (page 184 and page 295) round out this dish extraordinarily well. Peas and pearl onions also nicely underscore the spring theme. In addition, morel mushrooms are a wonderful springtime addition that complement the artichokes and beans. If you'd like to serve this with a sauce, try the Simple Herb Sauce (see Sidebar, page 33).

Basil Butter

MAKES ABOUT ¹/₂ CUP (A 4-INCH LOG)

15 large basil leaves (1 ounce)

8 tablespoons (1 stick) unsalted butter, at room temperature

2 tablespoons almond flour (page 375 for mail order source)

2¹/₂ teaspoons Dijon mustard

1 small garlic clove, mashed to a paste with a sprinkle of coarse salt

¹/₄ teaspoon chopped fresh marjoram leaves

1 teaspoon coarse salt

¹/₂ teaspoon coarsely cracked white peppercorns

THIS HERB BUTTER IS unusual because it uses almond flour, which gives it a consistency not found in other compound butters.

Bring a small saucepan of lightly salted water to a boil over high heat. Add the basil leaves and cook for 15 seconds. Drain and transfer to a bowl of iced water to stop the cooking and set the color. Let stand for 1 minute. Drain the basil again, gently squeezing out all excess liquid, and coarsely chop.

Transfer to a blender or food processor fitted with the metal blade. Add the remaining ingredients and process, stopping often to scrape the butter from the sides onto the blade, until the butter is pale green, about 2 minutes or more.

Scrape the butter out onto a piece of plastic wrap, form it into a 4-inch-long log, and wrap tightly. Refrigerate until firm, at least 2 hours.

Loin of Venison with Rosemary Poached Pears, Root Vegetables, and Pumpkin Puree

MAKES 4 SERVINGS

Thinking Ahead: The sauce must be made in advance. The pears and baby pumpkins may be prepared 1 day in advance and held in their cooking liquid. The spinach, vegetables, and puree may be prepared up to 4 hours in advance. All should be stored covered and refrigerated.

THIS VISUALLY ALLURING entrée pays tribute to fall by uniting the fruits, vegetables, and game of the season. I've included it here, and on the Gotham's menu, because cooks today can avail themselves of farm-raised venison, which has a more moderate flavor than the traditional, wild variety. Poaching the pears with rosemary makes them a savory foil for the meat. (Playing pears and game off one another is a time-honored convention.) Salsify, carrots, spinach, and pumpkin create a virtual cornucopia on the plate, an effect that we amplify at the Gotham by actually presenting the pumpkin puree in a carved-out baby pumpkin. Slicing the venison thin and fanning it out balances the presentation.

ROSEMARY POACHED PEARS

3 cups water

$2/3$ cup sugar

1 cup dry white wine

1 sprig rosemary

$1^1/2$ teaspoons whole black peppercorns

1 cinnamon stick

4 Seckel or Forelle pears, peeled, halved lengthwise, and cored

In a medium saucepan, bring all the ingredients except the pears to a boil over high heat. Add the pears and reduce the heat to low. Place a clean, folded kitchen towel directly on the pears to keep them submerged. Simmer until the pears are still firm but partially cooked, about 5 minutes. Remove the pan from the heat and let stand until the pears are tender when pierced with the tip of a knife, about 15 minutes. Refrigerate the pears in their cooking liquid until ready to use, and reheat if necessary.

BABY PUMPKINS

4 (6-ounce) baby pumpkins

1 tablespoon unsalted butter

Coarse salt and freshly ground white pepper to taste

Cut the tops off the baby pumpkins and reserve them to make lids.

Using a small spoon, scoop out and discard the seeds from each pumpkin. Scrape out the flesh, leaving ½-inch-thick shells.

Place the baby pumpkins and their tops in a medium saucepan and add enough cold water to cover. Add the butter, salt, and pepper. Bring to a boil over high heat. Reduce the heat to low, and simmer until the baby pumpkins are barely tender when pierced with the tip of a sharp knife, no more than 3 minutes. Drain the baby pumpkins and set aside.

PUMPKIN PUREE

1 (3-pound) cooking pumpkin, such as sugar pumpkin, acorn or Hubbard squash, cut in half, seeds discarded

½ cup water

2 tablespoons unsalted butter

Coarse salt and freshly ground white pepper to taste

2 tablespoons pure maple syrup (Grade B is preferable)

Preheat the oven to 375° F. Place the pumpkin halves, cut side down, in a baking dish. Add the water, 1 tablespoon of the butter, and season with salt and pepper. Cover tightly with foil. Bake until the pumpkin is tender when pierced with the tip of a sharp knife, 50 minutes to 1 hour. Cool slightly.

Using a large spoon, scoop out the pumpkin flesh into a medium heavy-bottomed saucepan, discarding the skin. Place the flesh over medium heat and mash. Cook, stirring often to avoid scorching and to evaporate excess moisture, 5 to 10 minutes. Off the heat, whisk in the maple syrup, the remaining tablespoon of butter, and season with salt and pepper. Cover and keep warm at the side of the stove, or refrigerate and and reheat if necessary. (If making in advance, don't add butter until you reheat.)

SALSIFY AND CARROTS

1 large (6-ounce) salsify, peeled and cut in half crosswise

Juice of ½ lemon

Coarse salt and freshly ground white pepper to taste

2 medium carrots, cut into ¼-inch dice

1 teaspoon unsalted butter

Place the salsify and lemon juice in a medium saucepan, add enough water to cover, and season with salt and pepper. Bring to a boil over high heat. Reduce the heat to medium-low and simmer until the salsify is still firm but partially cooked, about 5 minutes. Remove from the heat and cool and finish cooking in the liquid, at least 15 minutes. When ready to use, remove and cut into ¼-inch dice.

Place the carrots in another medium saucepan, add enough water to cover, and season with salt and pepper. Bring to a boil over high heat. Reduce the heat to medium-low and simmer until just tender, about 3 minutes. Drain and set aside, or refrigerate if necessary.

When ready to use, reheat the salsify and carrots in a medium saucepan with 2 tablespoons of water and the remaining tablespoon of butter, seasoned with salt and pepper.

ASSEMBLY

2 tablespoons vegetable oil

1½ pounds boneless loin of venison

Coarse salt and freshly ground white pepper

1 tablespoon unsalted butter

1 pound fresh spinach, well rinsed, tough stems removed

Red Onion Marmalade (recipe follows), warmed

Sauce Poivrade (recipe follows)

Rosemary sprigs, for garnish

In a 12-inch nonstick sauté pan, heat the oil over medium-high heat. Season the venison with salt and pepper and cook until nicely browned on all sides, turning occasionally, 10 to 12 minutes total. The venison should be medium-rare: An instant read thermometer inserted in the center of the loin will read 125° F. Remove to a plate, tent with foil, and let stand for 5 minutes before slicing.

When the venison is almost cooked, bring a medium saucepan to a boil over high heat with 1 inch of water and the butter. Stir in the spinach, and season with salt and pepper. Cook just until wilted, about 1 minute. Drain, cover with foil, and keep warm. Fill the baby pumpkins with the warmed puree.

Gotham Presentation: Using a sharp slicing knife, cut the venison into ¼-inch-thick slices. On each of 4 warmed dinner plates, arrange slices in an overlapping pattern toward the bottom of the plate. Place some spinach in the center, then a baby pumpkin at the "ten o'clock" position. Spoon a little red onion marmalade at the "two o'clock" position, and rest the pear halves against it. Spoon the salsify and carrots at "twelve o'clock," and spoon the sauce around the edge of the plates. Garnish with rosemary sprigs.

Everyday Presentation: For a family-style feast, present the pears and venison on the same platter, place the pumpkins on a serving tray, and pass the vegetables, sauce, and marmalade in individual bowls. Even in this format, the colors of the season will make a strong impact.

Red Onion Marmalade

MAKES ABOUT 1 CUP

2 tablespoons unsalted butter

2 medium onions, thinly sliced

2 cups dry red wine

THIS SIMPLE RECIPE produces a marmalade that is more of a condiment than a side dish. It adds another note of interest and complexity to game dishes.

3 tablespoons red wine vinegar

3 tablespoons balsamic vinegar

Coarse salt and freshly ground white pepper to taste

In a medium saucepan, melt the butter over medium-low heat. Add the onions and cover. Cook, stirring occasionally, until they are softened without browning, about 10 minutes.

Add the wine, red wine and balsamic vinegars, and continue cooking until the cooking liquid is thick and syrupy, about 30 minutes. Season with salt and pepper. Serve warm or at room temperature.

Sauce Poivrade

MAKES ABOUT 1 ½ CUPS

THIS IS A CLASSIC sauce for game and roasted beef. I normally make it with brown stock, but this relatively quick version works just fine.

3 tablespoons unsalted butter

¼ cup chopped shallots

2 teaspoons whole black peppercorns

8 juniper berries

1 sprig thyme

1 cup dry red wine

3 cups White Chicken Stock (page 33)

1 sprig rosemary

Coarse salt and freshly ground white pepper to taste

In a medium saucepan, heat 1 tablespoon of the butter over medium-low heat. Add the shallots and cook, stirring often, until they're browned, about 5 minutes. Add the peppercorns, juniper berries and thyme and stir until fragrant, about 2 minutes. Add the wine and bring to a boil over high heat. Boil until the wine is reduced to about 2 tablespoons, 12 to 15 minutes. Add the chicken stock, bring to a boil, and cook over high heat until reduced to about 1½ cups, 30 to 40 minutes. During the last 5 minutes, add the rosemary. Strain the sauce, pressing on the solids. Return the sauce to the saucepan and, still off the heat, whisk in the remaining butter, 1 tablespoon at a time. Season with salt and pepper.

Flavor Building: Farm-raised venison is mild enough for a white chicken stock to succeed here, but the Brown Chicken Stock (page 34) would be even better. Of course, if you have access to the necessary bones, venison stock would be the *ideal* base for this dish.

Grilled Rack of Venison with Grilled Nectarines and Dandelion Greens

MAKES 4 SERVINGS

VENISON AND NECTARINES

2 racks of venison (about 1 pound, 6 ounces each), bones frenched

1 tablespoon canola oil

Coarse salt and freshly ground black pepper

2 ripe large (10-ounce) nectarines, halved and pitted

1 tablespoon unsalted butter, melted

Build a charcoal fire in a grill, banking the coals to one side, and let them burn until covered with white ash. Lightly oil the grill grate.

Brush the venison with the oil, and season generously with salt and pepper. Grill directly over the coals, turning once, until the meat is seared, 8 to 10 minutes total. Move the venison to the other side of the grill, away from the coals. Cover the grill and cook until a meat thermometer inserted in the thickest part of the venison reads 125° F. (for medium-rare meat), 10 to 15 minutes more. Place the venison on a platter and let it rest for 10 minutes before carving.

While the venison stands, brush the nectarines with the butter and season with salt and pepper. Grill the nectarines covered, cut sides down, until lightly browned, about 5 minutes. Turn, and continue cooking until heated through and tender, about 5 more minutes.

DANDELION SALAD

1 (2-pound) bunch dandelion leaves or arugula, tough stems removed, washed and dried

Lemon Vinaigrette (page 60)

Coarse salt and freshly ground white pepper to taste

In a large bowl, toss the dandelions with the vinaigrette. Season with salt and freshly ground white pepper.

ASSEMBLY

Cut the racks into double rib chops. In the center of 4 warmed dinner plates, place mounds of the salad. Stand up a pair of chops in the

GRILLING FRUIT IS A simple way to create the highly unusual combination of rich sweetness and smoky flavor. The fruits should be cooked over a very low heat so their natural sugars do not caramelize too quickly and become bitter. The fruits will take on a deeper color, at which point they should be moved to the edge of the grill.

In the spring, you can buy wild dandelion greens, and these days some markets carry cultivated ones. I can remember, as a child, when my grandfather would stop the car, get out, and pick them from the side of the road. (If you ever pick them yourself, you must be very careful that they are not growing in an area that has been treated with pesticides or other chemicals). Also, when foraging for dandelions, remember, the larger the dandelion, the more bitter the greens. Pick the tiny, tender, youngest shoots. If dandelion greens are not available, arugula will work well as a substitute.

This impressive entrée is remarkably easy to prepare,

(continued)

thanks largely to the ease with which venison cooks. It's a very lean cut of meat that sears quickly over high heat. But be careful to keep an eye on it so that it doesn't overcook and dry out. Medium-rare yields the best texture and flavor.

center of the plates, interlocking the bones. Garnish with the nectarines.

Variations: The dandelions may also be cooked with excellent results following the instructions for Braised Escarole (page 300). Peaches, apricots, pears, and plums would all make excellent stand-ins for the nectarines. If you'd like to try something in place of the dandelions, try wilted escarole. You might also try Grilled Vegetables (page 303) to create a different dynamic.

Flavor Building: Green Peppercorn Sauce (page 266), Sauce Poivrade (page 320), or even the Red Wine Butter (page 292) works very well with the venison.

Bollito **Misto**

MAKES 8 TO 12 SERVINGS

WHEN WE MAKE THIS dish at my house, it's a celebration. It is best made in a large quantity, designed to yield some leftovers, which provide days' worth of interesting lunches. The Italians usually serve this dish in courses, the first being a deep, steaming bowl of the broth with plump tortellini floating in it. The second course is meats, with green sauce and little pots of coarse salt, which is an essential seasoning. In this recipe, the vegetables are cooked separately and in advance and then reheated in the broth, for less last-minute preparation. This last step is also an improvement over the traditional technique in which the vegetables are cooked together in the broth so long that their flavors become muddled.

Thinking Ahead: The bollito misto and the vegetables may be prepared as much as 6 hours in advance. The horseradish sauce may be prepared as much as 1 day in advance. Both should be stored covered in the refrigerator. Make the green sauce as close to serving as possible.

Special Equipment: very large stockpot (at least 16 quarts), a huge platter or 2 large platters, large colander or china cap strainer

MEAT

1 (3$\frac{1}{2}$-pound) beef brisket

1 (2$\frac{1}{2}$-pound) unsmoked beef tongue

3$\frac{1}{2}$ quarts White Chicken Stock (page 33)

2 quarts water

3 pounds oxtail, sawed into pieces about 1$\frac{1}{2}$ inches long

3 pounds veal shanks (osso buco), sawed into pieces about 1$\frac{1}{2}$ inches thick

2 pounds beef short ribs

2 medium onions, coarsely chopped

1 medium celery rib, coarsely chopped

1 medium carrot, coarsely chopped

1 medium head garlic, halved crosswise

3 sprigs thyme

3 sprigs flat-leaf parsley

2 dried bay leaves

1 tablespoon whole black peppercorns

Coarse salt

1 (3$\frac{1}{2}$-pound) whole chicken, trussed with kitchen twine

1$\frac{1}{2}$ pounds kielbasa sausage, pricked with a fork

1$\frac{1}{2}$ pounds white sausage, such as brockwurst or boudin blanc, pricked with a fork

Place the brisket and tongue in the stockpot and pour in the stock and water. Bring to a boil over high heat. Reduce the heat to low and simmer, uncovered, skimming off any foam that rises to the surface, for 1½ hours. Add the oxtail, veal shanks, short ribs, onions, celery, carrot, and garlic. Tie the thyme, parsley, bay leaves, and peppercorns in cheesecloth with kitchen twine and add to the stockpot. Add salt generously to taste. Return the liquid to a boil over high heat, then reduce the heat to low and simmer, uncovered, for 1 hour. Add the chicken and continue cooking until all the meats are tender and pulling away from the bone, about 45 minutes.

About 20 minutes before the meats are tender, ladle about 3 cups of the broth into a large pot and add the kielbasa and white sausages. Cover and bring to a simmer over medium heat. Cook until the sausages are heated through, about 15 minutes. Transfer the sausages to the stockpot, and discard the sausage cooking liquid—it's too smoky and salty to serve.

Remove the tongue from the broth and, when cool enough to handle, cut off and discard the base of the tongue. Make a shallow incision through the tongue skin, peel off and discard the skin. Return the tongue to the broth. (The bollito misto will keep warm for up to 1 hour, removed from the heat. If necessary, reheat it before serving.)

VEGETABLES

1 pound green beans, trimmed

1 pound carrots, cut in half lengthwise and then into thirds

1 pound parsnips, cut in half lengthwise and then into thirds

4 medium turnips (1 pound total), peeled and quartered

6 small leeks, white part only, well washed between the layers to remove grit

1 medium (2½-pound) cabbage, quartered

1½ pounds small new potatoes, unpeeled

Coarse salt

Horseradish Sauce: Mix 2 cups crème fraîche or sour cream, 2 tablespoons red wine vinegar, 1 tablespoon freshly grated peeled or prepared horseradish (or to taste), and season with coarse salt and freshly ground white pepper to taste. Makes about 2 cups.

Bring a large pot of salted water to a boil over high heat. Place a large bowl of iced water near the stove. Each of the vegetables will be individually cooked in the water until tender, then removed with a skimmer or slotted spoon and transferred to the iced water to stop the cooking. Cook the vegetables in the boiling salted water in the following order, so the strong-flavored ones are cooked last: Green beans—cook until tender, about 3 minutes; carrots—cook until tender, about 5 minutes; parsnips—cook until tender, about 5 minutes; turnips—cook until tender, 10 to 15 minutes; leeks—cook until tender, 5 to 7 minutes; cabbage—cook until tender, 10 to 12 minutes.

Drain the cooked, cooled vegetables well and transfer them to a large bowl.

For the potatoes, bring a medium saucepan of lightly salted water to a boil over high heat. Add the potatoes and cook until tender, 15 to 20 minutes. Drain and cool. Set the potatoes aside.

ASSEMBLY

Coarse salt and freshly ground white pepper to taste

Horseradish Sauce (see Sidebar, page 325)

Green Sauce (recipe follows)

When ready to serve, use a skimmer or slotted spoon to transfer the meats from the broth to a cutting board. The oxtail, veal shanks, and short ribs can go directly to a large warmed platter. Cover them with foil to keep warm. Strain the broth through a fine sieve into a large pot. Let stand for 2 minutes, then skim off the clear fat that rises to the surface. Taste and season with salt and pepper, if needed. Return to a simmer and add the vegetables and potatoes to reheat, approximately 8 minutes. Cut the tongue crosswise into thin slices. Cut the brisket across the grain into thin slices. Carve the chicken into serving pieces and slice the sausage. Transfer to the meat platter.

Remove the vegetables from the broth with a slotted spoon and arrange them on the same platter or transfer to one of their own. Ladle over some of the broth to moisten them. Serve with the green sauce and horseradish sauce on the side with a small bowl of coarse salt for seasoning the meat.

If you like, you can serve the broth as a first course, garnished with tortellini, as the Italians traditionally do.

Green Sauce

MAKES ABOUT 3 CUPS

4 large egg yolks, hard boiled

A generous $1/3$ cup chopped fresh flat-leaf parsley

A generous $1/3$ cup red wine vinegar

2 tablespoons finely chopped capers

2 tablespoons chopped fresh tarragon

2 tablespoons chopped fresh chives

2 tablespoons chopped fresh chervil

6 garlic cloves, peeled and finely chopped

2 salt-packed anchovies, soaked, rinsed, and filleted (see Sidebar, page 64)

$1^{1}/3$ cups extra-virgin olive oil

Coarse salt and freshly ground black pepper to taste

THIS SAUCE SHOULD BE made as close to serving time as possible. Because of the vinaigrette, the sauce's bright color will fade on standing.

In a food processor fitted with the metal blade, or in a blender, combine all the ingredients except the oil, salt, and pepper. With the machine running, gradually add the oil until the sauce is emulsified. Season with salt and pepper.

10 Desserts

Warm Chocolate Cake with Toasted Almond Ice Cream

Lemon Cake with Crème Fraîche and Warm Berry Compote

Marbled Pumpkin Cheesecake and Pumpkin Seed Brittle

Apple-Calvados Tarts with Maple Ice Cream and Cranberry Confit

Strawberry Tart with Mascarpone and Aged Balsamic Vinegar

Chocolate Banana Strudel with Vanilla Ice Cream and Caramel Sauce

Bittersweet Chocolate Bread Pudding with Whipped Cream

Ginger Crème Brûlée with Warm Plum and Raspberry Compote

Panna Cotta with Fresh Raspberries and Spearmint

Cherry and Berry Fruit Compote with Mint Tea Infusion

Passion Fruit Granité with Tropical Fruits

Zinfandel Granité with Poached Bosc Pears

Champagne Granité with Strawberries and Grand Marnier

Poached Winter Fruit Compote in White Wine Syrup

Honey Tuile Cookies

Langues-de-Chat

Lemon-Pistachio Biscotti

Restaurant desserts can be as complex and time-consuming to prepare as a main course, but I strongly believe in simplifying desserts in a home setting. I myself am not a highly trained pastry chef with years of experience, so I rarely prepare elaborate desserts at home. In this chapter, I've tried to provide dishes that can be made without a master's degree in pastry. A few of the following recipes *do* require baking, such as the Warm Chocolate Cake (page 331), but others are simple enough that just about anyone should be able to make them.

Consider, for example, the simple process that yields the three granités that follow (pages 360 to 365). These simple desserts, more sophisticated and uncommon than sorbet, can be transformed into an elegant affair by serving them in stemmed glasses and pairing them with interesting fresh or poached fruits.

Because fruits are such naturally pleasing sweets, I've incorporated many of them into these recipes. In addition to the granités, a Strawberry Tart with Mascarpone and Aged Balsamic Vinegar (page 347) offers rich, simple flavors, while the Poached Winter Fruit Compote (page 367) features a combination of naturally sweet dried fruits in white wine. These, too, are desserts that may be prepared by amateur home cooks.

I've also included some recipes that are variations on classic desserts, such as the Ginger Crème Brûlée with Warm Plum and Raspberry Compote (page 354). For years, cooks have engaged in an ongoing and heated debate over what constitutes the perfect crème brûlée, from the amount of sugar to the ratio of milk to cream, to the depth of the serving container, to the type of sugar that should be used to caramelize the top.

For a while, I was caught up in this debate myself. As a purist, I proudly had the words "Classic Vanilla Crème Brûlée" on my menu. But I gradually began experimenting and have since made a wonderful coffee-flavored crème brûlée, a maple crème brûlée with pure Vermont maple syrup, and even a pumpkin crème brûlée. I think Wolfgang Puck may have been the first to use ginger in this dessert in 1984; my only contribution is to serve it with poached plums and cookies.

Making a crème brûlée is not as difficult as its legend might suggest; it's certainly easier than making a crème anglaise. The cooking and thickening of the custard takes place in the oven. The "brûlée-ing" part is the most difficult, and, if you're seriously interested in mastering the craft, you should invest in a propane torch from a hardware store.

I've also provided a recipe for Bittersweet Chocolate Bread Pudding with Whipped Cream (page 353), which elevates the traditional bread pudding through the use of brioche and fine

chocolate. (I recommend Valrona, Callebaut, or Lindt for this recipe and for the Warm Chocolate Cake).

As with the recipe selection in other chapters, I've tried to provide some seasonal desserts, like the Marbled Pumpkin Cheesecake and Pumpkin Seed Brittle (page 338), an autumn novelty. Try it instead of pumpkin pie next Thanksgiving. Also, the Cherry and Berry Fruit Compote with Mint Tea Infusion (page 358) is ideal for summer entertaining.

Since we all associate desserts with childhood, I've adapted some of my own childhood favorites here. The Chocolate Banana Strudel with Vanilla Ice Cream and Caramel Sauce (page 350) is a sophisticated version of a banana split. It's a delicious warm fruit dessert made with store-bought sheets of filo dough, so you won't have to make your own. I use bananas in this recipe, but the technique can be used for blueberries, pear, and apple, as well. (If you want to make this with fresh dough, you might try to secure some from a local pastry shop; they are often willing to sell you plain sheets.)

I've augmented another childhood favorite, cake and ice cream, in the Warm Chocolate Cake with Toasted Almond Ice Cream, a deceptively simple looking dessert packed with layers of rich flavor. And, as the ultimate nod to childhood, I've included a recipe for Vanilla Ice Cream and a few variations.

At the restaurant, we make and serve all of these desserts in individual portions, often using small molds and time-consuming plating techniques. In a home setting, I'd encourage you to relax, serve family-style, and enjoy one of these simple, sweet endings.

Warm Chocolate Cake with Toasted Almond Ice Cream

MAKES 12 SERVINGS

Thinking Ahead: This cake cools in a turned-off oven for 2 hours, and should be refrigerated for at least 4 hours. It can also be frozen for up to 1 week, wrapped well in plastic wrap and then aluminum foil. The ice cream has to be prepared at least 4 hours before serving and frozen.

Special Equipment: one 10-inch round springform pan (optional)

1 pound high-quality bittersweet chocolate, preferably Callebaut or Lindt, finely chopped

3 ounces high-quality unsweetened chocolate, finely chopped

1/2 cup plus 2 tablespoons strong brewed coffee

6 large eggs, at room temperature

3/4 cup sugar

1 cup heavy cream

Preheat the oven to 325° F. Lightly butter the inside of a 10-inch-round cake pan. (You can use a springform pan, if the bottom is tight-fitting.) Line the bottom of the pan with a circle of parchment paper.

In the top part of a double boiler or in a large metal bowl set over a medium saucepan of simmering, not boiling, water, melt the bittersweet and unsweetened chocolates with the coffee.

Meanwhile, in the bowl of a heavy-duty electric mixer, whisk the eggs and sugar. Set the bowl over a medium saucepan of simmering, not boiling, water, and whisk until the mixture is warm to the touch and the sugar is dissolved, about 2 minutes. Rub a little of the mixture between your thumb and finger to test it. Attach the bowl to the mixer and beat at medium-high speed until light and almost tripled in volume, about 3 minutes. Reduce the speed to medium-low and continue beating for another 2 minutes. Set aside.

In a chilled bowl, beat the cream just past the soft-peak stage, un-

IF YOU HAVE NOT VISITED the Gotham and tried our Warm Chocolate Cake, then imagine reaching the end of a wonderful meal comprised of dramatic and complex dishes. Then, a small slice of unassuming, simple, dark chocolate cake arrives at your table accompanied only by a scoop of ice cream. Anticlimactic, right? Any thoughts of disappointment are shattered, however, by your first taste, as it melts over the tongue, revealing itself to be extremely light, moist, and complex. Not so bad after all!

Because of this reversal of expectations, I've always felt that this deceptively simple-looking Gotham favorite boasts one of the most effective presentations at the restaurant. And, as impressive as this effect is in that setting, on those occasions when I've cooked it at home, the response has been even more appreciative.

This cake also lends itself to home entertaining because it can be kept warm in the oven prior to serving. Bring the cake to room temperature and, after

(continued)

til it dollops nicely and holds its shape when dropped from a spoon onto a plate. If the whipped cream is too soft, the cake will be airy. If too firm, the cake may be dry.

Fold a quarter of the egg mixture into the chocolate mixture. Fold this lightened chocolate mixture back into the remaining egg mixture. Fold in the whipped cream. Transfer to the prepared pan, smooth the top, and tap the filled pan lightly on the work surface a few times to settle any air pockets.

Place the pan in a larger baking pan and put in the oven. Add enough hot water to the baking pan to come halfway up the sides of the cake pan. Bake for 30 minutes. Open the oven door for 30 seconds to release any excess moisture that builds in the oven. Continue baking until the center of the cake feels somewhat firm when pressed lightly with your fingers, another 20 to 30 minutes. Let the cake cool in the turned-off oven for 2 hours.

Run a warm knife around the inside of the pan, and carefully unmold the cake onto a 10-inch cardboard round or an ovenproof serving platter. Peel off the parchment paper. Wrap the cake tightly in plastic wrap and refrigerate until well chilled and firm, at least 4 hours or overnight.

Using a thin-bladed slicing knife dipped into hot water, cut the chilled cake into 12 wedges. Wipe the knife clean between slices. Do not separate the slices. Rewrap the entire cake in plastic wrap and refrigerate or freeze.

Remove cake from refrigerator or freezer and allow it to return to room temperature (allow 4 hours if frozen). At least 1 hour before serving the cake, preheat the oven to its lowest setting, (or lower the temperature if you have used the oven for other cooking). Place the plastic-wrapped cake on a baking sheet. Transfer it to the oven and let the cake slowly warm through, at least 30 minutes and up to 3 hours. It will remain perfectly fine in the oven throughout dinner and be ready when needed.

cooking the main course, lower the oven temperature to its lowest setting and place the cake in the center rack. It must be heated for at least 30 minutes, but may remain at this temperature for up to 3 hours. It's as appropriate to cap off a formal meal as it is after a simple family dinner. Of course, a dollop of sweetened whipped cream can be a simple addition to, or substitute for, the toasted almond ice cream.

Here it is . . . the most requested recipe in the Gotham's history.

ASSEMBLY

Unsweetened cocoa powder, for garnish

1 recipe Toasted Almond Ice Cream (recipe follows)

To serve, unwrap the warmed cake and sift cocoa powder over the top. Transfer the slices to dessert plates. Garnish each serving with a scoop of the ice cream.

Variations: Other ice creams may be substituted for Toasted Almond. At the Gotham, we sometimes use espresso ice cream, but feel free to use your favorite flavor.

Whipped cream or Crème Anglaise (page 342) may be used in addition to or in place of the ice cream.

Toasted Almond Ice Cream

MAKES ABOUT 1 QUART, ENOUGH FOR 12 SERVINGS WITH THE CAKE

Special Equipment: ice cream machine

DEEPLY TOASTED almonds, and lots of them, infuse this ice cream with an intensely nutty flavor. Don't be afraid to let the almonds get good and brown, but be careful not to burn them.

1^3/$_4$ cups (6 ounces) sliced almonds

2 cups heavy cream

1 cup milk

^{3}/$_4$ cup plus 2 tablespoons sugar

8 large egg yolks

Preheat the oven to 350° F. Spread the almonds on a large baking sheet. Bake, stirring often, until the almonds are evenly, deeply, browned, about 15 minutes. Transfer to a medium saucepan.

Add the cream, milk, and 7 tablespoons (or half) the sugar. Bring to a simmer over medium heat. Cover, remove from the heat, and let steep for 30 minutes. Strain through a fine wire sieve into a medium bowl, discarding the almonds.

Rinse out the saucepan and set it aside. In a medium metal bowl, combine the egg yolks and the remaining sugar; whisk until smooth. Gradually whisk in the warm almond-infused cream. Transfer the mixture to the clean saucepan and return to the stove. Stirring constantly with a flat-bottomed wooden spatula over low heat, cook until the mixture is thick enough to coat the spatula, 3 to 5 minutes. Strain through a fine wire sieve into a medium metal bowl. Place the bowl in a larger bowl of iced water and let stand, stirring often, until completely cooled.

Transfer to the container of an electric ice cream machine and freeze the ice cream according to the manufacturer's directions. Scrape the ice cream into a covered container and freeze until firm, at least 4 hours or overnight.

Lemon Cake **with Crème Fraîche and Warm Berry Compote**

MAKES 8 SERVINGS

Thinking Ahead: The cake can be made as much as 1 day in advance, covered tightly with plastic wrap, and stored at room temperature. The cake may also be served warm. The raspberry compote sauce can be prepared up to 1 day in advance and reheated gently, but fold in the strawberries and blueberries just before serving.

Special Equipment: one 9-inch springform pan

LEMON CAKE

1 cup cake flour (not self-rising)

1/3 cup almond flour (see page 375 for mail order source)

1/2 teaspoon baking powder

1/2 teaspoon baking soda

1/8 teaspoon coarse salt

12 tablespoons (1 1/2 sticks) unsalted butter, at room temperature

1 cup granulated sugar

2 large eggs, at room temperature

Grated zest of 1 orange

Grated zest of 1 lemon

1/2 teaspoon almond extract

1 teaspoon vanilla extract

2/3 cup crème fraîche (see Sidebar, page 337) or sour cream

ASSEMBLY

Confectioners' sugar, for garnish

Sweetened whipped cream, for garnish

Warm Berry Compote (recipe follows)

Mint sprigs, for garnish

THERE ARE NOT MANY baked desserts easier to make than this citrus-scented cake. Its soft, moist crumb comes from the recipe's crème fraîche and the use of almond flour which give a tender, melt-in-your-mouth quality. You can use sour cream instead of the crème fraîche with equally good results. The warm berry compote is a delicious partner to the cake, as the cake soaks up the compote juices, making each bite a composite of summery fruit flavors. If you like, serve it with a dollop of whipped cream or a big scoop of Vanilla Ice Cream (page 352).

Position a rack in the center of the oven and preheat to 350° F. Lightly butter and flour the inside of a 9-inch springform pan.

In a medium bowl, whisk together the cake and almond flours, the baking powder, baking soda, and salt to combine, and set aside.

In another medium bowl, using an electric mixer set at high speed, beat the butter and sugar until light in color and texture, about 2 minutes. One at a time, beat in the eggs, beating well after each addition. Beat in the orange and lemon zests, and the almond and vanilla extracts. Reduce the mixer speed to medium-low, and gradually add the dry ingredients, scraping down the sides as needed, and mix until smooth. Mix in the crème fraîche until well blended. Pour into the prepared pan and smooth the top.

Bake until the top springs back when pressed in the center, 30 to 40 minutes. Cool on a wire cake rack for 10 minutes. Remove the sides of the springform pan. Invert the cake onto a rack and remove the pan bottom. Turn the cake right side up and cool completely on the rack.

Sift confectioners' sugar over the top of the cake. Slice the cake into wedges, top with a spoonful of whipped cream, and spoon the compote next to each piece of cake. Garnish each serving with mint sprigs.

Crème fraîche is a thick, fermented cream, similar to American sour cream, but with a more pronounced tang. Chefs prefer it to sour cream for 2 reasons. First crème fraîche won't separate when stirred into a hot sauce. Second, although you can substitute sour cream for crème fraîche in baked goods, the latter has more flavor and character. Crème fraîche can be found in the refrigerated section of specialty food shops.

Warm Berry Compote

MAKES ABOUT 4 CUPS

¹/₂ pint raspberries

2 tablespoons sugar

1 tablespoon fresh lemon juice

1 pint strawberries, hulled and halved (quartered if large)

¹/₂ pint blueberries or blackberries

In a blender or food processor, puree the raspberries and strain through a wire sieve to remove the seeds. In a medium saucepan, stir the raspberry puree, sugar, and lemon juice over low heat until the sugar is dissolved and the sauce is hot. Gently fold in the strawberries and blueberries.

Marbled Pumpkin Cheesecake and Pumpkin Seed Brittle

MAKES ONE 8-INCH CHEESECAKE (8 SERVINGS) OR 6 INDIVIDUAL CHEESECAKES

THIS SEASONAL indulgence combines the creamy texture of cheesecake with the autumn flavors of pumpkin and the spices most often used to underscore pumpkin's distinct flavor.

You may be surprised to learn that I recommend using canned pumpkin in this recipe. I don't use it at the Gotham because I have access to a large selection of fresh cooking pumpkins just 2 blocks from our front door at the Union Square Greenmarket. But, for the home cook, canned pumpkin promises a consistency that is difficult to attain with fresh pumpkin because the moisture content varies so drastically. The pumpkin seed brittle is a dramatic, colorful way to add a crunchy component to the dish, as well as a final visual flourish.

Thinking Ahead: The cheesecake should be prepared at least 8 hours in advance, and may be prepared as much as 2 days in advance, wrapped in plastic, and chilled. The pumpkin seed brittle may be prepared as much as 1 day in advance, if the weather isn't humid. The crème anglaise will hold for 2 days in the refrigerator.

Special Equipment: one 8-inch springform pan or six 3^1/2- × 2-inch metal entremet rings

SPICED COOKIE DOUGH

1 cup all-purpose flour

^{3}/4 teaspoon ground cinnamon

^{1}/4 teaspoon freshly grated nutmeg

^{1}/4 teaspoon ground fresh ginger

^{1}/8 teaspoon ground cloves

^{1}/8 teaspoon ground cardamom

^{1}/8 teaspoon freshly ground white pepper

^{3}/4 teaspoon baking powder

^{1}/4 teaspoon salt

4 tablespoons unsalted butter, at room temperature

^{1}/3 cup sugar

1 large egg yolk

2 tablespoons water

Sift the flour, spices, white pepper, baking powder, and salt onto a sheet of waxed paper. Set aside. In a medium bowl, using an electric mixer, beat the butter and sugar until light and creamy, about 2 minutes. Beat in the egg yolk and water. Stir in the dry ingredients. Gather the dough, wrap it in plastic, and press it into a flat disc. Chill

until firm, at least 2 hours or overnight. Before rolling out the dough, let it stand at room temperature until easy to roll without cracking, about 15 minutes.

To make a large cheesecake, preheat the oven to 350° F. Lightly butter the inside of an 8-inch spring-form pan. Roll out the dough ³/₈ inch thick, and cut out an 8-inch round of dough. (You will have left-over dough to cut into cookies, if you wish.) Fit the dough into the bottom of the pan. Bake until firm and lightly browned, about 20 minutes. Leave in the springform and cool completely on a wire cake rack. Reduce the oven temperature to 275°.

To make individual cheesecakes, lightly butter the insides of the metal rings. On a lightly floured work surface, roll out the spiced cookie dough about ³/₈ inch thick. Using a metal ring, cut out 6 rounds of dough. Arrange the rings on a parchment paper–lined baking sheet, and fit the dough into the bottom of the rings. Bake until the cookie dough is set and lightly browned, about 20 minutes. Cool the cookie rounds in the rings on the baking sheet, about 15 minutes.

CHEESECAKE FILLING

12 ounces cream cheese, softened

¹/₂ cup granulated sugar

³/₄ cup heavy cream

¹/₂ cup crème fraîche (see Sidebar, page 337) or sour cream

1 large egg plus 1 large egg yolk

2 teaspoons fresh lemon juice

¹/₂ teaspoon vanilla extract

1¹/₄ cups canned pumpkin

¹/₃ cup packed light brown sugar, rubbed through a wire sieve

1 teaspoon ground cinnamon

¹/₂ teaspoon ground fresh ginger

¹/₂ teaspoon ground cloves

In a medium bowl, using an electric mixer set at medium speed, beat the cream cheese and sugar until smooth. Beat in the heavy cream, crème fraîche, egg, egg yolk, lemon juice, and vanilla, scraping down the sides of the bowl often with a rubber spatula. Measure out 1 cup of the batter and set aside. Add the pumpkin, sieved brown sugar, cinnamon, ginger, and cloves to the larger portion of batter and beat well.

If making 1 large cake, pour the pumpkin batter into the pan on top of the crust. Add dollops of the plain batter, and swirl it with a table knife to create a marbled effect. Bake until the sides of the cheese-cake are slightly puffed and feel set (the very center will still be a little loose), about 1 hour, 20 minutes. Allow the cheesecake to cool for 30 minutes at room temperature, then run a sharp knife around the in-side of the pan, release the sides, cover with plastic wrap, and refrigerate until well chilled.

If making individual cakes, prepare the filling as directed, and divide among the metal rings over the crusts. Spoon about 2 generous tablespoons of the plain batter into the center of each. Using a table knife, swirl the 2 batters into a marble pattern. Bake until the sides of the cheesecakes look set (the centers will still be slightly loose), 35 to 45 minutes. Cool the cheesecakes at room temperature for about 30 minutes, then cover with plastic wrap and refrigerate until well chilled, at least 4 hours or overnight.

ASSEMBLY

1 recipe Pumpkin Seed Brittle (recipe follows)

1 recipe Crème Anglaise (recipe follows)

To serve, use a hot, wet knife to slice the cheesecake. Garnish each slice with a piece of pumpkin seed brittle and some crème anglaise. For individual cakes, run a sharp knife around the inside of each ring and lift it up to unmold. Transfer the cakes to dessert plates and garnish with pieces of pumpkin seed brittle and the crème anglaise.

Pumpkin Seed Brittle

MAKES ABOUT 8 TO 12 PIECES

$^1/_2$ cup water

1 cup sugar

$^2/_3$ cup shelled unsalted pumpkin seeds

Lightly butter a baking sheet (or use a nonstick baking sheet) and set aside. Pour the water into a small saucepan. Add the sugar and bring to a boil over high heat, stirring to dissolve the sugar. When the syrup boils, stop stirring and cook, washing down the sugar crystals as they form on the sides of the pan with a pastry brush dipped in cold water, until the syrup has caramelized to a golden brown, 3 to 5 minutes. Remove from the heat, add the pumpkin seeds, and swirl the pan to combine.

A DEPARTURE FROM peanut brittle, this recipe raises the seasonal effect of the marbled pumpkin cheesecake. Do not make it if the weather is humid as it will become sticky upon standing.

Immediately pour out onto the prepared baking sheet. Let the brittle stand until slightly cooled but still warm, about 2 minutes. Using your fingers (protect them with rubber gloves, if you wish), pull and stretch the mixture to make a sheet of brittle as thin as possible. Cool completely. Break the brittle into long shapes. Store at room temperature in an airtight container.

Crème Anglaise

MAKES ABOUT 1 ¼ CUPS

1 cup heavy cream

½ cup milk

1 vanilla bean, split lengthwise

3 large egg yolks

½ cup sugar

In a medium saucepan, combine the cream and milk. Using the tip of a small sharp knife, scrape the tiny black seeds from the vanilla bean into the saucepan, and add the bean. Bring to a simmer over very low heat.

In a small bowl, whisk the yolks and sugar. Gradually whisk in the hot cream mixture. Return to the saucepan. Stirring constantly with a flat wooden spatula, cook over very low heat until the mixture is thick enough to coat the spatula, 1 to 2 minutes. (An instant-read thermometer will read 180° to 185° F.) Strain through a fine wire sieve into a small bowl. Cool completely, then cover tightly and refrigerate until well chilled, at least 4 hours.

Apple-Calvados Tarts with Maple Ice Cream and Cranberry Confit

MAKES 8 TARTS

Thinking Ahead: The apple chips and cranberry confit can be prepared up to 3 days in advance, covered, and refrigerated. The tartlets can be prepared as much as 8 hours in advance and reheated.

Special Equipment: six $3^1/2$- × 1-inch tart rings, or one $10^1/2$-inch tart pan with a removable bottom; dried beans or rice, for weighing down the dough; A mandoline-type slicer

SWEET PASTRY DOUGH

$1^1/2$ cups all-purpose flour

1 tablespoon almond flour (see page 375 for mail-order source)

1 tablespoon confectioners' sugar

$1/8$ teaspoon salt

10 tablespoons (1 stick plus 2 tablespoons) unsalted butter, at room temperature

$1/3$ cup granulated sugar

2 tablespoons milk

1 large egg yolk

In a small bowl, whisk the flours, confectioners' sugar, and salt until combined; set aside. In a medium bowl, using an electric mixer set at medium-high speed, cream the butter and granulated sugar until light in color. Beat in the milk and egg yolk. On low speed, add the dry ingredients and mix just until the mixture begins to pull together. Gather up the dough into a ball, wrap it in plastic wrap, and press it into a thick disc. Refrigerate until well chilled but still pliable, 1 to 2 hours.

Preheat the oven to 400° F. If making individual tartlets, place the tart rings on a baking sheet. On a lightly floured work surface, roll out the dough to about $1/4$ inch thick. (If the dough cracks, it is too

THIS COMBINATION OF smooth custard and firm chunks of apple is topped off by an eye-catching apple chip—a versatile garnish that's easy to make. At the restaurant, we make and serve this dessert in individual tartlets. This allows for a most striking presentation, and it also enables me to heat each serving to order. Nevertheless, I have also provided a recipe for 1 large tart.

At the Gotham, the pastry chefs place a scoop of ice cream in a tuile cookie, so it won't melt by the time it reaches the customer, but this is really unnecessary at home. Also, the tart cranberry confit with hints of orange may be viewed as a restaurant-designed indulgence, but it is worth the effort.

cold. Let it stand for a few minutes to soften, then try rolling again.) Cut out as many 5½-inch rounds of dough as possible. Carefully ease and fit the dough rounds into the tart rings, pressing them securely into the corners. Trim the dough flush with the tops of the pastry rings. Gather up the scraps and refrigerate briefly until firm. Roll out and repeat the procedure until all the dough is used and the rings are lined. Firm in the freezer for several minutes. Line the inside of each tart with a piece of aluminum foil and fill with beans or rice to weigh down the dough.

To make a large tart, roll out the dough ¼ inch thick and carefully line the pan with the dough, trimming it flush with the top of the pan. The dough is very tender; if it cracks, make sure the cracks are sealed so the filling won't leak. Firm in the freezer several minutes, then line with foil and weight with beans.

Bake either individual tartlets or the larger tart until set, about 6 minutes. Remove the foil and beans. Continue baking until the pastry is more firmly set but not browned, 6 to 10 more minutes. Remove from the oven and set aside until ready to fill.

APPLES, CALVADOS FILLING, AND STREUSEL

4 tablespoons unsalted butter, at room temperature

4 medium tart apples, such as Granny Smith, peeled, cored, and cut into ¼-inch-thick wedges

⅓ cup plus 1 tablespoon granulated sugar

½ teaspoon ground cinnamon

¼ cup crème fraîche (see Sidebar, page 337) or sour cream

¼ cup milk

1 large egg plus 1 large egg yolk

2 teaspoons Calvados or apple brandy

1 teaspoon vanilla extract

½ cup packed light brown sugar

¼ cup chopped walnuts

2 tablespoons all-purpose flour

In a medium sauté pan, heat 2 tablespoons of the butter over medium heat. Add the apples and sprinkle with 1 tablespoon of the granulated sugar and the cinnamon. Cook until the sugar has caramelized lightly and the apples are tender, about 1 minute. Cool completely.

In a medium bowl, whisk the ⅓ cup granulated sugar, the crème fraîche, milk, egg, egg yolk, Calvados, and vanilla until smooth. Set the Calvados filling aside.

In a small bowl, using your fingertips, work the remaining 2 tablespoons of butter with the brown sugar, nuts, and flour until well combined and crumbly. Set the streusel aside.

CRANBERRY CONFIT

$^1/_2$ cup water

$1^1/_4$ cups sugar

$3^1/_2$ cups fresh cranberries

$^1/_2$ cup fresh orange juice

Zest of $^1/_2$ medium orange

Place the water in a medium saucepan and add 1 cup of the sugar. Bring to a boil over medium heat, stirring often to dissolve the sugar. Add 2 cups of the cranberries and return to a boil. Reduce the heat to very low and cook for 1 minute. Do not allow the cranberries to burst. Pour into a bowl and cool completely. Drain the cranberries and set aside.

In another saucepan, bring the remaining $1^1/_2$ cups of cranberries and $^1/_4$ cup of sugar, the orange juice, and orange zest to a boil over medium-high heat, stirring to dissolve the sugar. Cook until the cranberries have burst, about 5 minutes. Remove from the heat and cool completely. Rub the cranberries through a coarse wire strainer set over a bowl, discarding the solids in the sieve. Stir the drained whole cranberries into the cranberry sauce.

APPLE CHIPS

2 cups sugar, plus additional for sprinkling

1 cup water

1 medium tart apple, such as Granny Smith, unpeeled, cored, and cut on a mandoline-type slicer into the thinnest possible rounds

Preheat the oven to its lowest setting. In a medium saucepan, bring the 2 cups sugar and the water to a boil over high heat, stirring constantly to dissolve the sugar. When it reaches a boil, stop stirring and cook for 1 minute. Add the apple slices and cook until they turn translucent, about 1 minute. Using a slotted spoon, lay out the apples without touching each other on a nonstick or parchment paper–lined baking sheet. Sprinkle lightly with sugar.

Slowly bake (if the oven seems too high—above 200° F.—leave the door ajar) until the syrup has evaporated and the apples feel leathery, about 8 hours or overnight. Cool for 5 minutes, then carefully peel the apples from the baking sheet or parchment paper, laying them back on the sheet to cool completely. Store in an airtight container. You will have about 20 apple crisps.

ASSEMBLY

8 cone-shaped Honey Tuile Cookies (page 369, optional)

$^3/_4$ quart Maple Ice Cream (page 352)

Preheat the oven to 350° F. Arrange the apple slices close together in the pastry shells or shell. Place on a baking sheet in the oven, and carefully ladle or pour the Calvados filling over the apples. If the apple slices move, press them down. Crumble the streusel on top. Bake until the filling is set, 15 to 20 minutes for the tartlets, 35 to 40 minutes for the large tart. Remove the tart from the rings or pan while still hot, or the tarts will stick.

Place the warm individual tarts on dessert plates, and serve with a honey tuile cookie filled with a scoop of maple ice cream, and garnished with apple chips and cranberry compote.

To serve a large tart, slice and serve on individual plates, adding accompaniments in the same manner.

Strawberry Tart with Mascarpone and Aged Balsamic Vinegar

MAKES ONE 10½-INCH TART, 8 SERVINGS

Thinking Ahead: The crust may be made in advance and tightly wrapped in plastic and stored at room temperature. Fill it just before serving to preserve its crispness.

Special Equipment: 10$^{1}/_{2}$-inch tart pan with a removable bottom; dried beans or rice, for weighing down the dough

PASTRY

1 recipe Sweet Pastry Dough (page 343)

Preheat the oven to 400° F. On a lightly floured work surface, roll out the dough into a circle, about 13 inches in diameter and ¼ inch thick. (If the dough cracks, it is too cold. Let it stand for a few minutes to soften, then try rolling it again.) Carefully roll up the circle of dough onto the rolling pin. Place the pin over the tart pan, and unroll the pastry over the pan. Ease the dough into the pan, fitting it securely into the corners. If the dough cracks, just press it back together. Trim the dough flush with the top of the pan. Firm in the freezer for several minutes. Line the inside of the tart with a piece of aluminum foil and fill with beans or rice to weigh down the dough.

Bake until the dough is set, about 6 minutes. Remove the foil and beans and continue baking until the pastry is fully cooked and lightly browned, 10 to 15 minutes longer. Cool completely on a wire cake rack.

BALSAMIC STRAWBERRIES

3 pints strawberries, hulled

¼ cup best-quality balsamic vinegar

2 tablespoons sugar

WHEN TIRAMISU BECAME a culinary fad in the '80s, mascarpone, the primary ingredient in this rich Italian dessert, became more familiar to U.S. diners and pastry chefs. This creamy indulgence boasts a thick, buttery texture that makes it a viable alternative to a labor-intensive pastry cream. In northern Italy there is a tradition of serving strawberries mascerated in quality aged balsamic vinegar; the berry's flavor is dramatically heightened in the process. If you are using a common supermarket-quality vinegar, balance its acidity with more sugar.

In a small bowl, combine all of the ingredients, tossing gently to help the sugar dissolve. Cover and re-frigerate, gently stirring occasionally, until well chilled, up to 2 hours.

MASCARPONE FILLING AND ASSEMBLY

1 pound mascarpone cheese

$^3/_4$ cup heavy cream

$^1/_3$ cup plus 1 tablespoon sugar

1 tablespoon vanilla extract

Grated zest of 1 medium orange

Just before serving, make the filling. In a medium bowl, whisk together all the ingredients just until smooth; be careful not to overbeat or the filling will separate.

Spread the filling evenly in the cooled tart shell. Drain the berries well and arrange them in concentric circles over the top of the filling. Serve immediately.

Chocolate Banana Strudel with Vanilla Ice Cream and Caramel Sauce

MAKES 6 SERVINGS

Thinking Ahead: The vanilla ice cream can be prepared as much as 2 days in advance and frozen. Make the strudel right before serving—it is best warm.

Special Equipment: ice cream maker

STRUDEL

Nonstick vegetable cooking spray, for baking sheet

8 tablespoons (1 stick) unsalted butter

3 ripe large bananas, cut into $1/4$-inch-thick rounds (3 cups)

$3/4$ cup toasted, coarsely chopped walnuts (see Sidebar, page 351)

$1/2$ cup coarsely chopped high-quality bittersweet chocolate

Six (12- × 17-inch) sheets filo dough, thawed if necessary

Position the oven rack in the top third of the oven and preheat the oven to 425° F. Lightly spray a baking sheet with the nonstick cooking spray.

In a small saucepan, melt the butter slowly over medium-low heat. Remove from the heat and let stand for 1 minute. Skim off any foam from the surface. Decant into a small bowl, leaving any white solids in the bottom of the saucepan.

In a medium bowl, combine the bananas, walnuts, and chocolate. Set aside.

Keeping the remaining filo sheets covered with plastic wrap to avoid drying, place 1 sheet on a work surface, long side facing you, and brush with some of the melted butter. Stack with another sheet, and brush with butter. Repeat with all the filo, brushing each sheet with butter. Spoon the banana mixture down the center of the filo stack, leaving a 2-inch border at both short ends. Fold in the short ends of the filo to partially cover the filling. Starting at a long end, roll up to form a thick cylinder. Place, seam side down, on the prepared baking sheet and brush with the remaining butter.

Bake until deep golden brown, 25 to 35 minutes. Partially cool on the baking sheet, 20 to 30 minutes before serving.

CARAMEL SAUCE

²/₃ cup sugar

¹/₄ cup water

²/₃ cup heavy cream

Place the water in a medium saucepan, and add the sugar, swirling the pan so the sugar is completely moistened. Bring to a boil over high heat. Cook, washing down the sides of the pan with a pastry brush dipped in water, until the syrup turns a deep golden brown, 3 to 5 minutes. Remove from the heat. Gradually stir in the cream (be careful, as it will boil up). Keep the caramel sauce warm by placing the skillet in a pan of hot water over low heat.

ASSEMBLY

³/₄ quart Vanilla Ice Cream (recipe follows)

Fresh mint sprigs, for garnish

Using a serrated knife, trim off the unfilled ends of the strudel, then cut the strudel into 6 pieces. Transfer to dessert plates and add a scoop of ice cream to each serving. Garnish with mint sprigs and spoon the warm sauce around.

Variations: Substitute your favorite fruit for the banana. My favorite alternatives are apricots and pears.

Toasting nuts brings out their flavor and crisps them slightly. To toast walnuts, pistachios, or almonds preheat the oven to 350° F. Spread the nuts on a baking sheet and bake, stirring occasionally, until the nuts are lightly browned and fragrant, about 10 minutes. (Note that the almonds for the Toasted Almond Ice Cream [page 334] are well toasted for a deeper flavor.) Cool completely before chopping.

Vanilla Ice Cream

MAKES ABOUT 1 ½ QUARTS

2 cups heavy cream

1 cup milk

1 cup sugar

1 vanilla bean, split lengthwise

8 large egg yolks

In a medium saucepan, bring the cream, milk, ½ cup of the sugar, and the vanilla bean to a simmer over low heat. Remove from the heat.

In a medium bowl, whisk the egg yolks with the remaining ½ cup of sugar. Gradually whisk in the hot cream mixture, including the vanilla bean. Return to the saucepan and cook over low heat, stirring constantly, until the custard is thick enough to lightly coat the back of a wooden spoon, 3 to 5 minutes. Strain through a fine wire sieve into a bowl. Place the bowl in a larger bowl of iced water and let it stand, stirring occasionally, until chilled, about 20 minutes. Remove the vanilla bean halves. With the tip of a small knife, scrape the tiny black vanilla seeds back into the custard, discarding the bean.

Transfer the custard to the container of an ice cream machine. Freeze the ice cream according to the manufacturer's directions. Scrape the ice cream into a covered container and freeze until firm, at least 4 hours or overnight.

Variations: Maple Ice Cream: Delete the vanilla bean and substitute 1 cup Grade B (amber) maple syrup for the sugar.

Bittersweet Chocolate Bread Pudding with Whipped Cream

MAKES 6 SERVINGS

Sweetened Whipped Cream: In a chilled medium bowl, whisk ¹/₂ cup heavy cream (preferably pasteurized, not ultra-pasteurized), 1 tablespoon sugar, and ¹/₄ teaspoon vanilla extract just until the cream forms soft peaks. Do not overwhip.

1¹/₂ cups heavy cream

¹/₃ cup milk

4 large egg yolks

3 tablespoons sugar

5 ounces finely chopped, high-quality bittersweet chocolate, such as Callebaut or Lindt

6 packed cups ¹/₄-inch cubes of day-old brioche or challah, crusts trimmed before cubing

Sweetened whipped cream, for garnish (see Sidebar)

Position a rack in the center of the oven and preheat to 325° F. Lightly butter the inside of a 1¹/₂-quart soufflé dish.

In a medium saucepan over medium heat, bring the cream and milk to a simmer. In a medium bowl, whisk together the egg yolks and sugar. Gradually whisk in the hot cream mixture. Add the bittersweet chocolate and let stand until the chocolate melts, about 3 minutes. Whisk until smooth.

Add the bread cubes and let stand for about 5 minutes, occasionally folding the bread and chocolate custard together, until evenly soaked. Pour into the prepared soufflé dish. Place the soufflé dish in a baking pan and put the baking pan in the oven. Pour enough hot water into the pan to come 1 inch up the sides of the soufflé dish.

Bake until a knife inserted 1 inch from the side of the dish comes out clean, about 55 minutes. Remove from the oven and let stand for 10 minutes. Invert and unmold onto a serving dish. Serve warm, cut into wedges, with a dollop of sweetened whipped cream.

THIS DESSERT VARIES from the traditional bread pudding in 2 ways: It is prepared with brioche or challah bread, which lends it a richer, fuller texture that we preserve by using precisely cut cubes of bread. This recipe also uses first-rate chocolate, an important departure from the simple baker's chocolate most people associate with the dessert they enjoyed as children.

If you have easy access to a French bakery, buy brioche (a particularly egg-and-butter-rich dough) to make the pudding. Otherwise, use challah bread—if it is covered in seeds, don't worry, because you will cut off the crust. As a final option, choose a firm-textured sandwich bread, like Pepperidge Farm, but the result will not be the same. Don't be tempted to leave out the whipped cream, an essential foil to the richness of this dessert.

Ginger Crème Brûlée with Warm Plum and Raspberry Compote

MAKES 8 SERVINGS

THOUGH THE CRÈME brûlée and the fruit compote are served in separate containers at the Gotham, they are meant to be eaten together, or at least in alternating mouthfuls. The tart sweetness of the fruit cuts the richness of the cream, while the ginger, plum, and raspberry all leave ghosts of flavor with each bite, dazzling the palate with bright sensations.

Thinking Ahead: The custards and the compote may be prepared as much as 1 day in advance, covered, and refrigerated. Caramelize the custards right before serving.

Special Equipment: eight 6-ounce ovenproof ramekins

CRÈME BRÛLÉE

4 cups heavy cream

½ cup chopped fresh ginger

12 large egg yolks

1 cup sugar

Position a rack in the center of the oven and preheat to 325° F. Place the ramekins in a large baking pan.

In a medium saucepan, bring the cream and ginger to a simmer over medium heat. Reduce the heat to very low and simmer gently for 30 minutes.

In a medium bowl, whisk the egg yolks and sugar. Gradually whisk in the cream. Strain through a wire sieve into a bowl, and discard the ginger. Place the baking dish with the ramekins in the oven, and carefully ladle or pour the mixture into the ramekins. Using a teaspoon, skim off any foam that forms on the surface of the custards.

Pour enough hot water into the baking pan to come ½ inch up the sides of the ramekins. Bake until the custards seem firm (the centers will be slightly loose), 40 to 50 minutes. Remove from the water bath and cool completely. Cover each ramekin with plastic wrap and refrigerate until ready to serve.

WARM PLUM AND BERRY COMPOTE

2 tablespoons unsalted butter

3 ripe dark-skinned black or Santa Rosa plums, pitted and cut into sixths

2 to 3 tablespoons sugar, depending on the sweetness of the plums

$^{1}/_{4}$ cup fresh orange juice

$^{1}/_{2}$ pint fresh raspberries

In a medium saucepan, heat the butter over medium-low heat. Add the plums and sugar. Cook, stirring occasionally, until the plums begin to release their juices, 3 to 4 minutes. Add the orange juice and bring to a boil over high heat. Cook until the orange juice is slightly thickened, about 2 minutes. Remove from the heat and fold in the raspberries. Spoon the warm compote into small serving dishes.

ASSEMBLY

$^{1}/_{3}$ cup packed light brown sugar (see Sidebar)

Position a broiler rack about 6 inches from the source of heat and preheat the broiler. Rub the brown sugar through a wire sieve to cover each custard with a dusting of the sugar. Put the ramekins on a baking sheet and broil, watching carefully to avoid scorching, until the brown sugar has caramelized, 1 to 2 minutes. On a large plate, place a crème brûlée and a small dish of the compote.

For the best, thinnest sugar crust, rub the brown sugar through a wire sieve onto a baking sheet and spread it out. Let stand overnight to dry.

At the Gotham, our pastry chefs prefer to glaze the crème brûlée with a hand-held propane torch, available for relatively little cost at hardware stores. Wave the ignited flame in a circular pattern about 2 inches above each brown sugar–dusted custard, and let the flame melt the sugar, which will only take a few seconds.

Panna Cotta **with Fresh Raspberries and Spearmint**

MAKES 8 SERVINGS

Thinking Ahead: The panna cotta may be prepared up to 1 day in advance, covered, and refrigerated. Unmold just before serving.

Special Equipment: eight 6-ounce ramekins

2 tablespoons (2 envelopes) unflavored gelatin

1 cup milk

3 cups heavy cream, pasteurized, not ultra-pasteurized

$1/2$ cup sugar

2 vanilla beans, split lengthwise

1 pint fresh raspberries

2 tablespoons chiffonade of fresh spearmint (page 44)

Lightly butter the insides of the ramekins and place them on a baking sheet.

In a small bowl, sprinkle the gelatin over $1/4$ cup of the milk. Let stand until the gelatin softens and absorbs the milk, about 5 minutes.

Meanwhile, in a medium saucepan, heat the remaining $3/4$ cup of milk with the cream, sugar, and vanilla beans over medium heat, stirring occasionally, until simmering, about 5 minutes. Remove from the heat. Add the gelatin mixture and stir until the gelatin is completely dissolved, about 1 minute. Strain into a 1-quart measuring cup or medium bowl. Press hard on the vanilla beans to extract all the flavor, then discard the beans.

Pour or ladle the mixture into the prepared ramekins. Cover with plastic wrap and chill until set, at least 4 hours or overnight.

To unmold, fill a shallow dish with about $1/2$ inch of very hot tap water. One at a time, place the ramekins in the dish for about 15 seconds. Remove from the water and dry the outside of the ramekin. Press the panna cotta around the edges to loosen it from the sides of the ramekin, and invert onto the center of a dessert plate. Scatter the raspberries and spearmint chiffonade around the panna cotta.

THE RENOWNED ITALIAN dessert panna cotta, which literally means "cooked cream," is the ultimate vanilla pudding. Actually, despite its name, this trembling little custard is hardly cooked at all . . . just enough to dissolve the gelatin that holds the cream and milk together. Surrounded with ripe raspberries and leaves of fresh-picked spearmint, this dessert becomes a complex version of simple berries and cream.

Variation: Any ripe summer fruits, alone or in combination, will work very well with this.

Cherry and Berry Fruit Compote with Mint Tea Infusion

MAKES 6 TO 8 SERVINGS

IN ADDITION TO MANY other accomplishments, my father-in-law, William, is an accomplished and sophisticated home cook. Whenever there's a family party, he can be counted on to bring a bowl of this luscious summer fruit soup. To really succeed, the recipe depends on obtaining the best possible fruits: red currants, white cherries, golden raspberries, sliced plums or peaches, huckle- or boysenberries can all be used to make this soup into a reflection of the best that summer has to offer.

Thinking Ahead: The compote must be chilled for at least 2 hours or up to 1 day before serving.

$^1/_2$ cup water

2 bags of mixed fruit or four fruit tea, or 1 tablespoon loose tea leaves

3 large mint sprigs, plus additional for garnish

$3^1/_4$ cups (one 750 ml bottle) dry white wine

$^2/_3$ cup sugar

2 vanilla beans, split lengthwise; or 1 teaspoon vanilla extract

1 pound black cherries, halved and pitted (2 cups)

1 pint strawberries, hulled and halved lengthwise ($1^1/_2$ cups)

$^1/_2$ pint blueberries (1 cup)

$^1/_2$ pint raspberries (1 cup)

$^1/_2$ pint blackberries (1 cup)

In a small saucepan, bring the water to a boil over high heat. Add the tea bags and mint, cover, and remove from the heat. Let steep for 10 minutes.

Meanwhile, in a large saucepan, bring the wine, sugar, and vanilla beans to a boil over high heat, stirring to dissolve the sugar. Strain the tea mixture into the syrup. Add the fruits and remove from the heat.

Pour the compote into a large bowl set in a sink full of iced water. Let stand, stirring gently and often, until cool. (The compote must cool quickly, or the fruits will continue to cook and soften.) Cover and refrigerate until well chilled, at least 2 hours or overnight. Remove the vanilla beans.

Ladle the compote into dessert bowls, garnish with mint sprigs, and serve chilled with crisp cookies or biscotti, such as the Lemon-Pistachio Biscotti (page 372).

Passion Fruit Granité
with Tropical Fruits

MAKES 6 TO 8 SERVINGS

GRANITÉS ARE wonderfully convenient desserts on which to rely for those times when you simply don't want to bake anything. These cool, sophisticated ices are suitable in formal or informal settings, and may be adjusted to use different fruits and liqueurs to accommodate the full range of seasons or occasions.

In this granité, passion fruit's unmistakable perfume and vibrant yellow-gold hue almost refreshes before it reaches the palate. But actually eating this somewhat unusual fruit in this frozen context is positively reinvigorating. Here, the passion fruit granité is accompanied by kiwi, mango, papaya, pineapple, and starfruit, but try combining it with any variety of ripe tropical fruits to experience its versatility for yourself.

A note about purchasing passion fruit: Don't pass them up if they are wrinkled; this simply indicates ripeness. Frozen passion fruit puree may also be found at Hispanic markets, but be sure to buy it unsweetened.

Thinking Ahead: The granité can be prepared as much as 1 day in advance, covered, and frozen. The fruits may be prepared as much as 8 hours in advance, covered, and refrigerated.

PASSION FRUIT GRANITÉ

2 cups water

$1^3/_4$ cups strained passion fruit pulp, or 1 (14-ounce) package thawed unsweetened passion fruit pulp

1 cup sugar

2 tablespoons fresh lemon juice

Place a 9- × 13-inch nonreactive metal pan in the freezer to chill.

In a nonreactive medium saucepan, combine the water, passion fruit, sugar, and lemon juice. Cook over medium heat, stirring constantly, until the sugar is dissolved. Pour into a medium bowl. Place in a larger bowl filled with iced water and let stand, stirring often, until cooled.

Pour into the chilled pan and freeze until the mixture is semi-solid and icy around the edges, about 1 hour. Using a large spoon, break up the icy edges and stir into the center. Freeze again until the edges are icy, about 1 hour. Repeat the mixing procedure. (This process helps the passion fruit stay evenly distributed throughout the mixture.) Freeze a final time until completely frozen and icy, about 2 or more hours.

TROPICAL FRUITS

2 kiwis, peeled and cut into $^1/_4$-inch-thick rounds

1 cup ($^1/_2$-inch) diced ripe papaya

1 cup ($^1/_2$-inch) diced ripe mango

1 cup ($^1/_2$-inch) diced ripe pineapple

1 starfruit, sliced

In a medium bowl, combine all the fruits. Cover and refrigerate until well chilled, at least 2 hours.

ASSEMBLY

Mint sprigs, for garnish

Using the tines of a fork, scrape the granité into large crystals, spoon it into chilled wineglasses, add equal amounts of the fruit, and top with a sprig of mint.

If you have children, make granités in ice pop molds. They're fun and taste just as good.

Zinfandel Granité
with Poached Bosc Pears

MAKES 6 SERVINGS

ZINFANDEL GRANITÉ

$^1/_2$ cup water

$^1/_2$ cup sugar

1$^3/_4$ cups Red Zinfandel wine

$^1/_3$ cup fresh orange juice

$^1/_4$ cup fresh lemon juice

ZINFANDEL'S BERRY, citrus, and spice notes make a perfect foil for the sweet velvety pears. This dessert is perfectly suited to autumn entertaining.

Place a 9- × 13-inch metal baking pan in the freezer to chill. Meanwhile, in a small saucepan, bring the water and sugar to a boil over high heat, stirring to dissolve the sugar. Place in a large bowl filled with ice water and let stand, stirring often, until cooled. Stir in the wine, orange and lemon juices.

Pour the mixture into the baking pan. Freeze until ice crystals form around the edges of the pan, about 1 hour. Using a spoon, scrape and stir the crystals into the center of the granité. Freeze again until crystals form, 1 hour. Repeat the scraping and stirring procedure. Freeze again until the granité is a solid mass of crystals, 2 or more hours.

POACHED PEARS

1 medium orange

1 medium lemon

4 cups water

1$^1/_2$ cups sugar

1 vanilla bean, split in half lengthwise; or $^1/_2$ teaspoon vanilla extract

3 medium ripe-firm Bosc pears, peeled and rubbed with lemon juice

Using a vegetable peeler, remove the zests from the orange and lemon. Cut the strips into julienne. Squeeze the juice from the orange and lemon, and place the juices and zests in a large nonreactive saucepan. Add the water, sugar, and vanilla bean (but not the extract) and bring to a boil over medium heat, stirring to dissolve the sugar.

Cut the pears in half lengthwise, and, using a paring knife, remove the cores. Place the pears in the syrup, and simmer over medium-low heat until they are barely tender when pierced with the tip of a small sharp knife, about 8 minutes. Remove from the heat and cool in the syrup to room temperature. (If using vanilla extract, stir it in now.) Cover and refrigerate until chilled, at least 6 hours.

ASSEMBLY

Mint springs, for garnish

Using the tines of a fork, scrape the granité into large crystals.

Spoon the granité into chilled coupe or wine glasses. Garnish each serving with a pear half. Finish with a mint sprig and serve immediately.

Variation: Use small Forelle or Seckel pears, allowing 1 for each serving, instead of the Bosc pears. Remove the tough core from the bottom of each small pear but leave the pears whole, following the instructions on page 367.

Champagne Granité with Strawberries and Grand Marnier

MAKES 6 TO 8 SERVINGS

Thinking Ahead: The strawberries may be prepared as much as 1 hour in advance. The granité should be made and frozen at least 1 day before serving.

CHAMPAGNE GRANITÉ

1 cup sugar

$^1/_2$ cup water

3$^1/_4$ cups (one 750 ml bottle) dry champagne (see Sidebar)

$^1/_2$ cup fresh orange juice

3 tablespoons fresh lemon juice

Place a 9- × 13-inch metal baking pan in the freezer to chill. Meanwhile, in a small saucepan, bring the sugar and water to a boil over high heat, stirring often to dissolve the sugar. Pour into a medium bowl, set in a larger bowl filled with ice water, and let stand, stirring often, until cool. Stir in the champagne, orange juice, and lemon juice.

Pour the mixture into the baking pan and freeze until ice crystals form around the edges of the pan, about 1 hour. Using a fork, scrape and stir the crystals into the center of the granité. Freeze again until crystals form, about 1 hour. Repeat the scraping and stirring procedure. Freeze again until the granité is a solid mass of crystals, 2 or more hours.

STRAWBERRIES

1$^1/_2$ pints hulled strawberries, quartered lengthwise

2 tablespoons Grand Marnier, or other orange-flavored liqueur

1$^1/_2$ tablespoons fresh lemon juice

1 tablespoon chiffonade of mint leaves (page 44)

2 tablespoons sugar, or as needed

FOR SOME PEOPLE, THE mere mention of strawberries and champagne evokes romance and elegance, and the effect is equally seductive when this special, sparkling wine is presented in crystalized granité form. In a wine or dessert glass, the play of light—especially candlelight—is exceptional.

And, as elegant as this dessert might be, it is equally simple. It may be mixed in minutes and frozen without an ice cream maker.

The strawberries are halved and splashed with Grand Marnier, which releases the juice of the berries. When spooned over the granité, the ice becomes tinged with red.

Because it isn't heated, the champagne will retain its true flavor. Be sure to use a quality label. Sparkling wine from France but made outside the Champagne region, or sparkling wine from Spain or California, are good choices.

In a medium bowl, combine all of the ingredients, adding the sugar to taste. (With luck, your strawberries will be perfectly ripe and sweet, and won't need much sugar.) Cover and refrigerate to chill and macerate, up to 1 hour. (No longer, or the strawberries will become soft.)

ASSEMBLY

Mint sprigs, for garnish

Using the tines of a large fork, scrape the granité into large crystals. Spoon into chilled coupe or wine glasses. Add the strawberries and a mint sprig. Serve immediately.

Variations: If you puree a few strawberries and stir them into the granité mixture before freezing, you will have created a lovely pink champagne.

You might also use other berries, such as raspberries, blackberries, or champagne grapes.

Poached Winter Fruit Compote in White Wine Syrup

MAKES 8 SERVINGS

Thinking Ahead: The compote should be prepared at least 4 hours in advance, but will become richer if allowed to sit for 1 or 2 days in the refrigerator.

WHITE WINE SYRUP

3$\frac{1}{4}$ cups (one 750 ml bottle) dry white wine

2 cups water

$\frac{3}{4}$ cup sugar

Zest of 1 medium lemon, removed in strips with a vegetable peeler

1 cinnamon stick

1 vanilla bean, split in half lengthwise

In a large saucepan, bring all the ingredients to a boil over high heat. Reduce the heat to low and simmer for 5 minutes. Remove from the heat and let stand until ready to use.

WINTER FRUITS

4 small Forelle or Seckel pears, peeled and rubbed with lemon juice

White Wine Syrup (see above)

24 dried apricots (about 3 ounces)

8 whole dried figs, preferably Kalimyrna

8 pitted Medjool dates

$\frac{1}{2}$ cup golden raisins

$\frac{1}{2}$ cup dried cherries

2 tablespoons dark rum

Using the tip of a paring knife, dig out the tough core from the bottom of each pear.

Add the pears to the prepared syrup. Cook over medium-low heat

LONG AFTER SUMMER fruits have become a distant memory, this assemblage of poached pear and dried fruits offers a naturally sweet and refreshing indulgence. It has a simple elegance that makes it an easy but appropriate dessert to conclude a complex meal. To heighten this quality, serve it from the center of the table in a fancy crystal bowl, or in stemmed dessert glasses. Not only can the compote be made ahead and kept in the refrigerator, but this actually works to its benefit, developing the rich, natural flavors of the fruit. Feel free to vary the ingredients to create your own version of this dessert.

If you find yourself with leftovers, enjoy them the next morning for a real breakfast indulgence. Serve with crisp cookies such as Lemon-Pistachio Biscotti (page 372) or a good store-bought variety.

until barely tender when pierced with the tip of a small sharp knife, about 10 minutes. Remove from the heat. Remove the vanilla bean, scrape the seeds back into the syrup, and discard the bean halves. Stir in the apricots, figs, dates, raisins, and cherries. Cool to room temperature. Cover with plastic wrap and refrigerate until chilled, at least 4 hours or overnight. Just before serving, drain all but about 1½ cups of the syrup from the compote and stir in the dark rum.

ASSEMBLY

　Mint sprigs, for garnish

Transfer the compote to a large glass serving bowl. Serve in individual coupe or wine glasses, being sure to include some of the syrup with each serving, and garnish with mint sprigs. Serve chilled.

　Variations: You may vary the fruits, using blueberries, dried strawberries, or currants.

Honey Tuile Cookies

MAKES ABOUT 1 DOZEN COOKIES

Thinking Ahead: The cookies may be made as much as 2 days in advance and stored in an airtight container. Do not try to make tuile cookies in humid weather because they will not hold their shape.

4 tablespoons unsalted butter, at room temperature

2 tablespoons strong, dark honey (see Sidebar)

½ cup all-purpose flour

½ cup confectioners' sugar

1 large egg white

3 tablespoons coarsely chopped sliced almonds

Position two racks in the upper third and center of the oven and preheat to 375° F.

In a medium bowl, using a hand-held electric mixer (the amount of batter is too small for most standing mixers) on medium speed, beat the butter and honey until combined, about 1 minute. Sift the flour and confectioners' sugar together, add to the butter mixture, and mix on low speed just until smooth. Beat in the egg white just until blended.

Spoon 1 tablespoon of batter onto a heavy nonstick baking sheet. Using the back of a spoon, spread the batter into a thin, freeform 5- to 6-inch round. Some areas of the batter will be a little thicker than others, which is fine—it will even out during baking. Don't get too involved with making the batter perfectly smooth, just do the best you can, realizing that by the time you get around to the last cookie, you will have improved immensely. You will be able to fit 2 or 3 cookies on each baking sheet. Sprinkle each cookie with about 1 teaspoon of the almonds.

Bake the cookies until golden brown, about 7 minutes. Halfway during baking, turn the baking sheet. Remove the baking sheet from the oven and cool the cookies slightly for about 2 minutes. Working

TUILE COOKIES PLAY A big role in any professional pastry department. Warm from the oven, they can be manipulated into a number of interesting shapes: Fluted cups, rolled cones, and curved "tiles" (hence the name, as they resemble clay roof tiles) are the most popular freeform shapes, but the unbaked batter may even be stenciled through a template onto a baking sheet to make distinct designs. When cooled, they harden into delicate, crisp cookies that we use at the Gotham to garnish a number of desserts. Our tuiles are flavored with a dose of strong, dark, clover-wild flower honey, which we buy from an apiary at the Union Square Greenmarket. Use the heartiest honey you can find or the taste won't show up in the batter.

quickly before the cookies harden, use a metal spatula to lift the cookies one at a time and form into the desired shape. If the cookies harden before they are shaped, return to the oven for a few seconds to warm and soften. Repeat with rest of the batter.

To make a cone, roll the cookie, almond side out. Hold the cone for a few seconds until it cools enough to secure the shape.

To make a cup, drape the cookie over an inverted tea cup, loosely pleating the cookie as needed.

To make the classic tuile shape, drape each cookie over a bottle or rolling pin.

Cool completely until crisp. Then store in airtight containers.

Langues-de-Chat

MAKES ABOUT 5 DOZEN COOKIES

Special Equipment: pastry bag fitted with plain $^5/_{16}$-inch tip

8 tablespoons (1 stick) unsalted butter, at room temperature

1 cup confectioners' sugar

4 large egg whites, at room temperature

1 teaspoon vanilla extract

1 cup all-purpose flour

Preheat the oven to 350° F. Lightly butter and flour 3 large baking sheets, or line them with parchment paper.

In a medium bowl, using a hand-held mixer (this amount of batter will probably be too small for most standing mixers) on high speed, beat the butter until creamy. On low speed, beat in the sugar until the mixture is combined and pale yellow. In 4 additions, beat in the egg whites, beating after each addition until smooth, then the vanilla. Add the flour and beat just to form a smooth batter—do not overmix.

Transfer the batter to a pastry bag fitted with a plain $^5/_{16}$-inch tip, such as Ateco number 3. Pipe out strips of batter, about 3½ inches long and ½ inch thick, and place 1 inch apart, onto the baking sheets.

Bake, 1 sheet at a time, until the cookies are golden brown around the edges but still pale in the center, 12 to 15 minutes. Cool briefly, then transfer to a wire cake rack to cool completely. They can be stored for 2 to 3 days in an airtight container at room temperature.

LANGUES-DE-CHAT (French for "cat tongues") are crisp, vanilla-scented cookies that are easily prepared from ingredients you probably already have on hand in the kitchen (although you will need a pastry bag.) They are delicious on their own with a cup of espresso or hot tea, but I like to use them as a garnish for other desserts as well. You can also use these long cookies as "edible spoons" for crème brûlée or ice cream.

Lemon-Pistachio Biscotti

MAKES ABOUT 3 ½ DOZEN COOKIES

SERVED SIMPLY WITH A glass of fine *vin santo,* biscotti offer a pleasant, understated conclusion to a casual meal. I like baking big batches; they make wonderful gifts, wrapped up with a beautiful bow.

Shelled pistachios are available at Middle Eastern and Indian grocers. Toasting them deepens their flavor, so don't skip this step.

Thinking Ahead: The biscotti may be made as much as 1 week in advance and stored at room temperature in an airtight container.

1½ cups (7 ounces) shelled pistachios

1½ cups all-purpose flour

1 cup plus 2 tablespoons sugar

1 teaspoon baking powder

Grated zest of 1 lemon

2 large eggs plus 1 large egg yolk, beaten

1 teaspoon vanilla extract

Preheat the oven to 350° F. Place the pistachios on a baking sheet and bake until fragrant and just beginning to brown, about 10 minutes. Cool completely, then chop coarsely.

Leave the oven on for baking the biscotti.

In a medium bowl, whisk the flour, sugar, baking powder, and lemon zest to combine. Make a well in the center and add the eggs and yolk, and the vanilla. Stir until the mixture comes together into a soft dough. Add the nuts and work them lightly into the dough.

Position 2 racks in the center and top third of the oven. Line 2 baking sheets with parchment paper.

Divide the dough into thirds. On 1 baking sheet, form two 12-inch-long logs, separating the logs by at least 2 inches. Form the remaining dough into a single 12-inch log on the other baking sheet. Bake, switching the positions of the baking sheets halfway through baking, until the logs feel firm and are lightly browned, 20 to 25 minutes. Cool slightly on the baking sheets.

Reduce the oven temperature to 325°. Remove the logs from the parchment paper. Using a serrated knife, cut on a slight bias into ½-inch-thick slices. Arrange the slices flat on the baking sheets and return them to the oven. Bake, turning the biscotti over halfway through baking, until crisp, 10 to 15 minutes.

Variations: Substitute toasted whole hazelnuts or almonds for the pistachios for a more traditional biscotti.

Appendices:
Recipes Within Recipes

Most of the dishes in this book are comprised of two or more component recipes. In many cases, these subrecipes can be used in other dishes. The Variations and Flavor Building tips offer much guidance on how you might use them to this end, but you should feel free to experiment to suit your own taste and inspiration.

Here is a quick reference list of the different recipes within recipes in this book:

Vinaigrettes

Balsamic Vinaigrette, 82
Caesar Vinaigrette, 99
Champagne Vinaigrette, 187
Charred Tomato Vinaigrette, 123
Citrus Vinaigrette, 66
Warm Coriander Seed Vinaigrette, 193
Curry Vinaigrette, 87
Creamy Garlic Vinaigrette, 97
Ginger Vinaigrette, 72
Lemon Vinaigrette, 58, 60
Lemon-Rosemary Vinaigrette, 194
Mustard Vinaigrette, 93
Black Olive Vinaigrette, 63
Walnut Vinaigrette, 76

Sauces

Apple Cider Sauce, 269
Artichoke Sauce, 203
Asian Duck Sauce, 260
Brown Butter Sauce, 230
Caramel Sauce, 351
Crème Anglaise, 342
Green Peppercorn Sauce, 266
Simple Herb Sauce, 33
Herbed Butter Sauce, 207
Merlot Sauce, 297
Sauce Poivrade, 320
Red Wine Sauce, 217

Romesco, 211
Scallop Butter Sauce, 244
Squab Pan Sauce, 273
Thai Curry Sauce, 252
Vintage Port Sauce, 189
White Port and Ginger Sauce, 234

Condiments

Aioli, 226
Ginger Aioli, 140
Basil Butter, 315
Bouilli Butter, 226
Herbed Garlic Butter, 231
Red Wine Butter, 292
Spiced Butter, 157
Apricot-Cherry Chutney, 74
Pineapple and Red Pepper Chutney, 253
Green Sauce, 326
Horseradish Sauce, 325
Red Onion Marmalade, 319
Basic Mayonnaise, 140
Ginger Mayonnaise, 140
Green Herb Mayonnaise, 115
Pickled Cipollini Onions, 79
Basil Pesto, 156
Green Herb Pesto, 258
Parsley Pesto, 149
Tapenade, 64
Gotham Tartar Sauce, 118

Side Dishes

Mail Order Sources

Aux Delices Des Bois
4 Leonard Street
New York, NY 10012
(800) 666-1232
(212) 334-1230
(212) 334-1231 (fax)
Suppliers of wild mushrooms, both fresh and dried,
as well as white truffle oil, and other ingredients

Balducci's
Mail Order Division
11-02 Queens Plaza South
Long Island City, NY 11101-4908
(800) 247-2450 (in NY State)
(718) 786-9690 (special requests)
One-stop shopping for such excellent products as
dry-aged beef and other prime meats and game,
white truffle oil, fine cheese, and other
provisions.

Bridge Kitchenware Corp.
214 East 52nd Street
New York, NY 10022
(212) 688-4220
Manhattan's famous kitchenware store, supplying
both professional chefs and passionate amateurs.
Look here for entremet rings, springform pans,
mandoline-type slicers, terrine molds.

The Cook's Garden
P.O. Box 65
Londonberry, VT 05148
(802) 824-3400
Call for their catalogue of culinary seeds.

D'Artagnan
399 St. Paul Avenue
Jersey City, NJ 07306
(800) 327-8246
(201) 792-0748
(201) 792-0113 (fax)
This company supplies the best restaurants in New
York, and can also provide you with the same
fresh game, foie gras, and free-range chickens.

Dean and Deluca
Mail Order Department
560 Broadway
New York, NY 10012
(800) 221-7714
(212) 226-6800
Another Manhattan food emporium that mail-
orders superior ingredients and equipment such
as aged balsamic vinegars, fine cheeses, pancetta,
prosciutto, salted anchovies, caper berries,
basmati rice, quick-cooking polenta, harissa,
hoisin sauce, and almond flour.

Jamison Farm
171 Jamison Lane
Latrobe, PA 15650-9419
(800) 237-LAMB
High-quality lamb.

Kitchen Arts and Letters
1435 Lexington Avenue
New York, NY 10128
(212) 876-5550
A bookstore and gallery devoted exclusively to
food and wine.

Morse Farms
Country Road
Montpelier, VT 05602
(802) 223-2740
Our suppliers for maple syrup, both fine Grade A
and the heartier-flavored Grade B (amber) that is
best for cooking.

New York Cake and Baking Supply
56 West 22nd Street
New York, NY 10010
(212) 675-2253
Offers a wide range of chocolate as well as baking
supplies.

Petrossian, Inc.
182 West 58th Street
New York, NY 10019
(212) 245-0303
World-renowned purveyors of impeccable caviar.

J. B. Prince
29 West 38th Street
New York, NY 10018
(212) 302-8611
Another source for excellent professional
equipment; where many New York chefs shop.

Shepherd's Garden Seeds
6116 Highway 9
Felton, CA 95018
(408) 335-5311
Also a reliable source for culinary seeds.

Index

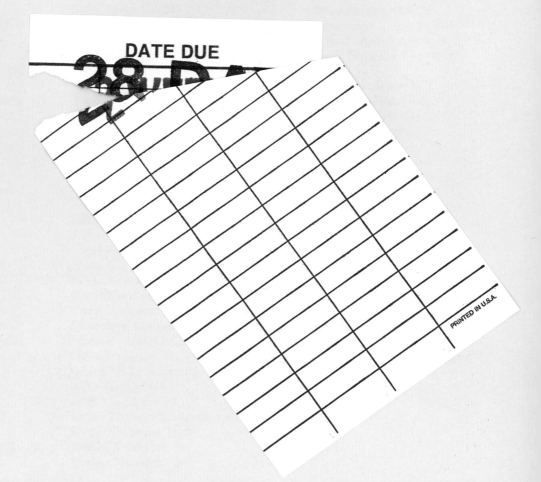

DATE DUE

28 D

PRINTED IN U.S.A.